Praise for

The Ball
in the Air

"*The Ball in the Air* tells the golf-related tales of three decidedly
non-high-profile figures. . . . Linking these tales is Mr. Bamberger's
own story and his conviction that golf has much to teach when
we open ourselves to the game's deepest, most subtle nature—the
unexpected emotions, the 'odd and beautiful playing fields,' the
intimate bonds that form among both friends and strangers.
The pleasure of *The Ball in the Air* is like that of an ordinary golf
round. . . . Mr. Bamberger's abiding love is for golf as it is experienced by everyday people."

—John Paul Newport, *The Wall Street Journal*

"I've devoured most everything from award-winning golf writer
Michael Bamberger, including his previous seven books, and his
latest offering may be his finest yet."

—Les Schupak, *The Met Golfer*

"*The Ball in the Air* is not your typical golf book. It doesn't revolve
around tour players, exotic trips to majestic courses, or the majors. Instead, Michael Bamberger introduces us to three individu-
als who love playing golf for the joy it brings them. . . . You don't
need to love the sport to be drawn to the characters who come to
life on the pages of this enthralling book."

—*Bookreporter*

"Bamberger knits together his subjects' golfing and life stories, showing how each found the game and their accomplishments and adventures. . . . Sparkling with details . . . The stories are heartwarming and affecting."

—*Kirkus Reviews*

"As beautiful as golf is on the outside, it's even better on the inside. In *The Ball in the Air*, Michael Bamberger intimately weaves four profoundly personal journeys with mesmerizing skill and leaves us with a deeper understanding of our own."

—Jaime Diaz, Golf Channel commentator and #1 *New York Times* bestselling coauthor (with Hank Haney) of *The Big Miss*

Also by Michael Bamberger

The Green Road Home

To the Linksland

Bart & Fay (a play)

Wonderland

This Golfing Life

The Man Who Heard Voices

The Swinger (with Alan Shipnuck)

Men in Green

The Second Life of Tiger Woods

The Ball
in the Air

A Golfing Adventure

MICHAEL BAMBERGER

AVID READER PRESS

New York • London • Toronto • Sydney • New Delhi

AVID READER PRESS
An Imprint of Simon & Schuster, LLC
1230 Avenue of the Americas
New York, NY 10020

First Avid Reader Press trade paperback edition March 2024

AVID READER PRESS and colophon are trademarks of
Simon & Schuster, LLC

Simon & Schuster: Celebrating 100 Years of Publishing in 2024

For information about special discounts for bulk purchases, please
contact Simon & Schuster Special Sales at 1-866-506-1949 or
business@simonandschuster.com.

The Simon & Schuster Speakers Bureau can bring authors to your
live event. For more information or to book an event, contact the
Simon & Schuster Speakers Bureau at 1-866-248-3049 or visit our
website at www.simonspeakers.com.

Manufactured in the United States of America

1   3   5   7   9   10   8   6   4   2

Library of Congress Control Number: 2023930579

ISBN 978-1-6680-0982-6
ISBN 978-1-6680-0983-3 (pbk)
ISBN 978-1-6680-0984-0 (ebook)

It's not often that someone comes along who is an outstanding golfer,
a gifted editor,
and a true friend.

This book is joyfully dedicated to
Jofie Ferrari-Adler.

The Ball
in the Air

Lee Trevino was throwing a party. He was on a driving range, putting on a show for an audience of two, a father and his son. Or three, if you count the ringmaster. With every word and swing, Lee Trevino was amusing himself, too. He was in his eighties. He was ridiculously boyish.

It was a warm December afternoon in central Florida, with Christmas in the air. Trevino was wearing long navy shorts and a black baseball cap, tufts of perfect silver hair spilling out from the sides and back. He was performing magic tricks with golf clubs.

The father, Tiger Woods, half Trevino's age, was entranced. By his example, he was inviting his son, closing in on thirteen, to watch this funny little magician in action.

Sunset was coming. Not that Trevino cared.

"Charlie," the old man said, trying to get the boy's attention.

Hee-hee-haw-haw-hee-hee.

Trevino was laughing at his good fortune—Tiger Woods was paying attention to him. He clapped his hands to punctuate his delight.

Trevino then played a slicing, spinning pitch shot, not with a wedge, as you might expect, but with a driver. He was practicing his art, showing off his dance moves, inventing swings, offering commentary all the while. His shots were coming out of his mouth, his eyes, his stout legs and round body, his meaty hands and nimble brain, the left side of it and the right side, too.

Tiger had already buried his father, said farewell to Arnold, stopped writing his own chasing-Jack story, too battered, in every way, to soldier on. He was a man in transition. To what, he couldn't know. His son was just starting out. And before them was this old puppet master. Trevino was deep into his back nine, but Tiger knew what all golfers knew, that Lee Trevino would go to his maker playing golf shots.

Three generations, right there, on that range. One starting (a first act), one turning (a second), one finishing (a third).

Golf runs in threes. Balls, new ones, come in sleeves of three. When you review your round in the trapped heat of a parked car, you count and rue your three-putt greens, don't you? All the while, you can't wait for another crack at it. Our game.

Tiger would have been an icon of golf even if he had quit playing in college. Charlie had been playing in junior events. But Trevino never played amateur golf at all.

He came to golf by way of a maintenance shed at a Texas golf course and was done with school by the tenth grade. Golf became his teacher. His desire to understand the game proved to be insatiable, so he stayed at it, a perpetual student. A lifer. Yes, the need for money drew him to the course. But then the game cast her spell on him. As she does.

"The greatest ball-striker there is, right here," Trevino said, motioning toward Tiger with the back of his bare right hand. He was stepping into a shot.

"Oh come on," Tiger said.

"You had power!" Trevino said.

Tiger knew better. Power comes and power goes. He'd learned that the hard way.

"You're the best I've ever seen," Tiger said, not loudly.

Trevino kept hitting shots, one rhythmic swing after another, the ball coming off the sweet spot of his club with something that sounded like joy.

I picked up a golf club for the first time in Mr. Greenlee's eighth-grade gym class at a public middle school where my mother later taught English, near the train station in the village of Patchogue, on the south shore of Long Island. We were in the gym, hitting plastic balls off plastic mats with real clubs, aiming for backboards. A couple of months later, the U.S. Open was played at Winged Foot, sixty-five miles and several light-years from my home. Our morning paper and bible, *The New York Times*, devoted many columns inches to it, with nods to Arnold Palmer, to Jack Nicklaus, to Lee Trevino. He was "the Merry Mex" that week, in the paper's smudgy black ink.

Eleven years later, I was caddying in the PGA Championship at Cherry Hills Country Club, near Denver. My player, the head pro from a club in Winged Foot's long shadow, made the cut and finished early. Later that Sunday I watched Hubert Green and Lee Trevino duke it out for the title. That night, I was driving with Al Geiberger and his wife and their young son to Al's next event, the Jerry Ford Invitational. Al's son said something about Hubie Green. Al said, "I think Mike was rooting for Lee." I don't know why he said it. I remember it because it was insightful and unexpected, and because I was in the thick of Act I. We all remember what that's like.

Fifteen years after that, Lee Trevino used a club I had designed while playing in his final British Open, in 2000, at the Old Course.

He wasn't playing to cash a check. His goal, at age sixty, was to shoot the lowest score he could, and that's why my little invention was in his bag, one of his fourteen clubs. (The E-Club, U.S. patent number 6,033,320.) He played with it, and he bragged to reporters and others about its special powers. If that's not the highlight of my second act in golf, I don't know what is. Trevino was then at the start of his third. Zero to thirty, thirty to sixty, sixty to ninety, if you start young and go deep. Trevino missed the cut, not that it mattered. Tiger won.

And then somebody flipped a switch, another twenty-one years passed, and there was Trevino, in his early eighties but otherwise little changed, standing on that driving range in central Florida, Tiger and Charlie Woods beside him. This was at the Father-Son tournament, as the founders used to call it. The broadcaster Roger Maltbie was on the scene. The Course Whisperer. I asked him, "Does anybody know more about the golf swing than Lee Trevino?" Rog thought for a half moment and said, "Nobody knows more about his own swing than Trevino knows about his."

Charlie's swing was pure youth. Long, fast through the ball, flowing. He was Gumby, as Tiger once had been. Tiger's swing was a grunt. Trevino's was the art of invention. He had moved beyond the professional ranks and tournament ambition. He seemed half-drunk (no, not literally), standing and swinging on that range, lifted by the satisfaction that comes with being relevant and alive. Later was later. Later, he came down. He was done with golf for the day, and he had turned surly and rough. But for a while there he had it in his hands, and the next day, maybe, he would have it again.

This golf. The game for a lifetime, old people said when I was a kid, and here I am, repeating their words. I'm not apologizing for the role it plays in my life anymore. Golf taught me to be punctual, among other things. To be courteous, to be aware, to try. Golf is hard. I cite that as a positive.

The people I have met along the way—it almost doesn't seem fair. Here are three. Pratima Sherpa, from Nepal, age twenty-three (eventually in these pages) and playing college golf in Los Angeles. My colleague Ryan French, from Alpena, Michigan, recovering fast-food restaurant manager who found a place in the game in his forties by writing about golf's dreamers, unearthing some miscreants while he was at it. And my friend Sam Reeves, pushing ninety, with a home in Pebble Beach but really at large in the world, wise beyond his years and still both at it and in it. I thought he might have a damn heart attack one morning as we stood on a driving range and he made these alarmingly aggressive warm-up swings with a headless shaft.

Here at the start, let me say this about Pratima and Ryan and Sam, and I could easily bring in Trevino and make it a foursome. They all know what it's like to marvel at a white ball in a high sky and get lost. What a gift that is. You know what I'm talking about, right?

STARTING

I want you to try and remember what it was like to have been very young. And particularly the days when you were first in love; when you were like a person sleepwalking, and you didn't quite see the street you were in, and didn't quite hear everything that was said to you. You're just a little bit crazy. Will you remember that, please?

—Stage Manager, *Our Town*, by Thornton Wilder

When she was six, Pratima Sherpa moved with her parents into the maintenance shed at the Royal Nepal Golf Club, where her parents worked. The club's leadership was looking for extra security for Royal Nepal's lawn mowers and rakes and the rest. The Sherpa family was looking for free digs. Talk about a win-win.

The low whitewashed cinder-block building was in the shade of a drunken conga line of short, unkempt trees. Its barnlike main door, with a cement ramp leading to it, was secured from the inside by a padlock. The dank interior space was crowded with the basic tools of course maintenance, including long bamboo poles used to remove morning dew and monkey dung off the greens each day, before the start of play. When there were no monkeys on the course, that meant leopards were making a rare appearance, which meant play was paused until they were chased off by the sound of gunfire. Golf at Royal Nepal in Kathmandu.

The Sherpas had turned a small section of the shed, an area measuring roughly twenty feet by ten, into living quarters. There were two beds covered by colorful blankets. The family's section was separated from the storage area by hanging curtains, as you might see in a college dormitory. The spigot for running water, cold only, was behind the shed. Water for bathing was heated over an open fire. There was an area to cook, another to sleep, and a third to congregate. There were nights when Pratima (*prah-TEE-ma*) fell asleep amid the aroma of cauliflower fried in a pan with her mother's spices. Her first smell in the morning was often "petrol" (Pratima's word) from the mowers as her father stood over them, red gas tank in hand.

And then there were the scents from beyond the shed's front door. A Hindu temple abutted the course, and there were days when Pratima could smell the smoke of festival fires and cremations. The family's backyard collection of animals—an inconstant population of goats and hens and dogs—provided its own bouquet. There was the smell of jet fuel from the national airport bordering the golf course on one side and exhaust fumes from the vehicles on the city's Ring Road on the other. Pratima Sherpa grew up in a pungent city.

Kathmandu was bustling in Pratima's girlhood. The city's narrow streets were dotted with giant puddles and piles of construction dirt. They were crammed with buses, mopeds, taxis, itty-bitty cars with the windows down, cows, beggars, hustling businesspeople, street kids, aristocrats, and various pilgrims, religious and otherwise. There was a lot of honking, yelling, no-signal lane changing. There were strolling Hindu holy men, the sadhus, their faces often covered with bright red and yellow paint. Almost every day, Pratima would see them, on a break from prayer and meditation, hanging their fingers on the club's chain-link boundary fence as they considered the odd cross-country game, imported from faraway Scotland. If Pratima had no money, which was typically the case, she would avoid them. If she had some rupee coins, she would receive a blessing and offer a coin. It was a way of life for Pratima, and anybody in Kathmandu.

For a Westerner, these sights, sounds, aromas, and customs might contribute to a bad case of sensory overload, but for Pratima and her parents, this was their daily life. The Sherpas had a TV with limited reception and an unreliable source for electricity anyhow. They had no internet connection in the shed. As a schoolgirl, Pratima had heard of Barack Obama but would have been hard-pressed to name another American.

The family ate all their meals together, a light one at sunrise, a bigger meal in late morning, and a third one after sunset. A thousand meals in one year, ten thousand in ten. Sitting on a rug on the floor, they ate these meals and their afternoon snacks with the fingers of their right hand, in the custom of their country. (The left hand is considered unclean and not suitable for such a sacred act.) Their plates were made of metal and had low border walls, the kind you might associate with camping. Pratima and her parents held their teacups with their palms, the steam warming their faces on cold winter mornings. The shed had no heating system. During the summer monsoons, nights could be terrifying.

"We've been through worse," Pratima's father would say when the wind and rain became so loud she could hardly hear herself talk. Sleep was impossible. "We're lucky to have this roof over our heads."

Pratima trusted her father. Still, she wanted to scream.

On school days, Pratima's mornings began in the dark, feeding the family animals before she had her morning tea and biscuit. Her public school was an hour away by bus, past Tribhuvan International Airport and through the chaos of the city's traffic. (There was a King Tribhuvan in Nepal for much of the twentieth century.) Pratima had no reason to go to the airport and neither did her parents, though they had friends who worked there. This was not an airport where you would see many, if any, holiday travelers wheeling golf bags, but you would see visiting mountain climbers with giant backpacks, a tiny percentage of them bound for Mount Everest. The Nepali name for Mount Everest is Mother.

Pratima's father, Pasang Sherpa, a tiny, lithe man with large glasses, was a Sherpa by birth (his family name), a Sherpa by ancestry (he descended from the Sherpa tribe in Tibet), and had been, as a younger man, a Sherpa by profession. He had worked, as did his father and grandfather, as a trekker, a guide to visiting mountain climbers. He had many relatives, close and distant, with his surname who worked as porters, guides, and pilots, among other jobs the mountain provided. All the jobs were dangerous. Pasang knew friends and relatives who had died leading groups on mountain passes in thin air and heavy snow, and he was relieved to find employment at the golf course, even if it barely kept him out of poverty. The English he learned as a trekker—"Look out for falling ice"—he would not need on the golf course. His work at Royal Nepal was far less challenging than his work in the Himalayas but also far less dangerous.

Pasang had met his wife, Kalpana Pokharel, at Royal Nepal. They were both in their early forties when they met, and neither had ever been married, and neither had ever had children. Their fellow course workers threw them together, and they went to a movie on their first date. Pasang was Buddhist. Kalpana was Hindu. Kalpana was from the Bahun caste. Her family was poor, but still they viewed Pasang as beneath her. For one thing, he had even less money, and his caste had lower status than hers. (You could live in Nepal for a hundred years and barely make a dent in your understanding of its caste system.) A marriage between Kalpana and Pasang would mix cultures, religions, regions, and backgrounds. There wasn't much precedent for it.

If it had been up to Kalpana's family, the marriage never would have happened. But Kalpana and Pasang had struggled all their lives, financially and otherwise, and they were happy to take a chance that their lives would be better as a couple. Their only wedding guests were a small group of fellow workers from Royal Nepal.

Two years after the wedding, Kalpana became pregnant. Nobody saw that coming. The only people not worried about the pregnancy and the future child were the expecting parents. Kalpana went through the pregnancy and delivery without any complications, but at birth Pratima had a serious and mysterious vision issue. At worst she was blind, and at best her eyesight was seriously impaired. A doctor thought the problem had been caused by an infection but was not at all sure. The only good that came out of the health scare was that it brought Kalpana's family back into her life. After about six weeks, the issue resolved itself. The miracle of modern medicine. Pratima's eyesight was fine and remained so.

She spent her early years in small, cramped, noisy apartments with playmates nearby. She was being raised with her mother's Hindu customs (many festivals) and her father's Buddhist ones (a lot of meditating). The two traditions coexisted in the house, and within Pratima.

The move to the maintenance shed came out of desperation, with the family on the verge of homelessness. In her mind, Pratima had moved from a safe apartment with an active little-girl social life to a terrifying jungle. She was close to her mother and father, her mother especially, but both parents had health challenges. Her father had persistent headaches, which he ascribed to his thin-air mountain climbing. Her mother had persistent stomach pain. Money was always tight. Also, they were her parents, not her friends. They were trying to raise their daughter. They worked long hours. They weren't young. This was a family of three trying to survive.

Even as a young girl, Pratima could see the big picture, as only children sometimes can. She was living in a dangerous jungle, and the family needed to stay together. There was safety in numbers.

One of Kalpana's jobs was to weed the golf course with the aid of a screwdriver, place the royal detritus in an enormous red sack, and carry the swollen pouch on her back to a dumping ground. She would also carry huge, cumbersome jugs of water to distant, thirsty greens. Royal Nepal was a course maintained by inexpensive manual labor wherever possible. Every adult golfer there, and sometimes even the junior ones, played with a caddie, a custom that created jobs in a population that needed them. Pratima's father mowed greens and raked bunkers. He patrolled the club's property as an unarmed security guard, keeping out trespassers, wild dogs, and wandering cows, the holy animal of Nepal. Pratima's parents knew the course, as a piece of ground, intimately. As a playfield, it was a mystery to them.

So were the golfers. Many of the golfers at Royal Nepal were members of Nepal's ruling class, well established in business, the military, or government, or they were heirs to the country's royal or aristocratic families. That makes the club sound vaguely British and far grander than it actually was. For one thing, the caddies—and there were scores of them, male and female—were allowed to play the course pretty much whenever they wished, which is not how these things customarily go. The nine-hole course was lush and beautiful but also unkempt. It was short in length but had narrow corridors, the fairways lined with tall trees and deep rough. If you wanted to play the course well, you needed to hit your golf ball straight.

Nobody would confuse Royal Nepal with a fancy Western country club, and it didn't aspire to be one. A Pepsi machine was trucked onto the course for tournaments. There was no snack stand, no fountain by the clubhouse, no valet parking, no dinner-for-four dining. It was a simple nine-hole golf course, the only course in Kathmandu.

From her front door, Pratima could watch golfers playing the par-3 third hole. She could watch the golfers play their tee shots and their delicate greenside shots. She'd see the strange body positions that signaled putting. Pratima could tell by the way the golfers walked and tended to the short grass below them that they had a special reverence for that part of the course. She did not yet know the term *putting green*.

She was a shy girl but a curious one, and before long she was walking the perimeter of the course. She'd see monkeys picking up lost golf balls and rejecting them after realizing they were hard as a rock with even less flavor. She noticed that few of the golfers were grown women. But she did see girls, her age or slightly older, playing or practicing. They were the daughters of members. In the vicinity of the maintenance shed, she began imitating them, using a random stick as a stand-in for a golf club.

Other girls in Kathmandu were playing badminton and volleyball in neighborhood parks, but there were no neighborhood parks near Pratima. Kids in rural Nepal, boys and girls, played a game called dandi biyo, a cousin to cricket that required stubby sticks. But Pratima didn't live in rural Nepal. She had no sport, even with golf in her backyard. The idea of their daughter becoming a golfer never occurred to Pratima's parents. It was an upper-class sport, and it was prohibitively expensive. Pratima was unaware of these obstacles. She had a collection of golf balls she had found in the rough. She had access to a course that was not usually crowded. In her mind, all she needed was a golf club. The sticks Pratima was swinging were too whippy to propel a golf ball anywhere. Her father saw that. But asking a Royal Nepal member or pro for one was not something he or his wife could do.

Pratima's father considered the problem, went into the woods with a machete, climbed a tree, cut down a modest limb, and turned it into a primitive club. It looked more like a field hockey stick than a golf club, but Pratima could hit balls with it. Pratima's first swings were left-handed, and the balls went scooting along the ground as if kicked by a midfielder. But she was hitting a golf ball. By way of a stick, she was propelling the ball forward. The starting point of the game.

Pratima's mother worked with other mothers who would bring their daughters to the course during the workday. Before long, those girls and Pratima were taking turns with the homemade club, making swings and hitting balls and giggling at the results. Pratima rebranded the maintenance shed in the jungle where her family lived. It became her golf house. *Come to my golf house, we'll play the golf!*

"I don't want to leave," one of the girls told Pratima. They spoke in Nepali and used their rudimentary English only while at their public school. "I want to live in your golf house, too!"

• • •

Sam Reeves was the father and Sammy Reeves was his son, riding his bike through town like he was the mayor. He was Sammy on the basketball court, on the football field, at church, and Mr. Sam's son when he arrived at the golf course, which got to be an everyday thing. Mr. Sam—Thomas Fambro (Sam) Reeves—was a cotton merchant, and cotton was king where the Reeves family lived, in the small Georgia textile town of Thomaston in rural Upson County, at the intersection of nothing and nowhere. The family was wealthy enough to have a swimming pool, one of three in town. That is, three operating ones.

Sammy Reeves was born in the family home on Thurston Avenue in 1934 and learned the game on a golf course on the outskirts of town about ten years later. The daily news then was all about World War II and, when it was over, the aftermath of war. War, and sports.

During the war, government-mandated rationing and recycling were central to life across Thomaston and across the country. Tired golf balls were sent to a factory in Acushnet, Massachusetts, to be refurbished. Bits of tinfoil from cigarette wrappers were recycled. Tires were recapped. Money was tight and workers were needed. In the summer of 1943, when he was eight turning nine, Sammy (as he would be known for years) started his first job, stitching together large pieces of remnant cotton at his father's cotton gin and warehouse, earning ten cents for each assembled five-hundred-pound bale. At the end of that summer, Sammy had saved $124. He bought shares of AT&T and Chrysler with his savings, on a hunch that someday every family would want a telephone in the kitchen and an automobile in the driveway.

The elder Sam Reeves, married and the father of two, was not in active service because he had "essential war employment," to use a phrase Sammy's mother knew well and used as needed. He was a cotton supplier to uniform manufacturers. Every family in Thomaston was shaped by the war. Many homes in town had a banner with a blue star hanging from a first-floor window, meaning that a family member was serving in the military. There were also banners with gold stars, for those who had lost a family member in the war. There was a gold-star banner on the Mitchum house, down the street from the Reeves house. Paul Mitchum had died in the Pacific while serving in the U.S. Navy. Sammy knew him as the best golfer in town and looked up to him in every way.

The golf course was the centerpiece and the only piece of the Thomaston Country Club. It had nine holes, six bunkers, and a practice green about the size of a large breakfast table. The club had a small wood-framed clubhouse, a tiny changing room, and one vending machine for crackers and another for pop, as everybody in Thomaston called soda. There were four slot machines, illegal in Upson County, but the sheriff didn't seem to mind—it was a modest income source for a club barely breaking even, and he was willing to look the other way.

Even though it paid low wages, the club had employees who stayed for decades. Mr. Pete, the caretaker. Mr. George, the greenkeeper. Mr. Mangrum, the club's longtime pro. Plus the many caddies.

The club was founded with lofty aspirations. A pool gave the club's founders all the permission they needed to drop *country* into the club name. But during the war, the pool had no water in it and weeds in its cracks. Thomaston Country Club was almost a public course in that any family with a hundred dollars could join, as long as the family was white. The schools were segregated, the churches were segregated, the ballfields were segregated, the country club was segregated.

But not the course itself, not as young Sammy got to know it. The two dozen or so caddies were all Black, except for Sammy Reeves, who was really more of a bag toter, working only for the pro and two or three other good players, not a true caddie like the others, grown men who could offer advice on distance and wry commentary on life. They zigzagged across the course carrying two bags and got three dollars for their efforts. Sammy might get a dollar or a little more for carrying a single bag while walking straight lines. But he was making money and learning the game's swing, etiquette, rules, and prominent names.

In the afternoons, the caddies would play and Sammy would join them, trying to copy their rhythm, those with good rhythm, but not the cross-handed grip many of the caddies preferred. That grip promoted straight shots but a lower ball flight, and it was not the grip used by elite players. Bobby Jones of Atlanta was a hero to Sammy and every golfer across Georgia. Jones wanted the left hand at the top of the shaft, turned clockwise so that you could see three knuckles. That was the gold standard. Sammy followed suit. A good grip was a mark of class, like a pressed suit on Sundays.

Golf was a major sport in Georgia. It wasn't embedded in the state's culture the way football, basketball, and baseball were, but it made the front page of the sports section on a regular basis. Sporting heroes were homegrown, the excitement for them whipped up by newspaper columnists, and the leading golfers from Georgia, amateur and professional, were stars. There was, of course, Bobby

Jones, but also his contemporaries, including the touring pro Sam Byrd (who had played on the Babe Ruth New York Yankees) and Charlie Yates and Alexa Stirling, amateur golfers who were close to Jones. The pro at the Thomaston course, Mr. Mangrum, had watched all of them and passed along to young Sammy Reeves what he saw, what he read, and what he knew.

Sammy's father was often out of state, driving a new car on dusty two-lane highways. He had a plant in Texas and another in Arkansas and could get gas during the war because his job required it. He was away from home half the year. He liked golf and played capably, but it was an occasional activity for the senior Reeves, as it was for most golfers then. Few people had the time or the money for regular leisure activities, not during the war and not in the first years after it.

Golf as a way of life came later, when the country was settling into its Eisenhower-era easy chair and Arnold Palmer arrived on the national golf scene, a working-class kid with a country-club background. He grew up at the club where his father was the pro. The sportswriters loved to tell his father-son story, just as they got a lot of column inches out of the Bobby Jones–Colonel Jones story. There was a lot of that in golf's lore, fathers handing the game down to their sons. Sammy knew all about Colonel Jones and his son, Bobby. Sammy knew he was never going to have with his father what Bobby Jones had with his. Sammy's dad was a busy man, keeping those plants going and the workers employed. In his life, Sammy played with his father only once. But he never forgot it.

● ● ●

When Ryan French was growing up, there were two major events each year at the Alpena Golf Club, the public course a couple of miles from Alpena's handsome but tiring lakefront downtown.

There was the city championship in midsummer and the club championship in late August. Ryan took up golf at six chiefly by hanging out with his father, Howard, on the course. By twelve, he was good enough and mature enough to play in the same Alpena events that his father was playing in.

Howard French was faintly famous in Alpena. He'd been one of the best basketball players Alpena High ever produced, and he was from an old Alpena family. (Not old and rich. Just old.) Howard's father was Bob French, who, by his retirement, had a coat-and-tie job at Alpena's biggest employer, Besser Company, concrete manufacturers. Bob French grew up in Alpena but was thrown out of his chaotic childhood home at thirteen by his father, with a kick and these words: "He don't look like me!"

Bob French never went to high school and spent most of the Depression living on the streets of Alpena or going from one friend's house to another. He was a baker at the Douville Bakery in Alpena for years and cooked on the industrial boats tied up at the docks before going to Besser's, where he spent most of his working life. Bob French was a gregarious man and ended up running the company's personnel department, which meant that anybody from Alpena who wanted a job at Besser's—and that was a hefty percentage of the population—came through his office. As for Bob, he was the exception that proved the rule: Nearly everybody who rose at Besser's from a shift job to management had a high school degree and some had been to college. But not Bob French.

Bob's youngest son, Howard, had been a *Detroit Free Press* second-team all-state basketball player as a senior at Alpena High in 1963. He was recruited to play basketball at Central Michigan and was set on going there until he made a springtime love-is-in-the-air decision to follow his high school prom date, Ginny Eustis, to Michigan State. His basketball days were over. His father was disappointed.

But in this case, son knew best. Howard French and Ginny Eustis married in 1966, as undergraduates. In 1973 they moved into a house on Eagle Drive with a view of the Alpena Golf Club course. By then, Howard had an MBA. Ginny and Howard celebrated their tenth wedding anniversary in high style, and nine months later their third child, Ryan Eustis French, was born. For his middle name, Ryan was given his mother's maiden name. In time, Ryan came to look like that grandfather, O. B. Eustis, a noted northern Michigan naturalist.

Ryan didn't inherit Howard's gene for speed, but he did get his father's gift for athleticism. Ryan played hockey in middle school. He played varsity tennis as a freshman and senior at Alpena High. He was on the varsity golf team all four years. Before he entered high school, he had played thousands of holes with his father, adding up the hundreds of fast-paced, nine-hole rounds they played, always walking. (Golf was never meant to be an all-day thing. Any Scottish golfer with haggis in the fridge will tell you that.) During summer in Alpena, sunlight bounces off Lake Huron and in the early evening the Alpena course becomes bathed in a soft orange glow that clings to life until nine p.m. or later. Howard played in an after-work men's league that waived its eighteen-and-older age requirement for Ryan. They played through dusk.

You know you have the golf fever when you wake up with a swing thought and you can't wait to give it a try. Ryan had the golf fever. He played regularly with his father, and when his father wasn't around he was happy to play by himself. On Mondays, any kid in Alpena could play four holes and use the driving range, no charge. A man on the range, Bill Peterson, gave free lessons. Bill was the best golfer in Alpena and owned a bar and restaurant called the Twin Acres 19th Hole, so while teaching he was also developing future customers. He taught Ryan to come from the inside on the downswing, release the hands through impact, clear left, and hit a draw. Everybody was encouraged to hit a draw. Wherever there is hockey, and Alpena was a hockey town, there are golfers hitting draw shots.

When the Alpena kids played that four-hole loop, they went out on the first and second and played in on eight and nine. Ryan joined them sometimes, but the free golf wasn't much of a draw for him. He could start on three, the par-3 in his backyard, pretty much any time he wished. He'd hit an iron off the tee, then go to the short par-4 fourth, a dogleg right, and hit another iron there. Even at thirteen, Ryan, a big, strong kid, could play the fourth with a 7-iron off the tee and a wedge into the green. That is, if the fairway would hold his tee shot. In summer, when the course was baked, it was hard to get your tee shot to stop. One day, tired of seeing another boring layup shot wind up in the trees down the left, Ryan did what all golfers playing alone do: He tried something else. He applied critical thinking and athletic skill to the problem at hand. He attempted to hit a driver over the trees on the right and found that it wasn't hard at all. He had turned the hole into a par-4 he could almost drive. Risk-reward, risk-reward, risk-reward. Golf's eternal balancing act, and its siren song. At thirteen, without adult supervision, Ryan had figured out a better way to play the fourth hole at Alpena.

Most of Ryan's golf was with his father, which meant a lot of golf with his father's friends, too. Their golf was casual, and the rules were more like suggestions than laws. Howard French wasn't any sort of rules expert, but he did teach Ryan golf's basic values. You don't step on an inconvenient branch to give yourself an unencumbered swing. Unless the ball is sitting almost on the lip of the hole, there are no gimmes. If a ball is out of bounds by a quarter-inch, it's out. There is no such thing as winter rules, even on the first day of the season, April 1, when the grass is still dormant and the bunkers are a mess. Howard's golf buddies thought all that was ridiculous, but Howard had an intuitive sense of golf's Calvinist roots, and that's how he raised Ryan in the game. Ryan thought his father was being a hard-ass.

Howard's golf buddies didn't change their behavior just because a kid was around. Ryan found that he could be as profane as he wished and nobody cared. He was in a position to hear and see things that most kids growing up in Alpena would not. He listened without talking (hard for him!) as his dad and his friends discussed various Alpena affairs, financial, political, and carnal. He saw and heard occasional scorekeeping disputes. He heard comical outbursts over missed three-footers and shanked irons. He'd see a club get hurled now and again. He saw men being men. It was workingman's golf, with guys playing in T-shirts and work pants. Even at the other course in town, the private Alpena Country Club, things were casual. (When the country club gave up its private status, the owner put a sign near the entrance with this peculiar use of quotation marks: *"A Public Course."*) These were Ryan's wonder years, playing the two Alpena courses, going to the range, playing on his high school golf team. But all through those years, Howard's buddies had a message for Ryan: *You could get out of this town.*

In addition to all that golf, Ryan played dozens of rounds alongside his brother, their father, and their paternal grandfather. Golf brought three generations of French men together in a way other families in Alpena, including his own, got together through hunting and fishing. O. B. Eustis (Ryan's maternal grandfather) was a well-known trapper, hunter, and fisherman in Alpena County, and he tried to lure his children and grandchildren into field and stream. Ryan, like his mother, was sometimes required to eat meat from muskrats trapped by his grandfather. The meat was oily, black, and repulsive, and baked muskrat did not endear Ryan to O. B.'s Thoreau-like life. Neither did the squirrel brain he put in his stew. (O. B.'s dense but beautiful book, *Notes from the North Country,* makes his outdoorsman's life seem more appealing, but the book doesn't reek of dead animal.) Ryan hunted some with his father and paternal grandfather, but only when they shamed him into it, and even then he spent most of his time in various deer blinds playing Game Boy. He could hunt, and he did, but it wasn't for him. He was a golfer.

Ryan's mother, Ginny French, was the biggest sports nut in the French house, always able to name names in the Detroit Tigers bullpen and the Michigan State backfield. Every year during the Masters, Ginny and Howard and any of the kids who might be around would go to her in-laws' house in Alpena and watch the Sunday finale. Bob and Annette French had something in their home that Howard and Ginny French did not: a working television. In 1983, as Ryan and his parents and siblings watched an NHL Stanley Cup game, the family TV started spewing smoke and shooting sparks. It was a goner. Howard and Ginny didn't decide to live without a TV, they just didn't get another one.

Ryan was the second-biggest sports fan in the French family. Growing up in a house where there was no access to ESPN forced him to become a reader in one narrow area. Every morning, Ryan, an early riser, would get the *Detroit Free Press* out of the raised yellow plastic box on the front curb and devour the sports section at the kitchen table. He spent many hours studying the golf results and knew the names of hundreds if not thousands of golfers, male and female, amateur and professional, from Michigan and the rest of the world. He could tell you all about the senior golf career of Mike Hill from Jackson, Michigan. He was familiar with the various Michigan club pros good enough to play in the Michigan Open each year. He sought out any information he could find about Greg Kraft, a golfer from Detroit trying to find a home on the PGA Tour. The game's biggest star, Greg Norman, made almost no impact on Ryan. Ryan read Mitch Albom religiously, especially when Albom was writing *Free*

Press columns about obscure players doing big things at the Buick Open, played each year on the outskirts of Flint, Michigan.

Ryan went to the tournament starting as a kid and right through his late twenties. He was more interested in the Friday-at-dusk cutline than the Sunday-afternoon leaderboard. One year he saw a tour journeyman named Kent Jones eating breakfast alone at the Bob Evans restaurant in Flint. He said hello to Kent by name. "If you know who I am, you need a new hobby," Kent said pleasantly. Kent Jones was Ryan's kind of guy. He had gone from the Canadian Tour to the Hooters Tour to the Nationwide Tour to the PGA Tour. He was never going to be a star. But he was in the bigs long enough to get a cup of coffee at the Bob Evans in Flint during the Buick Open. His name was on the Thursday/Friday tee sheet. No professional golfer is promised the weekend. You earn those tee times like you earn everything in professional golf.

Ryan was drawn to golf's stepping-stone system and the fairness at its core: Shoot the scores, move on up. When one player was heading north, another player was going south, if not out: the birthplace of the phrase *Every shot makes somebody happy.* Ryan had a black-and-white view of the world, so golf's dependence on numbers, and all the heartless accounting that came with it, was natural for him. It didn't matter who was playing: Professional golf, as long as it was played by the rules, was cutthroat and brutal but also fair. Ryan would sometimes tell his high school golf coach how close Greg Kraft or some other player was to getting his tour card. Ryan saw the toll and the work behind the numbers. He knew, from his own experience, that there was a story behind every score. Ryan's coach said to him, "Too bad you can't make a living from all this random stuff you know."

Though the morning paper was a font of information, no American sports-mad kid wants to grow up in a house without a working TV. Welcome to Ryan French's world. Without a TV, watching must-see sporting events required planning. So the French family, led by Ginny and with Ryan, would go to Grandma and Grandpa French's house to watch the Detroit Lions on Sundays or the NCAA basketball final on the first Monday night in April. Mother and son bonded over sports. When Magic Johnson, the Michigan State and state of Michigan basketball legend, announced his abrupt retirement from the NBA in 1991 after testing positive for HIV, Ryan and Ginny were both shaken. Before long, they were talking about Spartan pride, hero worship, AIDS. Ginny had some safe-sex tips for her son. She had a big heart and a real-world brain. Her mother, sister, and brother all had profound addiction issues, and Ginny made sure her kids knew. She was an expert in genetic predisposition.

Six months after Magic's announcement, the French family returned to Grandma and Grandpa's, and Ginny watched and rooted for Fred Couples at the 1992 Masters. Ryan could tell that his mother was drawn to Fred, in multiple ways. Ryan wasn't an introspective kid—how many fourteen-year-olds are?—but he could be insightful. Fred won, Ginny was happy, *60 Minutes* came on, and the French family headed home.

• • •

A course worker at Royal Nepal, a friend of Pratima's father, saw her swinging as a lefty with a club that looked like something you'd see in a golf museum. He knew it would be difficult to find left-handed clubs in Nepal, where there were a thousand active golfers, if that. He had a right-handed club, a pitching wedge, a short and lofted iron, and he gave it to her. At night, Pratima kept it under her bed. Later, a Royal Nepal member invited Pratima to attend a Saturday-morning junior clinic. She did. Her very first shot went straight up in the air. The next one was a ground-ball duff. Still, that first shot.

An assistant pro at the club, a man named Sachin Bhattarai, showed Pratima the interlocking grip, which (for a right-handed golfer) entwines the small finger of the right hand and the index finger of the left. It's not the most commonly used grip, but it is the grip that Tiger Woods has used all his life. Pratima was ten.

With her lone club in hand, Pratima started taking her mother to the hole beside their house, the par-3 third. Pratima's mother would sit on the green as Pratima played shots to it. If the shot was a dud, Pratima's mother sat there, silent and still in her colorful blouses and scarves, her spectacular face, bronzed and lined, showing nothing. When Pratima's shot landed on the green, Kalpana would smile and clap. On their way back to the house, as Pratima's mother talked about their next meal, Pratima was thinking about the shots she had just played.

She was drawn to the golf course. The tranquility it offered, the endless sky above, its unexpected hollows with their pockets of cool air. As she walked a fairway, heading for her ball, happiness would wash over her. You could say that she was becoming a golfer, but it was more than that. Nepal is patriarchal by ancient tradition, and the world beyond the Royal Nepal fence was telling her to know her place. Golf meant freedom to Pratima. She had her golf house. She had her golf course. She had a golf group, her golf teacher in Sachin, her golf mentors from the club. Within the club's boundary fence, she had it all. She was leading a golfing life.

From the Ring Road, you could glimpse Pratima's house. One day after school, Pratima and another girl were walking by. The girl said, "That's where you live, in that shit?" It was a wake-up call for Pratima. Her golf house, she knew, would always be a maintenance shed to those who didn't understand. Some people could see that the shed was a home, that the poor parents in it gave love without reservation, that they were raising a daughter who wasn't afraid to dream. But most people were blind to all that.

Pratima took her mother's Hindu customs to the course. Books, in the Sherpa home, though not plentiful, were considered instruments of learning and, by extension, instruments of the gods. On that basis, books were not to make contact with your feet or legs, as they were considered unclean body parts. Such contact, even when accidental, was considered disrespectful. The act of atonement was to hold the book in your hands, then place the fingers of your right hand on your forehead. Pratima took a version of that ancient tradition to the golf course: If her club made contact with her legs or feet, she would hold the club for a moment and then bring the fingers of her right hand to her forehead. As for the common Western custom of kicking a disobedient golf club, Pratima never had even the urge. She was playing Eastern golf.

Sachin, the Royal Nepal teaching pro, and some members assembled a collection of used clubs for her. In the United States, such sets are yard-sale staples, sometimes on the giveaway table by the end of the day. Pratima would have known nothing about that. She thought, *My own clubs.* If the course meant freedom to her, her clubs represented the game's challenges. When her shots were poor, Pratima blamed herself, not her clubs.

As a petite girl of eleven, Pratima played in her first golf events. Not tournaments but competitions with rules, designed for the kids in Royal Nepal's Saturday-morning junior program. None of the other girls came from a background anything like hers, but golf, despite its elitist reputation, levels playing fields as few sports do. The ball doesn't know a thing about your parents, about where they went to school, how much money they have, what they do. Coming from a family with money might give a young golfer opportunity, but you can't buy drive and desire. The World Golf Hall of Fame roster is loaded with former country club kids, like Bobby Jones and Jack Nicklaus and Tom Watson, but more players who came out of the caddie yard, like Walter Hagen and Ben Hogan and Seve Ballesteros.

In one Saturday-morning junior event at Royal Nepal, each young golfer was given ten balls to chip or pitch into a circle from a short distance. This is an important golf skill to learn and one you can develop only by repetition. The winner would be the golfer who got the most balls in the circle. The other golfers were the children of members. The first-place prize was a box of candy and a small trophy. Pratima walked into her house with the goods. Her mother knew immediately what that meant and began to cry with joy. She told her daughter, "I work on the golf course. I met your father on the golf course. You were raised on the golf course. Now you have a trophy *from* the golf course." In a city with a chasm between rich and poor, and in a country with an entrenched caste system, Kalpana's daughter had found, at least for a morning, a way to even things out. Pratima was discovering the joy that her golf could bring her parents. Her golf skill was improving, her confidence was rising, and so was her sense of responsibility.

At twelve, Pratima played in a junior event in Nepal that was part of the Faldo Series, a group of international events started by the English golfer Nick Faldo. The winner would be invited to play in China at a much bigger event. On the last hole, Pratima had a forty-inch putt. A putt of that length in a tournament can be hard, terrifying, or impossible, depending on the golfer's putting skill and level of anxiety. You can never take a forty-inch putt for granted.

"If you make this putt, you'll win," Pratima's caddie said to her.

She said nothing. The caddie meant well, but it would be hard to imagine a less useful thing for a caddie to say. (When in doubt, keep quiet.) Pratima imagined the ball going right into the hole, and then with one simple stroke that's what happened. She knocked it right in and didn't show a thing.

Pratima never showed much emotion. By this point, she had heard of Tiger Woods. She had seen YouTube clips of his miraculous shots and fist pumps. She was mesmerized by them. But such outward displays of emotion were not for her. Right from the start, the satisfaction golf gave Pratima came from a place she could not reach or even identify.

• • •

The only time Sammy Reeves played golf with his father, they played six afternoon holes at the Thomaston course. Sammy was thirteen. They played the first three holes, then created a fourth hole by dropping balls and playing to the fifth green. They played the sixth and then the ninth on the way back to the car. They eyeballed their invented fourth hole at 230 yards, and Sam the father knocked his shot onto the green with a Spalding driver, a Bobby Jones model with a bleached head. It was a draw shot, and just about perfect. Father and son walked quietly to their balls. The father took a quick look at his twelve-footer and made it on a green slower than their sitting room rug.

Sammy wasn't surprised to see his father make this unlikely 2. He knew his father to be good at anything he attempted. But now he had now more proof: His father could even play golf.

There wasn't much chitchat over those six holes. For one thing, it was golf, and golf took concentration. For another, Sammy didn't talk much as a kid, especially on the course, where he was accustomed to being around much older golfers. More than anything, it was a quiet era. Quiet fathers, quiet sons, quiet dinners, quiet nights. Sam Reeves and his son were reserved people in a time and place when reserved was the norm.

• • •

When Ryan French was growing up in Alpena, his father was the CEO of Nemroc, a small nonprofit company that placed people with physical and mental disabilities in a range of jobs. It was a rewarding but difficult position that paid modestly, despite the big title. A lot went right, but things went wrong, too, of course. Workers lost fingers in sawmills. There was a fight between two workers wielding nail guns. Funding the program was a constant struggle. Ryan could see his father's professional woes in their after-work golf games.

Howard French was often hard on himself. If he hit a poor shot, he would sometimes smash his club into the turf and say, "You are such a fuckup." But on other days, golf washed him in joy. Ryan never knew what mood he would find his father in. Howard won the Alpena Country Club title over a far better golfer by making a mile of putts, and he apologized gleefully for that. But a week later, he was cursing that putter out. He was like that, up and down, down and up.

When Ryan was in high school, his brother and sister were out of the house, and Ryan was like an only child. Father and son spent a lot of time together. Howard watched Ryan in a high school tennis match, saw Ryan throw a racket, and pulled his son off the court. He was a senior, and it was embarrassing. Howard used their time together on the golf course to talk to Ryan about the importance of getting a college degree. (Inspiring.) When Ryan's grades were poor in his junior year, his father said to him, "I will not stand for this." (Pointless.) Then there were the times when Ryan came home with an improved report card. When he kept his composure in the goalie's net. When he was in control of the flight of his golf ball. On all these occasions and many more, his father was supportive, kind, generous. But one day to the next, you didn't know which Howard you would get.

Ginny French's job as a district manager for the WeightWatchers in Alpena required her to work on Thursday nights. That meant Howard was in charge of dinner. But Howard didn't cook. Father and son played golf through dusk on those nights. Most of the time they went to the Bird's Nest, a diner in town where Ryan would get a house specialty, a chicken offering called Wing Dings. But sometimes Howard, uncharacteristically, wanted to live large, and on those nights, they went next door to a restaurant called the Thunderbird, with views of Lake Huron. One of the Frenches might order a steak, and sometimes they both did.

Howard was an engaged father. Once a year, he and Ryan made a special trip to play the long tree-lined courses at the Garland Lodge and Golf Resort, an hour from Alpena by car. Their foursome included Howard's brother, Dan, and their father. Dan was rough around the edges but funny. Howard was a hugger. Uncle Dan, by way of greeting, preferred to punch you in the stomach. Ryan loved him.

They were in a cart at Garland one day when Uncle Dan made a turn that was far too sharp on a slippery fairway. Ryan fell out of the cart and to the turf. He and Dan started laughing. Howard was mad. "Jesus Christ, what are you dumbasses laughing about? Now he's got his best pants all stained." Uncle Dan and Ryan could not contain their glee.

• • •

Pratima's father was an athletic, limber man. His daughter was athletic and limber, too. Golf is a litmus test for athleticism and flexibility. Before Tiger started to resemble the Michelin Man, he was like a yoga master, he was so flexible. He was also loaded with eye-hand coordination, as was his baseball-playing father. One year, walking off the range at the Masters, Tiger casually picked up a broken tee with the toe of a club, bounced the tee stub off the clubface, and flicked it away as if hitting a tennis ball to a child. You know how he can bounce a golf ball off a clubface like he's dribbling a basketball? Most elite golfers can do that. Elite golfers are superb athletes. It's a harsh truth that many 95 shooters don't want to recognize. Having good eye-hand coordination helps the beginning golfer immeasurably. If you start young and have good coordination and dedicate yourself to the game, you can quickly develop into a competent golfer, able to shoot in the 80s or better within a year or two or three. Yes, that quickly. (Golf takes ridiculous amounts of patience.) If you're good at making free throws or shooting pool, you'll likely be able to play reasonable golf. If you have strong hands, that's a big plus. Being a good dancer is another leading indicator of golfing promise. Formal instruction is overrated. You can learn the basics of the grip, a necessary and unnatural starting point, from an instruction book or a YouTube video or a friend who plays well. Or a pro, like Pratima's Sachin. But the swing itself is more instinctive than anything else. You copy what other people are doing and modify it to your body type and personality. "You already have such a nice swing," a Royal Nepal member told Pratima when she first started making full swings at the club's junior clinics. Yep, she had it in her.

After five years, Pratima also had Malcolm Gladwell's ten thousand hours of practice (and play). The club had given her permission to play as she wished, and she wished to play a lot. When playing alone, as she often did, Pratima did what all golfers playing alone do after a bad shot: Drop another ball, try to figure out what went wrong, and attempt the shot again. When she wasn't on the course, she could be found on the cramped Royal Nepal driving range, where plastic mats were glued to the cement floor. She never ran out of balls. If she did, she went out into the field, picked them up, and placed them on her practice mat.

You will frequently find an obsessive-compulsive strain in serious golfers, but Pratima didn't exhibit such tendencies. She found it calming to hit balls, one after another after another. The repetition of it put her in a pleasant, dreamy trance. More was happening than Pratima realized. She was quickly becoming Royal Nepal's best female junior golfer, and the power of positive reinforcement was raining down on her. Before long, the few shelves in her golf house were crammed with ribbons, cups, trophies, and medals. Beating the other kids didn't bring her any joy. What she liked were the spoils that came with her wins. She liked the trophies. She liked seeing her parents happy.

Over time, Pratima came to understand that competitive junior golf in Nepal was nothing like competitive junior golf in China or Korea or the United States. But golf in those countries existed only in her imagination. When she made that forty-inch putt to win the Faldo Series event, that qualified her to play in an international tournament in China. She couldn't do it. Her father didn't have a birth certificate, did not know his precise age, couldn't say for sure where he was born. In Nepal, children inherit citizenship from their father. Passport control in Nepal is a famously bureaucratic division of a government that is notorious for being bureaucratic. If Pasang couldn't prove he was Nepalese, how would his daughter ever get a Nepali passport?

"I'm so sorry," father said to daughter.

Pratima said she understood.

"Everything happens for a reason," Pratima's mother said.

Pratima said she knew.

She didn't imagine playing golf beyond Nepal. It seemed like too much.

Then, one day when she was sixteen, a representative of the world beyond Nepal came to her. The representative was a tall, skinny, energetic New Yorker named Oliver Horovitz.

Oliver Horovitz was a member of a family brimming with talent. His father was a prolific playwright, and Oliver was a writer, too. His mother was an elite marathon runner, and Oliver was a good runner, too. A brother (half brother, if you must) was a Beastie Boy. A sister (yes, point-five) was a producer of the movie *Moneyball*.

Oliver was an adventurer. After high school and before starting at Harvard, and for some summers after college, he worked as a caddie in St. Andrews and wrote a book about his time there. Later, he wrote a magazine piece about golf in Iceland. After that he began working on another unlikely story, this time about golf in Nepal. His first stop was Royal Nepal, where he immediately learned about the girl who loved golf and lived with her parents in the club's maintenance shed. He met Pratima.

He met Pratima's parents. He visited the family home. Horovitz made arrangements not to play with Pratima but to caddie for her. He saw Pratima's natural swing and her passion for the game. He could see that she wasn't an elite junior player, not by American or Korean standards. But he also felt that with the right resources, she could develop into an NCAA Division I golfer.

When he returned to his apartment in New York City, Horovitz wrote a piece about Pratima for *Golf Digest*. With two friends, he started a fundraising campaign to help Pratima get an intense junior-golf experience, with regular instruction and tournaments and high-quality range balls and all the rest. His piece about Pratima—not a great big thing but imbued with information and heart—ran in the November 2016 issue with an iconic cover photo of Arnold Palmer, who had recently died. It ran online, too, with a link to Oliver's fundraising efforts. Talk about advocacy journalism.

Tom Rinaldi, an ESPN reporter, read the Horovitz story, as did some of his colleagues. They started talking about how they could tell Pratima's story in documentary form. A family of three near Ojai, California—the Montanos, a mother and father and their golf-playing daughter—read the Horovitz piece and wrote to Horovitz to learn more about Nepal, golf in Nepal, and this remarkable young female golfer in Nepal. Tiger Woods read the Horovitz story and was so impressed by her unlikely path to golf that he wrote her a letter.

Dear Pratima,

Hi, it's Tiger.

I wanted to tell you how proud I am of all your accomplishments. To play at such a high level, and to inspire others, especially young women, is very admirable.

My Pop had an expression that I think of often. He said, "You get out of it what you put into it." That means that if you work hard you'll be successful, but if not, you don't deserve it. It's great to see you have the commitment, dedication and talent to do great things in the future.

Take care, and I know you'll have many more achievements in the game and in life.

Sincerely yours,
Tiger Woods

The letter was delivered to Pratima at her golf house by a friend of Horovitz's who was visiting Nepal. Pratima was overwhelmed. She gathered herself and read it a second time, aloud and in translation, for her parents.

"He is the best golfer in the world, is he not?" Pratima's father said.

"He is, Father."

Pratima turned seventeen a few weeks after the *Golf Digest* article appeared. Fall turned into winter and winter into spring. Nothing really changed for Pratima. You can play golf all year long at Royal Nepal, except during the monsoons, and Pratima did. She kept hitting balls, playing golf in her backyard, returning at dusk to her house, where she would do her homework, eat an evening meal with her parents, and fall asleep with the scent of her mother's cooking in her nose. That had been her life since the age of twelve, and she didn't see it changing. It was exciting, meeting Oliver from New York City, having a write-up in an American magazine. But Pratima still couldn't imagine playing golf outside Nepal. How could she ever get a passport if her father didn't even have a birth certificate?

In her dreams, Pratima would come off a plane in some faraway airport, show a passport to an immigration official, and be whisked away to a tournament. Then she would wake up.

• • •

Each summer, Sam Reeves and his son would drive from Thomaston, Georgia, to Harlingen, Texas, where Mr. Reeves had merchandising offices. It took three days. Sammy was fourteen the first time they made the trip. He had no license but helped with the driving anyhow. At a red light in a small Texas town, with Sammy behind the wheel, another car rear-ended their new wood-paneled Plymouth station wagon. Sam and Sammy and the other driver gathered at their joined bumpers. Their wagon was damaged but operable. "No worries," the elder Reeves told the other driver. Sammy looked at the other driver, whose face was frozen in shock and relief. The senior Reeves got behind the wheel, and father and son skedaddled on out.

Sammy learned by watching, in golf and beyond. The caddies and the workers at the club lived payday to payday at best, and the senior Reeves helped them as much as he could without making them feel like charity cases. He'd bring a club employee a pair of shoes and say, "Could you break these in for me?" then hand them over and never ask about them again. He'd bring a spare set of clubs to the course greenkeeper and say, "I can't hit these, maybe you can do better with them."

Sammy took his father's example to heart. You don't play the trumpet when giving a gift (Matthew 6:2). The Reeves family went to church every Sunday, at the First United Methodist of Thomaston, near Sam's school. Most every family went to church on Sundays. There was something for everyone, pretty much. Right in town were Trinity Baptist and First Presbyterian. Also a Mennonite church, a Catholic church, an Episcopal church, an AME church (African Methodist Episcopal), and, out in the country, a score of one-room Black churches.

About the closest Thomaston came to separate-but-equal was a monument in front of the county courthouse in town, dedicated to the men from Upson County who had lost their lives in World War I, with one column of names marked WHITE and the other COLORED. But Sammy knew the ugly truth, that there were men in town who found themselves on the wrong end of a gun, vile words and spittle raining on them, for the crime of having dark skin. Sammy's father would have nothing to do with these bigots. He wasn't Miss Lillian, the progressive Lilly Gordy of Richland, Georgia, who became famous as Jimmy Carter's mother. But love thy neighbor was the code of life in the Reeves home.

There was a Black nanny in the Reeves home named Miss Mag who was like a second mother to Sammy and his sister, Martha. Also a Black cook in the home, Allan. He could not read, but the Reeves family members ascribed much of their good health to Allan's cooking and the fresh ingredients he used. Every night, he got a ride home from Mr. or Mrs. Reeves and sometimes both. When they discovered that Allan lived in a single room with no running water, they added a bathroom to their home so that Allan could bathe in privacy. Sammy once used a harsh and haughty tone with Allan within earshot of his parents. Mother and Father let him have it: *Do you think you're better than anyone else? Any person in our home is our guest.*

The public high school in Thomaston, for white kids, was named after Robert E. Lee, and its sports teams were called the Rebels. Sammy played everything in its season: football in fall, basketball in winter, golf in spring. In summers, he worked for his father, attended sleepaway camp, went on family vacations in rented beach houses in northern Florida. Sammy would spend hours in the water there, swimming and bodysurfing. Thomaston had a few lakes, but nothing like the wildness and openness of the ocean. He played golf wherever and whenever he could.

There were tournaments sprinkled throughout the summer, typically two-day events, twenty-seven holes a day. If you were playing a nine-hole course, and that was often the case, you got to know every inch of every hole after playing each one six times over two days.

Sammy played a lot of pretty good golf and collected a lot of modest hardware at the smaller events, but got skunked in Georgia's bigger statewide junior tournaments. There was a kid from Cedartown—like Thomaston, a speck on the state map—who won everything. You might get a driver or a putter from the Georgia State Golf Association for winning, and Doug Sanders would sell his bounty on his way to his car. (A decade later, he was contending in majors and giving Jack Nicklaus a run for his money.) Doug Sanders shot scores that were out of Sammy's league, but Sammy could hang with him or anyone, on the right course and on the right day.

Golf was a good fit for him. He was too tall (north of six feet and still growing) and too skinny for football. But that didn't stop him from trying, and his parents were proud to see their son's name in the glossy program for the Rebels' Friday-night season opener in the fall of '49: Sammy Reeves, sophomore back, 140 pounds, the last five of them all benefit of the doubt. By physique and temperament, Sammy was better suited to basketball. He could shoot, and over the course of four seasons, he started far more often than not. He enjoyed standing on Robert E. Lee's polished gym floor, looking at the packed stands, and knowing every last face. As a senior, he was the team captain. The weekly paper, *The Thomaston Times*, was part of the town's lifeblood, and having your name in it for scoring twelve points during a Friday-night win raised your profile and status in town. The final-buzzer cheering in your ears, the attaboy backslaps in the school hallways, the write-ups in the paper—it was all intoxicating.

But all the while, Sammy couldn't wait for spring. In football and basketball, you couldn't really quantify your contribution. After the war, the emphasis, in Georgia and across the country, was on team sports, on giving yourself up in the name of others. Sammy understood and appreciated that. But he needed something else, and golf offered it. In golf, at the end of the day, there was a two-digit number attached to your name. It was tidy and efficient, not open to debate. In golf, at the end of the round and the end of the day, it's all on you, and that's how Sammy liked it.

And even if he couldn't shoot the scores Doug Sanders could shoot while half-asleep, he did manage to go around one day in 72, even par and his best tournament score ever. That was at the course in Barnesville, up the road from Thomaston. Sammy knew the course was a pasture with holes in the ground, but he also knew that 72 was 72 and that the score was his. So were his 82s, and there were many more of those. But every time Sammy played a stroke-play event, where you counted each shot, he had a goal he could quantify: to shoot the lowest score possible. That day at Barnesville, he went around in level 4s for the first time, and he left the course thinking it could have been lower. The golfer's lament is the golfer's disease.

Sammy figured out what some but not all golfers figure out: You can make any excuse you want for what happened and why it happened, but nobody cares, and in the end, you're just fooling yourself anyhow. Whatever you shoot, it's all on you. Sammy played tennis, and he liked it and was better than decent. But in tennis, the better player controls the weaker player, and before you know it, it's game, set, and match. In golf, you control yourself, or you try.

When he wasn't playing with the caddies, Sammy played a lot of his golf alone. Some of those solo games were played during polio outbreaks in town, and the course was an easy place to isolate, in the phrase his mother used. Also, not many kids in Thomaston played golf. Sammy didn't mind. Playing alone, Sammy did what all golfers playing alone do: Hit a bad shot, drop another ball, sort through what went wrong, and then try the shot again.

Sammy was ten, twelve, fifteen, seventeen. He turned eighteen the summer after he graduated from high school. Golf was already teaching him the value of being honest with yourself, understanding what you can do and what you can't. The path to improvement was clear to him: Admit you have a problem, try to find your own solution, ask for help if you can't. Yes, there are applications beyond golf.

· · ·

Howard French, in the manner of all serious athletes, never let his son win during their many games on the Alpena golf course. The opposite. *You're one up with three to play. Maybe this will be the first time you beat me. But I doubt it.*

When he was fifteen, Ryan did. He ran home to tell his mother, who disliked her husband's competitive streak with their son. Ryan wrote the score on a piece of paper in red marker and taped it to the basement door.

When Ryan played in the Alpena Golf Club club championship at eighteen, his father insisted on caddying for him. He had caddied for Ryan before but hadn't mastered the fine caddying art of saying nothing. ("How could you three-putt there?") Howard French was one of the few caddies on the course for this second and final major of the Alpena golf season. Most players carried their own bag, pulled a cart, or drove a gas-powered cart. Ryan could imagine what the other players were thinking: *Look at this fucking kid with his old man carrying those shitty Top Flite irons.* But Ryan wasn't going to tell his father he wasn't on the team. There was no way. Golf was their thing.

It was a two-day, thirty-six-hole event played over a weekend in late August. Ryan would start his senior year of high school right after Labor Day. There were plenty of golfers in Alpena better than Ryan, but he had a chance. After a first-round 73 on Saturday, he was in the thick of it.

When Ryan returned home after the first round in midafternoon, his girlfriend, Margot (as she is being called here), was in the driveway in her car. They were an unusual couple. Margot was one of the best students at Alpena High, and disciplined in everything she did. Ryan, most decidedly, was neither of those things. Yes, opposites attracting, same as forever. They had been boyfriend and girlfriend through most of their high school years.

Ryan saw that Margot was crying, and quickly found out why: She was late. Ryan could not even process the implication. *Well, if you are pregnant, maybe it will just go away?* He was a man-child. He struggled to keep track of his homework. How could he possibly manage golf and school and fatherhood? He went into a hole. Margot went into one of her own.

Ryan, normally so open with his parents, didn't say anything on that Saturday night, about Margot or really anything else. On Sunday morning, the day of the second round of the club championship, the same. Howard and Ginny knew something was off. They had seen the young couple in the driveway. Their guess was that a breakup was in the works, likely at Margot's initiative. They could do the math of high-school romance: Why on earth would Ryan break up with her?

On Sunday, in that second round, Ryan went around the Alpena course in a state of total distraction, and 72 shots. He was thinking about everything but the shot he was playing, and shot the round of his life. At the end of two rounds, he and Gerry Kneeshaw, several years older than Ryan and a better golfer, were tied at 145. They began a sudden-death playoff.

Ryan faced a six-foot putt on the first hole to keep the playoff alive. He gave it no thought and holed it. He faced a five-footer on the second hole to keep the playoff going. Stepped right up and knocked that one in, too. The two golfers came to the par-3 third hole, with the French home off to its right. Ryan's mother was watching in a cart, on the course with her father-in-law. There were about twenty spectators watching. Everybody had a rooting interest. Except for Ryan. He only wished he could go backward in time.

Ryan had played the third hole hundreds of times, most often with his trusty Top Flite 6-iron. He reached for it.

"It's a five," Ryan's caddie-father said.

Whatever.

Ryan grabbed the 5-iron and played a 173-yard shot. It finished within two feet of the hole. He tapped in for a birdie and the win. Gerry Kneeshaw was annoyed but hid it. That's part of the game, at every level. In victory, Ryan felt—nothing.

"Let's have a party!" Ginny French said. Her son was the Alpena Golf Club champion while still in high school. Ryan had clinched his win in the vicinity of where he was conceived. She could call some friends and have them come to the house.

"No, Mom, we're not gonna have a party," Ryan said.

He and his parents went back to the house. Ryan put the trophy on the kitchen table. He sat his parents down. They were bathed in fluorescent light. He told his parents about what Margot had said in the driveway, and his greatest fear.

Howard, a committed agnostic, reached for his preferred all-purpose commentary, reserved for whenever he felt overwhelmed, which was a regular thing. *Jesus Christ, Jesus Christ. Gee. Zuss. Christ.*

His mother said, "We will help you navigate this."

Ryan sat there, raw, empty, silent.

• • •

Tanya and Michael Montano lived on the outskirts of Ojai, California, in a large modern house. When she was home, their daughter, Sophia, lived there, too. In the fall of 2016, when Oliver Horovitz's story on Pratima Sherpa was published, Sophia was a sophomore at Pitzer College in Claremont, California, and a member of its golf team. As a senior in high school, she had made a three-week school trip to India. Now, as an undergraduate, Sophia was looking for more adventure education. She was searching the internet for study-abroad programs in Kathmandu. That's when she stumbled onto Horovitz's story about Pratima. She was struck by the similarities between her family of three and the Sherpa family of three. But there were stark differences, too. Sophia's mother was a medical-field communications executive. Her father was a commercial photographer. Sophia had more golf clothes and equipment than she knew what to do with.

The family began to make inquiries, asking if Pratima might be interested in spending the summer of '17 with the Montano family in their home in Southern California. It would be five weeks of golf immersion, American-style, along with trips to the beach, to museums, to Disneyland, to anywhere else she might want to go. The Sherpa family was interested.

Sophia enrolled in a semester-abroad program in Kathmandu. At the end of it, Tanya and Michael came to visit her. While they were there, they arranged to visit the Sherpa family in Pratima's golf home. While Pratima and Sophia played golf, Pasang and Kalpana served tea and cookies to Tanya and Michael. By the end of the visit, Pasang and Kalpana said they were comfortable with Pratima going to the United States and staying with the Montanos. They gave the trip their blessing. At the family's request, Sachin Bhattarai, the Royal Nepal teaching pro, would join Pratima on her flight to the United States and look in on her during her stay. Somehow—wonder of wonders!—Pratima got her passport. It was happening. For the first time in her life, Pratima would be leaving Nepal.

In early July, Pratima and Sachin flew from Tribhuvan International to LAX. Eight thousand air miles. Twenty-four hours on a plane.

The Montanos were at LAX to greet them. From there, they made the ninety-minute drive north on the 101 to their home near the Soule Park Golf Course. When Pratima first saw the house she thought it was a hotel.

"These are the Topatopa Mountains," Tanya said, waving a hand in the direction of the Ventura County wilderness. All Pratima saw was hills.

She entered the house. She had never been in one like it. The big windows. The shiny appliances. The many faucets and all that hot water. The Montanos showed Pratima to her bedroom. She started eating eggs and toast for breakfast.

A few days after arriving, Pratima and Sophia were in the Ojai Fourth of July parade, sitting together on a flatbed trailer turned into a float for Sophia's old school, Oak Grove. They went to an ocean beach, a first for Pratima. When Tanya learned that Pratima didn't know how to swim, she immediately enrolled her in lessons. Pratima played golf almost daily at the Soule Park course. She hit balls and received professional instruction. At her first tournament, playing competition far more experienced than any she had encountered before, Pratima saw that her hands were shaking. She played poorly. But over the course of five weeks, Pratima played five junior events in Southern California, competing against girls her age, many of whom had hopes of playing college golf, and her play steadily improved. She won one of the events. The Montanos were on hand for all of it. By the end of her five-week stay, Pratima was referring to her American sister, her American mother, her American father—her American family.

ESPN camera crews dropped in now and again to document Pratima's summer in Southern California. They were gathering string for a possible documentary. On her last full day, the Montanos threw a party for Pratima in their home and in the backyard. The party wrapped up, the ESPN crew left, and Tanya Montano found herself crying. Her only daughter had always wanted a sister. And for five weeks, she'd had one.

The ESPN people finished their labor-of-love project. It took a small and dedicated army, but they got it done. In April 2018, they invited Pratima to attend the premiere of *A Mountain to Climb*, a twenty-five-minute ESPN documentary about the life and times of Pratima Sherpa, the golfer who grew up in a maintenance shed in Kathmandu. Within hours of her arrival at JFK, Pratima was walking across Central Park with Oliver Horovitz, asking him if there were monkeys in the park. Yes, Horovitz said, but only in the park's zoo. Later, when his piece about Pratima's second visit to America was posted on GolfDigest.com, Horovitz put that exchange at the top of his story. He was chronicling Pratima's life while shaping it.

On that trip, paid for by ESPN, Pratima saw New York as few do. She stayed at a boutique hotel on the Upper West Side, and Horovitz, a lifelong New Yorker, took her to Zabar's, a gourmet deli (if those two words can coexist). The ESPN documentary was shown downtown as part of the Tribeca Film Festival. Upon arrival, Pratima posed for photos with Tom Rinaldi, the ESPN reporter who narrated the film, and the documentary's director, Kristen Lappas. The red carpet and Pratima's lipstick nearly matched.

Rinaldi got Pratima popcorn and a Sprite. Pratima took a seat in the packed auditorium. The lights went down, and Pratima and a house filled with strangers watched the story of her life on a screen in front of her. About six minutes into it, her tiny father, with his strong, lined face, filled the screen, a shoulder-and-head shot taken in front of the maintenance shed, by its main door. He spoke in Nepali. There were subtitles below him. He looked pensively at an off-camera interviewer. A simple and haunting score, for piano and violin, played in the background. The captions read, *People may question, "How are they living in these poor conditions?" But we don't have the power. There's not much I can do to change this. If I had money, I would have done many things. In reality, I don't have much money and I can't do much. I feel bad.* Pratima had never heard her father say those things. She watched, listened, and cried. All the while, an unspoken story was being told, one about the strange power of happenstance. Oliver Horovitz and the Montano threesome were all in the theater. Four agents of happenstance.

Some minutes after Pasang Sherpa spoke in the documentary, Tanya Montano appeared on the screen and said, "The Montano family always jumps in without ever thinking about anything. And we jumped in." The footage at that moment showed Tanya making a toast (with a water glass) to Pratima during the backyard farewell party at the end of Pratima's five-week stay.

The documentary's clips showed Pratima leading a life that looked ordinary, though it was not. Pratima playing golf in shorts for the first time. (In Nepal, with its conservative dress code for women, she could not.) Pratima seeing the ocean for the first time. (Nepal is landlocked.) Pratima on a bike for the first time. (The Sherpa family didn't have one.) You could see Pratima's casual confidence as she talked to the other guests at the farewell gathering. She was seventeen, with a golf-course tan, a sparkling smile, and long, shiny hair. Had you walked into the screening during that scene, you might have guessed that Pratima had been going to garden parties like that one all her life.

The documentary ended. The house lights came up. In the lobby, Oliver Horovitz said hello to a friend, David Fontanilla, a donor to Tiger's foundation. David had been crying. He told Oliver that he was flying to South Florida the next day, for a clinic being sponsored by Tiger's foundation. He said Pratima and her people should come, too.

On the day after the Tribeca Film Festival premiere, Pratima, Sophia Montano, and Oliver Horovitz flew to South Florida to attend a clinic that Woods was putting on for donors to his foundation. Pratima was told she would get a grip-and-grin with Tiger, and that was more than enough for her.

While waiting for Woods at Medalist Golf Club, Pratima put her hand on her heart and took a deep breath. When Tiger arrived, Pratima gave him a red Royal Nepal hat. He thanked her for it and asked Pratima if she wanted to hit balls. She caught her breath and said yes. They went to a quiet spot on the back of the range. Pratima took off her sandals and started making swings with a club she was borrowing from Tiger Woods. Tiger was watching closely. Pratima thought, *Is this really happening?*

She hit a choked-down pitching wedge, clipped and perfect. At impact, her knees were practically touching, her hips had cleared, her head was back, her hair was flying. Some people have swings that are filled with art. You can't teach it.

"Beautiful swing," Tiger said, almost to himself. Pratima could barely hear him.

At the end, Tiger had a few suggestions for Pratima, about posture and course strategy, about the importance of having a plan for practice, a strategy for play. She was hanging on Tiger's every word.

"Golf is a mind game," he said.

• • •

Sammy Reeves graduated from Thomaston's Robert E. Lee High School in June 1952, spent most of the summer working for his father in Texas, and then, after a twelfth-hour change of heart, enrolled at the University of North Carolina at Chapel Hill. He had been planning to attend Washington and Lee in Virginia, but late in the summer he realized that UNC offered a trifecta he could not find elsewhere. His sister, Martha, two years his elder, would be there. It had excellent golf and academics. And it had an Air Force ROTC program. Sammy had already done four years of Army ROTC in high school. He wanted to come out of college and be able to join the Air Force as a commissioned officer. Sammy was ready to serve, like many young American men of his generation, not that there was a choice in the matter. But if his government wanted him to serve in Korea, Sammy Reeves didn't want to be on the ground. He wanted to serve from the air.

Because of his late decision to enroll at UNC, and with his arrival in Chapel Hill further delayed by playing in a late-summer golf tournament, Sammy missed freshman orientation for the Class of '56. He was shut out of the dormitories, so he rented a room in a home on Green Street, near campus. He didn't have access to the home's kitchen, or a cafeteria meal plan on campus, or a car, so he walked to the Carolina Inn every morning and had breakfast there. Sammy knew nobody in Chapel Hill except his sister, also a new arrival. Martha took him around. Martha saved him. But golf helped.

Sammy made the freshman golf team and was its number two or three player through the season. His golf game helped him find a path to a fancy-pants fraternity, SAE. He was mocked all through rush for his rural Georgia accent, but still he got tapped. Now and again, he was introduced as somebody's "new redneck friend," and Sammy kind of laughed without finding it at all funny. But he quickly made one true friend, another SAE pledge and a fellow golf-team member named Billy Armfield. Billy, a prep-school sophisticate, urged Sammy to retire his tan sport coat from home and invest in one good blue blazer from Julian's College Shop in Chapel Hill. Sam did. Things were looking up.

• • •

Well, Ryan was right. It just went away. Margot's scare was for naught. She wasn't going to need a babysitter anytime soon, and Ryan wasn't going to have to learn how to change a diaper as a senior in high school. No baby was coming. Margot's college application process continued apace. There wasn't a four-year school in Michigan that *wouldn't* want her. As for Ryan, if he could find *any* four-year school in Michigan to admit him, that would be an accomplishment.

They went to their senior prom together, just as Ryan's parents had done. They graduated from Alpena High together, just as Ryan's parents had done. By outward appearance, they were a committed high school couple. They had grown up together, and had been together too long to break up. But their pregnancy scare had extinguished the pilot light of young love, and they had no manual to show them how to relight it.

• • •

The first time I saw Pratima was through Tiger's eyes. That was in February 2019 at Riviera Country Club in Pacific Palisades, California, at the Genesis Invitational, a tournament that Trevino and the generations before his all called L.A. That week, Woods was named as the tournament host, its first since Glen Campbell. As Arnold Palmer and Jack Nicklaus had invitational events, Woods would now have one, too. His educational foundation would become the tournament's main beneficiary.

You almost can't overstate Tiger's commitment to his foundation and to education. Earl Woods, Tiger's father, grew up in Manhattan, Kansas, in difficult circumstances. He had ten siblings, full and half, and his parents died before he turned sixteen. And still he was able to graduate from Manhattan High School at seventeen and then, four years later, Kansas State, where he played baseball and was in ROTC. Earl was a career .400 talker, and he spoke regularly about how his college experiences, good, bad, and otherwise, improved his life. Tiger was raised on that. He had an affinity for young people trying to find their way in the world against heavy odds, as his father had.

After six long days at Riviera and a lot of wet, cold, lousy weather, Woods was exhausted by Sunday afternoon, when the tournament was mercifully wrapping up. He wearily climbed the fifty or so hillside steps from the eighteenth green to Riviera's sprawling Spanish Revival clubhouse, where he would sign his final-round scorecard and do one last series of interviews with various rights holders, broadcast partners, and actual reporters. In the trade, we call this conveyor belt of chat "the car wash." His shoes seemed heavy.

Tiger's Sunday golf was workmanlike, and he had made up no ground on the leader. He posted a top-twenty finish. Ho-hum, for him. But the big picture of his golfing life was looking better. He was putting together the pieces he needed for what he hoped would be both an athletic comeback and a public-image makeover.

Five months earlier, after a trying and barren half decade—no wins, two surgeries, a case of the chip yips, a DUI arrest, plus other indignities—Woods had won his eightieth PGA Tour event. That was at the Tour Championship at East Lake in Atlanta. Tiger raised his arms in victory, and the ground shook. For many of his fans, Tiger's past was his past, and all that mattered was his now and his next.

The sanctuary of the Riviera clubhouse was right in front of him. Standing in his path was a young woman with a dark complexion and long black hair, about a foot shorter than Tiger. Not much gets Tiger to stop, but he did. He saw this young woman, and his entire face seemed to break into a smile. He hugged her, put his arm around her shoulder in a fatherly way, and invited her to walk with him as he made his appointed post-tournament rounds.

I was standing there. I had never seen this young woman and could think of only one other time when an unexpected face got such a warm response from Woods. (In that instance, Tiger's niece, Cheyenne Woods, had shown up at a tournament with no advance notice.) Was this mystery person a long-lost cousin? A Tiger Woods Foundation student? I had no idea.

I emailed Glenn Greenspan, Tiger's main PR person, hoping he could make an ID. Glenn wrote back immediately, and that was when I saw the name of Nepal's best female golfer for the first time: *Pratima Sherpa*.

He pointed me to the Oliver Horovitz piece in *Golf Digest* and Tom Rinaldi's ESPN documentary. I hadn't seen either. (For this report, I have mined their work, deeply, with gratitude and admiration.) In time, I learned about Pratima's first trip to the United States, when she spent those five summer weeks with the Montanos. And the second one, to New York for the premiere of the ESPN documentary, followed by the impromptu trip to Florida to see Tiger. And a third trip, where she was recognized by Billie Jean King's organization, the Women's Sports Foundation. Now Pratima was on her fourth trip to the U.S., living again with the Montano family, but enrolled at Santa Barbara City College and a member of its golf team. As an athlete at UCLA is a Bruin, an athlete at SBCC is a Vaquero, Spanish for cattle herder. Pratima was a Vaquero. She told all this to Tiger.

"No way!" Tiger said.

"Yes!" said Pratima.

Later, I began an email correspondence with Pratima, followed by text exchanges and phone conversations. I interviewed her in person. I got a driving-range lesson from her. *OMG* (to use one of her preferred phrases). Pratima was a force field of positive energy, without being kooky about it. I don't know about your experience, but in mine, that's a combination you seldom see.

As Pratima told me about her life and what she wanted to do with it, I was struck by how realistic and candid she sounded. How honest and straightforward. She had a dream, but she wasn't spouting dreamland stuff. All the while, you could sense her life-is-good spirit. You'd bottle it, if you could.

I asked Pratima, more than two years after the event, what she remembered about that Sunday at Riviera on the final day of the 2019 Genesis Invitational.

As Tiger was in the midst of another fresh start to his life, so was she, living with the Montano family again, but now in the United States on an education visa. She was trying to get a California driver's license, and her American father, Michael Montano, was giving her tough-love instruction. (*You're braking too fast. Stay in your lane. Look over your shoulder.*) Pratima was far more comfortable driving a golf ball on a narrow fairway than driving a car on California's freeways, and nobody was more surprised than Pratima when she passed her driver's license test on her first try.

Pratima secured a ticket for the last round of the tournament at Riviera and followed Tiger for all eighteen holes. She had hoped to say hi to him, but when she saw the size of the crowd following him, she realized that would never happen. Then Pratima, with help from one of Tiger's foundation people, got herself to the top of the steps beside the Riviera clubhouse, in a spot where all the players walked by. She was right where she needed to be when Tiger was two paces from the clubhouse. He stopped (rare!), looked her way, and said, "Pratima!" Pratima was describing what I saw, standing there that day. But she was adding things I could not have known. Her arms, she said, were tingling.

"I didn't think he'd remember my name," Pratima said. A reasonable assumption. Tiger had met her briefly, ten months earlier, on the other side of the country. He might have met a hundred or more people since then. But he had also read about Pratima, watched the ESPN documentary about her, and written her a warm and encouraging letter.

Pratima described how they walked together down a pathway beside the clubhouse. It was a vivid memory for me. Tiger said something like, "Wanna help me with my interviews?" And then he got swept away. The demands that come with being Tiger Woods.

Two months after the Riviera event, Woods won his fifth Masters. A hundred headline-writers reached for the same word: *comeback*. Two months after that, the U.S. Open was played at Pebble Beach. A friend of the Montano family invited Pratima to watch one of the practice rounds and play two nearby courses. A four-hour drive there. Three magical days of playing and watching golf. A four-hour drive back home. She couldn't get over the seventeenth hole at Pebble Beach, a long par-3 usually played into the wind. She imagined herself hitting driver there. She followed the tournament, won by Gary Woodland with a remarkable par on seventeen on Sunday, where he hit a pitch shot from the green for his second shot. Woods finished eleven shots back. After Pebble, Tiger and his family—his mother, his two kids, his girlfriend—went to Thailand, where Tiger's mother, Tida, was born and raised. June 2019. Tiger was on top of the world.

Twenty months later, two days after the conclusion of the 2021 Genesis Invitational, Woods drove off the side of a dry, empty suburban Los Angeles road while traveling at twice the speed limit. He never put his foot on the brake, an investigating officer said. The opposite. The accelerator, the police report said, was virtually floored when the car made impact with a tree, which caused the car to be upended. Tiger's car was mangled, and Tiger's body was, too. His career as a tournament golfer, by his own admission, changed forever that day. It cannot be easy, being Tiger Woods. Pratima doesn't pretend otherwise.

"I think he's had a lot of suffering in his life, but I also think he does a lot of meditating, and that must help," Pratima told me. She said that because she knew what her meditation did for her. In her meditative breathing, she said, she could actually hear the challenges of her life. Pratima seemed to have a keen sense of Tiger. I felt like she could see him and hear him in a way I did not.

"Buddhist teach go inside, deep to soul, and correct bad thing to be a good thing," Tida once told Doug Ferguson, the Associated Press golf writer. Tiger's mother was talking about how Buddhist practice and tradition could benefit her son. Tida didn't have the benefit of a university education, but she was smart, tough, and driven. Her path from Thailand to Augusta National, her green-coated son beside her, was about as likely as the one Pratima took from the Royal Nepal maintenance shed to the Medalist driving range, Tiger Woods standing beside her.

"My dad would say to me, 'Enjoy every moment of your life,'" Pratima said. Our conversation had shifted from Pratima's golf to her interior life, if that's a shift at all. "I said to my dad, 'How can you enjoy every moment? How can you enjoy being sad?' He said, 'You cannot know happy if you don't know sad. You have to understand both. When you know both, then you are mature, then you have balance, then you are good.' I will always remember that he said that. That's how I try to live."

When I watch the ESPN documentary about Pratima, one moment always stops me. It comes during Pratima's going-away party at the end of her five-week summer stay at the Montano house in the summer of '17, when she was seventeen.

An older gent with a vaguely British accent asks Pratima, "On the golf course, since you've been here, how did you do? Did you do okay?"

"Of course I won the tournament," Pratima says, laughing. It was a bit of a non sequitur, but in that setting, who could possibly care?

Pratima is the picture of contentment at that gathering. It is by no means her only mood. Michael Montano, Pratima's host father, captured, by way of photography and videography, other sides of Pratima during her stay: Pratima in the gym, Pratima at the driving range, Pratima taking a lesson. Pratima treating her game as work. But that afternoon was reserved for dessert.

"Oh, you did!" the older gent says, processing her on-course success. "Congratulations."

"Yeah," Pratima says, in that easy California way.

From those ten seconds, you might have guessed Pratima had been living in that house for seventeen years. We see what we see, and we extrapolate the rest. Right?

"Later that night, I was sobbing," Pratima told me. Just as Tanya Montano had been.

I asked Pratima why.

"Because it was hard to leave Nepal, and now it would be hard to go back," she said. "Because I would be leaving my American family. Because my parents never had a chance to see anything like what I was seeing."

• • •

As seniors at Chapel Hill, Billy Armfield and Sammy Reeves made a Christmastime road trip that Sammy could not have imagined in his Thomaston boyhood. Billy's father was in the textile business in Greensboro, North Carolina, and each winter, Billy's family rented a tall wood-shingled Victorian home between the golf course and the ocean at The Breakers, a resort in the heart of Palm Beach, Florida. The Armfields needed their Cadillac there and their steamer trunks, too. Billy picked up Sammy in Thomaston. They made their way to U.S. 1 and drove south down the Florida coastline. In a car that big, weighed down by all that luggage, you never drove over thirty-five miles an hour. A long trip and a good time.

Billy was short and dapper and smooth. Sam was tall and lean and earnest. The closest thing Billy had to a drink was TruAde, out of a bottle, through a straw. (What Yoo-hoo is to chocolate milk, TruAde was to orange juice.) Sam didn't abstain from alcohol (Billy did), but he never touched hard liquor. At their fraternity, SAE, that put them in a minority, decidedly so. They were both drawn to golf in ways most of their fraternity buddies could not understand. They both had a close relationship with a father who knew his way around the South and its cotton gins. They both read and knew there was a world beyond the Mason-Dixon Line. They had traveled to Europe together. They wanted to go places where people didn't speak English and didn't want to. In their crowd, that was not the norm.

Billy's father was a member at the Everglades Club, an elite club on Worth Avenue in Palm Beach, and knew people at Seminole Golf Club, with its pink clubhouse and oceanfront Donald Ross course. Seminole was about ten miles north of The Breakers, and Mr. Armfield helped arrange for his namesake son and his son's college friend to play it. Sammy had never seen a course anything like it, built through the dunes, on the ocean, your body and ball windblown from start to finish, every shot requiring shape, including every putt. He was struck by the way the midday sun illuminated the ocean by the seventeenth tee. It was translucent. In the weak light of early morning, when he and Billy had gone for a swim in the ocean by The Breakers, the water had been dark and unforgiving. He marveled at the change.

Sammy knew a thing or two about Seminole before he got there. The club's head pro was Claude Harmon, winner of the 1948 Masters. The club president was George Coleman, an industrialist and widely known golf personage. Every winter, Ben Hogan spent a month in Palm Beach, playing golf at Seminole and hitting balls on its range. When Billy and Sammy got to the course, there was Hogan, on the practice tee. Hogan! Sammy felt he was at the epicenter of golf.

Hogan was not one to make eye contact with strangers. He certainly wasn't going to make idle chat with a couple of college kids. Billy and Sammy knew that. This was a man with an aura. Billy and Sammy were scared out of their minds. They hit about three balls, where they could see Hogan but he couldn't see them, and then dashed to the first tee. The power of his presence was overwhelming.

Billy and Sammy were already connected, and sharing that experience—Hogan, Seminole, the finishing holes on the ocean—brought them even closer. Five weeks later, Billy's father was dead. Cancer, and it was quick. After that, they were like brothers.

•   •   •

Ryan's girlfriend, Margot, with her stellar academic record at Alpena High, got a generous financial offer from Michigan State and enrolled there. She hoped her undergraduate years would be a first step toward a career in health care. She was off to East Lansing.

Ryan tried to get the attention of some college golf coaches. A few Division III schools showed modest interest. Nobody was beating down his door. He could shoot even par on an easy course on a good day. But so could thousands of other high school golfers.

Ryan got himself invited to play with the Lansing Community College golf team in the summer after he graduated from Alpena

High. The two-year school had a much decorated coach, Tom Blake, who was named coach of the year by his peer group (coaches of two-year schools in Michigan) on a half dozen occasions. His name was in the Lansing paper regularly, for playing in county and city tournaments, for signing players, for holding open tryouts, for writing guest columns. In one piece, he wrote, *I try to instill in our players that it's a privilege to be playing the club we're at and at the end of the round the course should be in better shape than when we teed off.* Who could argue with that?

Ryan played well in that audition round, and Coach Blake told him on the spot he had a place on the team if he wanted it. Ryan wanted it. Years later, Coach Blake could still remember how well Ryan had played that day. He was a fast player, which meant he knew what he was doing. He was long, which meant he could reach par-5s in two shots. And he was strong, which meant he could play out of the rough.

Later that summer, Ryan and his father made a second trip to Lansing so that Ryan could sign up for classes, find an apartment, get himself settled, and start his college life. Life after Alpena. On that trip, he joined the team for a round, his first as a member. He played in a group with Coach Blake and two new teammates. They were playing golf gambling games that Ryan could barely understand for stakes he didn't know. Ryan's worry only increased when he saw that Coach Blake had a separate scorecard to keep track of all the action. Ryan's game fell apart.

His father came to the course to pick him up after the round.

"I need money," Ryan said, almost panicking. He told his father that he had lost about two hundred dollars gambling on the course. He had forty dollars in his wallet. He was on the hook for the rest, cash money, no IOUs allowed.

"*What?*" Howard said.

His son's staggering first-day debt offended Howard's frugal nature. In Howard's regular game at Alpena, if you lost or made ten dollars in a round, that was high rolling. More significantly, Howard had not brought Ryan to Lansing Community College, with its well-regarded golf team run by its well-regarded coach, so his son could piss away huge sums he didn't have.

Jesus Christ, Jesus Christ. Gee. Zuss. Christ.

Howard was in psychic pain. Still, he reached into his wallet and withdrew the balance Ryan owed.

That's Ryan's telling of the incident. (Coach Blake tells it differently.) Whatever happened, Ryan left the course with his account settled. That was the one thing he accomplished on his first day with the team.

• • •

Golf courses, when described by Pratima, sound like outdoor sanctuaries. She tends to talk fast, but when the subject turns to golf courses she knows and loves, the words tumble out, she is so happy. Soule Park, the public course near the Montano home, in the Topatopa Mountains. The two courses at the Monterey Peninsula Country Club, which she played when she attended the U.S. Open at Pebble Beach, with an emphatic nod to the various holes that sneak up on the Pacific. Royal Nepal in Kathmandu, between the city's Ring Road and the country's international airport: her home course and her home period, all cramped nine holes of it, the course she would play if she had only one round left. She'd go around twice or more, especially if the game fell during October and November, when the monsoon season is over, the humidity is low, overnight dew hangs on the juniper branches through midmorning, and your golf ball, sitting there in the fairway, practically shines.

"In Kathmandu, the air is dusty, it's polluted, but when I get on the golf course, I'm in heaven," Pratima said. "The air is clean. I can breathe. The smell of it—it gives me peace."

We were at Rio Hondo, a popular public course in Downey, California, two miles from the first McDonald's. There was a two-tiered driving range, and we were on its top deck, sitting on a metal bench.

It was a hot summer weekend day. Some of the golfers had umbrellas attached to their pushcarts. The electric carts all had roofs, for protection from the sun. They also had drink holders and spaces for food. There was a snack stand with an open window, cold beers and warm hot dogs coming through it at a steady clip. A golfer in a cart headed from the snack stand to the tenth tee while looking at his scorecard on the steering wheel, his front nine all marked up, the back nine a line of empty squares waiting for scores. There was a middle-aged woman behind the counter in the pro shop. Every ten minutes or so, the starter would call a foursome to the first tee over a speaker system and by surname. It was a United Nations of golfers. Pratima knew the whole scene intimately, right down to the kid on the practice putting green with three balls and a face that was all business. There was always a kid like that there.

On the driving range, on its second tier, there was another young woman, at least a half foot taller than Pratima, a few years younger, who was pounding one shot after another. But there was something off, even unsettling, about the way she was going about her work. Her backswing was out of a textbook, but there was a fierceness to her downswing, like she was looking to hurt something. Pratima had nothing like that in her swing. This tall girl had white earbuds in her ears, and she would stop to adjust them now and again, club leaning against her leg as if it were an appendage. Lots of young golfers Pratima knew practiced that way, listening to start-me-up music or a coach's instructions or white noise to block out the rest of the world.

Pratima wanted none of that. She didn't even like wearing a golf glove. She was trying to get as close to her golf ball as she could, in a manner of speaking. You know: *Stop thinking, let things happen, and be the ball.* Yes, *Caddyshack.* From the same scene: *Turn off all the sound.* Why would you want to bring *in* earbuds and all that sound? Nature was sacred to Pratima, and golf was nature. She wasn't trying to manipulate anything in her golf.

"People say, 'Oh, you play golf—that's nice,'" Pratima said. In other words, golf is a pleasant hobby, a good weekend activity. Nope, not for Pratima. "It's so much more than that. Golf is—"

Sorry to interrupt, but would you mind if we *didn't* commit Pratima to a definition just now? I've known people in their seventies and eighties and nineties who have spent their lives trying to finish that thought, trying to put into words what golf is. Ms. Sherpa was just twenty-two, on that day at Rio Hondo. Can we give her a few decades here?

• • •

In time, Billy Armfield introduced Sammy to Betsy Webb of Asheville, North Carolina. Betsy was enrolled at Duke, ten miles from Chapel Hill, when Sammy started dating her. Sammy was finding his get-the-girl charm gear. He became a talker, a storyteller, a bartender, a reader, a conversationalist. With his pressed blue Julian's College Shop blazer at hand, he was ready for anything, Betsy often beside him, along with Billy Armfield and Billy's girlfriend. The mid-fifties in America. Double-dating was a way of life. Car ownership was surging, and Sammy now had his own car, with Georgia plates. There were drive-in theaters, new interstate highways, and malt shops that stayed open late. You could place your order without ever leaving your car.

In his sophomore, junior, and senior years, Sammy did not go out for the varsity golf team at Carolina. Other players were miles ahead of him, and those guys, playing tournament golf all summer, were only getting better. Sammy wanted to work, and that's what he did, for and with his father. He continued to play golf, but it was more a now-and-then thing. Sammy's plan was to graduate from UNC right on schedule in May 1956 and join the Air Force as a second lieutenant (the major benefit of his Air Force ROTC program) with money in the bank. Marriage to Betsy, he hoped, would come after he had completed his Air Force service. His grades were good, and his test scores were excellent. All he needed to do was pass the physical.

• • •

Almost from the start of his days at Lansing Community College, Ryan found himself trying to amuse and shock his parents with his stories from the golf team under Coach Tom Blake. Fasten your seat belts, because the golf road in this next part gets a little bumpy. (Coach Blake's account of these same events appears at the end of this joyride.) Ryan and his brother both had the instinct to share and sometimes overshare. Ginny French had gone back to grad school and was now working as an addiction counselor. She encouraged people to be open and honest. "But that doesn't mean you have to tell me *everything*," she would sometimes tell her sons. That didn't seem to register with Ryan. He told the saga of his two years on the golf team at Lansing Community College in real time, and as an ongoing soap opera.

Ryan told his parents how often he smoked pot with various teammates. He told them how, while on a road trip in Indiana, Coach Blake tripped on a curb on his way out of a liquor store and dropped a case of liquor, breaking at least one bottle. He told them about all the gambling the team did. He told his parents about the team parties at Coach Blake's apartment and the copious amounts of underage drinking.

And then came the pièce de résistance, the season-ending trip to North Carolina for the National Junior College Division II golf championship, played on the Maples Course of the Woodlake Country Club, about twenty miles from Pinehurst. Five players, one coach, one van.

The trip came at the end of Ryan's second year at Lansing Community College. The second day of this four-day tournament fell on his twenty-first birthday. His parents drove to the tournament from Alpena, a fifteen-hour trip, to watch their son play and to celebrate his birthday. He shot a first-round 84. Terrible, but most of the field did not break 80 on that Monday.

At the stroke of midnight, Monday became Tuesday, and Ryan French became twenty-one. He was legal. He and his coach and others celebrated by going to a strip club, getting drunk, and closing the place at three in the morning.

Later that morning, but not much later, Ryan was over his first shot of the day. He had not hit a single warm-up shot. He could barely hear himself think through his raging headache. He had a driver in hand. The hole was a short par-4. He had one swing thought, and it was not a study in the power of positive thinking.

I could whiff this.

He didn't.

He caught it, long and straight. For his second shot, he had a wedge into the green. Standing over it, he had a new thought.

Maybe I'll be okay.

He sculled the shot. It was a line-drive screamer that went fifty or more yards over the green before dying in a lake. As he walked to the pond, trying to figure out where to drop, he had his third cogent thought of the day.

I'm not going to be okay.

By midafternoon, the temperature had reached 95 degrees. Ryan decided to take off his socks and shoes and play barefoot. More than once, he vomited in the woods. He said to a playing partner, a good player from Tyler Junior College in Texas, "Are you *ever* going to put back a fucking pin?" It was a bizarre comment from Ryan, as he was normally the most even-tempered person in his group, wherever he was playing. His parents were aghast at . . . *everything*.

Ryan shot 92, his highest tournament score in years and one of the highest scores shot by any player that day. He was *not* leaving the course in better shape than he had found it. There was no birthday celebration that night.

Tyler Junior College won the tournament. Lansing finished ninth of thirteen teams. The team loaded the van for the twelve-hour drive back to school, five players, one coach, all of them worse for wear.

To Ryan, the highlight reel of his Lansing Community golf-team experience was like a trailer for an *Animal House* sequel. That's how he shared these events with his parents.

But that's not how they took Ryan's stories. Ginny and Howard figured it was just luck that was keeping their son out of a jail cell or an emergency room. They were worried for the next group of kids on the team. After a lot of kitchen-table debate, and against Ryan's wishes, they called the president of Lansing Community College to tell him what they knew about the college golf team under Coach Tom Blake.

Over twenty years after he last saw Ryan, Tom Blake remembered Ryan well but their interactions differently. He said he had never heard anything about Ryan's parents calling the Lansing Community College president. If it happened, the college president didn't take up the matter with him. He said in his twelve years as coach, he never had any conversation with the college president. It was a part-time job. When Coach Blake was at Lansing Community in the late 1990s, the most he was paid was four thousand dollars a year. His main job was selling life and health insurance and retirement plans. His path to the Lansing Community College golf team was an unusual one. He had played on the team, as a student in his mid-thirties.

Coach Blake said of Ryan, "He had a strong personality, and sometimes it was tough to rein him in. He liked to be the center of attention and was outstandingly vulgar much of the time. I got to know his father some. The father might have been tough to deal with, and Ryan might have grown up a little angry and rebellious."

In that first gambling match, Coach Blake said, it was Ryan and the coach against two of his favorite returning players. He said that Ryan played well but the other guys played better, and with presses and the other wagering, the losses came to sixty dollars, not two hundred, and that he, not Ryan's father, had covered Ryan's losses. Regarding gambling on his team, he said, "I don't think it's illegal. It's probably not recommended. I want to see how a player is when he's losing, how he handles it emotionally."

Coach Blake did recall buying and breaking a single bottle of liquor while on a team trip to Indiana. "I bought a bottle of Maker's Mark that was probably ten dollars less than it would have been in Michigan. And as I'm unloading the trunk, unpacking to get into the hotel, I dropped the silly thing that I had just paid thirty dollars for. I'm like, 'Great, that was money well spent.' Just dropped it in the parking lot, and it smashed. So I had to clean up a mess, and I was out thirty bucks. So that's true. But it wasn't for the team's use. It was for me to bring back to Michigan."

Regarding team parties at the coach's home, Coach Blake said, "Did some of the guys come by and hang out? Yes. And if you want to have a beer or two with me, that's fine with me. Is that something that's technically illegal? Yeah, although some of the guys were over twenty-one, and some of the guys were not. So we're all together. We're here as a group."

Coach Blake remembered the night Ryan turned twenty-one, and remembered going to a strip club with him that night. "I don't want to offer too much, but another coach and I wanted to take him out to celebrate, along with another player," Coach Blake said. "We went to a local topless place, and we were there for like twenty or thirty minutes. He didn't get drunk with me because I'm not going to be buying expensive beers at a topless place. We just wanted to have a good time and hang out with the guys and then go back to our rooms. All the rest of anything there is total embellishment."

As for Ryan being hungover for the second round of the event, Coach Blake said, "That's on him. If he was hungover, I don't know where he got it, but I wasn't the provider, that's for sure."

The ride home was the ride home. Finishing ninth of thirteen teams, it is what it is. Pretty mediocre. Twelve hours in a van is twelve hours in a van.

• • •

Pratima spent a year and a half at Santa Barbara City College, a two-year school. Her golf was superb, and she shot a bunch of tournament scores in the mid-70s. To shoot in the mid-70s, pencil in hand and everything in the hole, is a significant accomplishment for almost any amateur golfer, playing in any kind of tournament. (Bobby Jones: "You may take it from me, there are two types of golf. There is golf—and tournament golf. And they are not at all the same thing.") For two seasons, she was the best or second-best player on the SBCC women's golf team. She was a star Vaquero. Those initial Saturday-morning clinics at Royal Nepal were now half her life ago.

There were many challenges. Extreme bouts of homesickness. The death, in a helicopter crash, of a prominent Nepali business-man who had shown keen interest in Pratima's golf and growth. Language barriers of a subtle nature. She had signed up for a public speaking class. She despised it and wanted to drop it.

And alongside the challenges, a series of successes. Her car driving was improving (though she never got the knack of paral-lel parking). She was majoring in business management, and her grades were excellent. Her favorite class turned out to be the one she initially wanted to drop, COMM 131, Fundamentals of Public Speaking. She was adapting to American life. She was getting ac-customed to her second culture.

On campus, Pratima saw her classmates stand up for themselves in ways that were new to her. In Nepal, your station in life pre-dicts how private disagreements get settled. Deference is built into the Nepali social system, based on a cryptic hierarchical formula that mixes caste, religion, wealth, and gender. In America, Pratima discovered, "stand your ground" is part of the national character. Maybe her sample pool was limited, but that was her take.

This broad subject showed up in Pratima's golf because ev-erything in her life showed up in Pratima's golf. During a college tournament in Los Angeles, Pratima encountered a scorekeeping problem that she could have filed under honest mistake. Disagree-ments of this sort can quickly get ugly, because before long, the real issue becomes a person's integrity. In this case, Pratima's opponent was claiming a score that Pratima knew to be wrong.

"You have to be careful with the rules," Pratima said. "The rules are like ethics. They give golf discipline. They can be tricky. Some-times you have a question like, 'Where did the ball cross the hazard, and where do you drop?' And the player says, 'You have to use rule blah-blah-blah and drop here.' And I'm like, 'Is that right?' But I'm cautious. I'll say, 'I think this is the rule.' I'll always say *think*." But this issue had nothing to do with parsing complex options in the rule book. It was about counting shots.

Pratima then described a scene that came at the end of a tournament round. She and another golfer, from another school, were comparing scorecards. That is a standard part of tournament golf. You compare cards, make sure everything is correct, and then sign and submit them. There are two signatures on a card that attest to its accuracy, from the player and the player's scorekeeper, who is another player in the group. Tournament golf is never played alone.

"The other girl marked six on a par-five where she had made seven," Pratima said. "People are like, 'What's the difference, a six or a seven?' But in golf, that one shot can be everything.

"So we're checking our scores, and I say, 'No, it was a seven.' And she says, 'No, it was a six.' Like that's the final word. So I say, 'Do you want to go out to the hole? I can show you where you hit every shot.' She says yes. We get in a cart. She's driving. We get out there. We get to the hole, and we're going around. I say, 'You hit it here, then you hit it here, then you hit it here,' and I go all the way to the hole, for seven. And she says, 'No, it was six.'"

Now, on some unspoken level, each woman is calling the other a liar.

"Are you getting mad at this point?" I asked.

"No, not mad," Pratima said. "I try not to get mad. It doesn't help. I learned that from my father."

But Pratima was not going to just let a shot played vanish into nothingness. That's not golf, at least not tournament golf.

They returned—two silent players in one cart—to the scoring area. Golfers and coaches were milling about. Pratima said to her opponent, "Do you want me to ask the other girls?" There were two other players in the group.

The question Pratima posed changed something. Maybe the girl was afraid of what the other players might say. Maybe she didn't want the circle of mistrust around her expanding. Whatever it was, her tune changed suddenly. "Then she was like, 'Oh, you're right. Oh my God, now I do remember.'" Her 6 became a 7.

"The whole thing was quite challenging," Pratima said. "I was actually kind of scared. I was new to everything then."

Pratima's handling of the situation was flawless. Of course, such a dispute shouldn't happen in the first place, but human nature is human nature. Some people can't handle facts, numbers, reality, unfavorable results. Those people really must be called out early, or they will become empowered. Yes, there are applications beyond golf.

Anyway, you hope the girl learned something that day. For Pratima, it was her first brush with stand your ground American-style. But every golfer has the responsibility to do what Pratima did. There's a phrase in tournament golf that covers this subject: *Protect the field.*

People describe golf as a game of honor. It is. Golfers call penalties on themselves that nobody else sees. But it's also a game where players police one another. Those two systems work in tandem, an internal do-the-right-thing mechanism and outside policing. They are the yin and yang of a kosher scorecard.

When Pratima's father spoke of what it means to be mature— *then you are mature, then you have balance*—it's as if he knew that playing golf ethically requires maturity. Pasang Sherpa wasn't a golfer, but he had picked up the essence of the game from his daughter, by osmosis. Golf had been part of Pratima's life for nearly all her life. That's one of the many good things that comes from starting golf at an early age: The sense of responsibility for the scorecard, your own or somebody else's, becomes ingrained. Really, it's a way of showing respect for others.

Jack Nicklaus learned this lesson at age eleven in a junior event in Ohio. An annoyed little Jack got hot and whacked away a ball without finishing a hole in a stroke-play event. His playing-partner buddy called him on it. Nicklaus never forgot. I love seeing kids play golf without an adult in sight. You know they're going to figure out ways to adjudicate any oddness that might come up. A guiding principle of golf's rule book is fairness.

Pratima did two years' worth of classwork at Santa Barbara in her eighteen months there. As 2019 turned into 2020, Pratima was looking for a new place to land—for a four-year school in Southern California where she could get a scholarship, play on the golf team, and finish her coursework for a bachelor's degree in business management. She found one school, and one school found her. All the while, a nasty virus was coming ashore by boat and plane, by foot and car. You couldn't see it, but it was everywhere.

• • •

Sammy Reeves flunked his Air Force physical. If you wanted to sit in the cockpit of a United States Air Force plane, you had to have perfect vision. Sammy didn't pass the eye test. His lifelong nearsightedness. With glasses, his distance vision was fine, but not without them. In ways, he viewed this handicap in a positive light. He knew he saw the world differently than other people did. His eyesight wasn't good enough for the Air Force, but it was good enough for the U.S. Army, and that was where he landed, by way of the draft. To the Army, Sammy's four years of Air Force ROTC and all the Tar Heel glory meant nothing. Ditto for his BS in business and his blue Chapel Hill blazer. In the Army, he'd be another buck private, another grunt, likely in a platoon with loads of other Georgia boys, the whole lot of them running and chanting "Sound Off" in their familiar brogues.

• • •

After finishing two years at Lansing Community College, Ryan French enrolled at Michigan State. Margot was in her junior year there, and now he was, too. They were still a couple. Margot lived in an off-campus apartment, and Ryan got one just down the street from her. In theory, he was a full-time student, although he was more devoted to tossing pizza doughs, clearing tables, and making money at Mark's Pizza on Grand River Avenue, the major thoroughfare in East Lansing. Before long, Ryan was one of Mark's prized shift managers.

For the first time since he was six, golf was not a high priority for Ryan, even though affordable golf was available to him. Michigan State had two golf courses, West and East, both with discounted green fees for students. West was considered far better than East. The West course was the home of the Michigan State golf team, it was more challenging than the East, and it was in far better condition. It was also more expensive. When Ryan played, which wasn't often, he played the East. Whatever he saved, he'd spend on Jack Daniel's and Cokes. But more significantly, he realized that golf with his father, and golf with teammates, was what he knew and liked. Without his father, without teammates, golf didn't mean much.

Margot graduated right on time and with distinction. Ryan did, too, minus the distinction. He was permitted to walk with the Class of 2000, but he still had coursework to complete. His major was Interdisciplinary Studies in Social Science, considered the easiest major at Michigan State. He went to graduation, did his last bit of makeup coursework, and his diploma showed up at his apartment. That same day, he received another university communiqué, a letter telling Ryan that he was being placed on academic probation. It's a big school.

The graduation ceremony had been in May. Three months later, Margot and Ryan got married.

• • •

All through her time at Santa Barbara City College, Pratima was aware of the ocean, the mountains, and the vast distance that separated California from Nepal and Pratima from her parents. But then the pandemic arrived, and what had been merely a vast distance became an impassable chasm. After finishing up her classes and golf season at SBCC in May 2020, Pratima had planned to fly home. But she couldn't. There were no flights into Nepal. The pandemic had stopped the world.

Pratima's parents were still living in the Royal Nepal maintenance shed. She wasn't even thinking of it as her girlhood "golf house" anymore. Golf didn't seem like golf. Golf didn't seem important. All that mattered to Pratima was her parents and their health.

Like millions of others during the pandemic, Pratima went into a mental funk. She wasn't depressed, not in the common clinical sense. She was active. She had been admitted into Cal State L.A., where Billie Jean King had gone to school. She was taking classes. She was hitting balls and playing. But she was going through the motions. She was in a daze. Pratima's worry about her parents was like a low-grade fever that wouldn't abate. A friend died. A relative died. All the news was about illness and death. If she heard from her father, her first thought was: *Is Mom alive?* If she heard from her mother, she had the same first thought but about her father. In the back of her mind, always, was a single question: *Will I ever see my parents again?*

All that California sunshine and freedom wasn't doing Pratima a damn bit of good. She had her American family to hold her hand, literally and otherwise. The Montanos and Pratima had developed a close bond. "I could tell my American mom anything," Pratima told me. She could tell her American mom things that she couldn't tell her actual mother because she didn't want her mother, eight thousand miles away, to worry more than she already was. But all Pratima really wanted was to hold her parents as they once held her. When she was a newborn who could not see. When she had returned from her first Saturday-morning clinic at Royal Nepal. When she was making her first trip to the United States at age seventeen. All Pratima wanted was to get home. Nepal home. *Home* home.

At her first chance, when Tribhuvan International Airport reopened for international travel, she did. Pratima got home and discovered that her mother was barely eating and was losing weight. She began monitoring her mother's oxygen level. The readings were dangerously low. Pratima knew her mother most likely had COVID-19, but she had no access to home test kits. She was in an impoverished country again. Not that Pratima ever thought of it that way. But you could fit a world in between where she had been (Southern California) and where she was, her family's isolated and repurposed maintenance shed on the Royal Nepal golf course.

Late one night, on the edge of panic, Pratima got her mother to a hospital. It was overwhelmed with patients, and Kalpana was put in a hallway. Pratima did not leave her side. Dead people on gurneys were passing by. Kalpana was tested, and she had COVID, but Pratima quickly realized that her mother would be better at home—as long as she could get oxygen there. She asked a doctor if that could happen. Doctors are gods in Nepal. They're not accustomed to being asked anything, especially by young unmarried women. But Pratima's American stand-your-ground experience was part of her now. A doctor relented. Pratima took her mother and an oxygen tank home.

Pratima was home. She was a college student in America. Her golf and intelligence and charm got her there, and the experiences were enriching her life immeasurably. But Nepal was home.

• • •

After graduation from the University of North Carolina, and before reporting for basic training at Fort Jackson in Columbia, South Carolina, Sammy checked in to a motel in Asheville, Betsy's hometown, and played in an invitational golf tournament at the Biltmore Forest Country Club, where Betsy's family had long enjoyed a membership. Billy Armfield, also Army-bound, was with him. They figured it would be their final golf fling for a long while, but that was secondary. For Sammy, the tournament and the events around it were all part of the courtship of Betsy Webb. That was his main reason for being there. Billy, who had thrown the young couple together in the first place, was his wingman.

If you wanted to marry a girl like Betsy from a family like the Webbs in a town like Asheville, you had to know how to navigate various and proper courting rituals. That was Billy's advice to his closest friend. The challenges of such courting, Asheville-style, quickly became evident to Sammy. Betsy's father, R. Stanford Webb, expected Sammy to be back in his room early each night, to get the rest he needed for the next day's play. Mr. Webb was an insurance man with a shooting range in his basement and was taciturn by nature. He was Stan to his friends and (of course!) Mr. Webb to Sammy. Stan's wife, who went by Gaga to Sammy from the start, was all about the fun, and she expected Betsy's suitors to be fun, too. Sammy knew there was some Mr. Webb in Betsy—and more Gaga. Gaga, Betsy, Sammy, and Billy stayed out late every night. The tournament went fine. The courtship was proceeding, and then some.

There was a blowtorch pointed at American golf, right about then. Arnold Palmer had won the U.S. Amateur in 1954 and, four years later, the Masters, kicking his leg and tossing his visor in victory. CBS showed it live, and the papers ran the photos the next morning. Everybody saw it. "Arnie's Army" quickly became a thing. Black golfers, many of them war veterans, were taking up golf in large numbers at public courses. The Hogan-Nelson-Snead trio had become a staple of the country's sporting landscape. Hogan was turning the golf swing into a science that anybody could study and master, which made the game seem more democratic. Eisenhower was slipping off to Camp David and playing a lot of duffer golf, and *that* made the game seem democratic. Three formidable American sporting-goods manufacturers (Wilson, Spalding, MacGregor) were going all in on golf equipment, trying to meet increasing demand. Courses were being built at a rate never seen before. Driving ranges, too. Robert Trent Jones, a Cornell graduate, became America's first homegrown celebrity course architect, and his thing was to work *big*. The Army spent millions of dollars (of taxpayer money) improving and expanding Army courses for the benefit of Army personnel. All of this was good news for Private Reeves.

Sammy had superiors who liked and knew golf and before long he was playing a lot of peacetime golf while drawing an Army paycheck. He was playing in Army golf tournaments, paired with Army men of every rank, from all over the country and from every imaginable background. A decade or so after he started playing afternoon golf with the Black caddies at the Thomaston course, Sammy was playing in Army tournaments with Black golfers, some of whom were fellow privates, while others were his chain-of-command superiors. Some of these Black golfers were loaded with game but had clubs held together by duct tape. Taking his cue from his father, Sammy helped where he could, but quietly. (*I can't hit this driver anymore.*) He played in high-stakes matches with Black partners who had a winning combination of manly grace and joie de vivre. A guy would hole a putt on the last, win all the loot for himself and his partner (often Sammy!), and make sure everybody knew about it. *Cry home to Mama!* (That would be a *tame* example.)

This was all a welcome wake-up call for Sammy Reeves. Nobody was talking like that at the Biltmore Forest Country Club.

Every golfer has had this experience: You see a player with a swing so good you can't help yourself. You have to stop and watch. Sammy experienced this repeatedly in his Army golf but with one golfer in particular, a Black paratrooper from North Carolina named Cliff Harrington. Sammy had never seen a golfer with a more beautiful swing or better rhythm and few golfers with more talent, style, and game. Reeves thought, *This guy could play with Arnold Palmer if he had the chance.*

It was a fantasy. The closest Cliff Harrington came to Arnold Palmer was as his caddie at Pinehurst one day when Palmer and his Wake Forest teammates were playing there. The PGA of America, which oversaw the series of weekly events for the leading touring pros (later known as the tour), prohibited Black golfers from competing. The U.S. Army had been integrated by Harry Truman in 1948, but the PGA of America was all white by its constitution and by its temperament. (It would remain so until 1961.) Had Harrington been white, his play in Army tournaments most likely would have been an apprenticeship for a career as a touring pro. That's what Army golf was for Orville Moody, Tom Nieporte, Billy Maxwell, and other outstanding golfers who weren't Black. In Army tournaments, which offered no prize money, Harrington regularly beat guys who later became rich playing the tour and playing for somebody else's money. On tour, the purses just seemed to magically appear, put up by a sponsor with whom the players shook hands at a cocktail party, if that. For Harrington to make money playing golf, he had to risk his own money. And he did. He knew what he could do and was happy to take his chances. But he also knew there was no pathway to the pro tour for him, not in the late 1950s, when he was in his late twenties and in his prime. He was handsome, lean, talented—and Black. Sammy had a generous thought, about Cliff Harrington and Arnold Palmer in the same tournaments, but it was definitely a fantasy.

Cliff Harrington was killed in 1965 in one of the first battles of the Vietnam War, a search-and-destroy mission known as Operation Hump. His death, at age thirty-four, was part of a U.S. offensive that claimed the lives of forty-nine Americans and hundreds of Viet Cong soldiers. Harrington was a U.S. Army staff sergeant, a hero to many, a gifted golfer, and a victim of time and place. Lee Elder, an Army golfer who later became the first Black golfer to play in the Masters, knew and admired Harrington as a golfer and a man. He said late what Sammy said early, that Harrington could have played with anyone. At the end of his short life, Cliff Harrington was serving in the U.S. Army by choice. But the path of his life, and his options, were defined by his race.

Sammy Reeves was long done with his military service when he heard about Harrington's death. He had played with him only once, on the Army course at Camp Gordon in Augusta, Georgia, during a qualifying round for the All Army Golf Championship. One round can tell you everything about a golfer, if you know what to look for. Reeves was mesmerized by Harrington's long, rhythmic swing, by the variety of his shots, and most especially by his gentlemanly, take-it-in-stride demeanor. Sammy admired Harrington first at close range and later from afar. The news of his death in combat was a jolt.

With every passing year, Sammy was becoming more aware of life's fundamental inequities, more dismayed by the human capacity for brutality. He was like a child sitting alone in shallow surf, wavelets of understanding washing over him. On the golf course, to most of his playing partners, these changes in Sammy were invisible. But he knew. Inside, he was shaking.

•   •   •

Ryan asked Margot to marry him. The Labor Day pregnancy scare was now a half decade old but had woven its way into every aspect of their relationship. On the other hand, being together was all they knew. Margot said yes. They were married in a church in Alpena that had two ministers, one of whom Ryan despised. A groom is famously a decoration at best at his wedding, but on this matter, Ryan was insistent, and the one guy was benched in favor of the minister Ryan could tolerate. For their wedding gift, Ryan's siblings—his sister, Dallas, and brother, Scott—picked up the tab for the honeymoon. The reception was at the civic center in downtown Alpena. Alpena's leading radio personality was the DJ. After a first night in the Alpena Holiday Inn, the newlyweds began their long journey to a Sandals resort in Jamaica. The hotel had a golf course and Ryan rented clubs, went out by himself, made some halfhearted swings, and quit after nine. The young couple returned to Michigan, got set up in a small apartment, and began their lives as husband and wife.

Margot and Ryan moved into a small apartment on Jolly Road in Lansing, behind a sports bar called Leo's Lodge. With his experience at Mark's Pizza under his belt, Ryan got a job as manager of a Qdoba in East Lansing. It was a franchise, one property in a Mexican-fast-food empire run by a man known as Lou Senior. His son, Lou Junior, was his deputy. Senior made the big moves, and Junior—a grown man in his mid-forties with a golf game, a wife, and a daughter—oversaw the many little ones. Senior and Junior liked Ryan's spunk, and by his first anniversary, he was managing three Qdobas. A half decade later, he was up to twelve and had a company car. He and Margot moved to Farmington Hills in suburban Detroit. Margot enrolled in a nursing program. She was a trim person and a careful eater. Ryan was starting to look like a middle-aged dad, though he was neither. He was several inches over six feet, ate a lot of food out of paper bags, wore metal-framed glasses without a nod to the style of the moment, shaved when he felt like it, and tucked in his shirt only when he was around Lou Senior.

Lou Junior, as Ryan saw it up close, had multiple lives. Ryan had been in Junior's house many times and had seen Junior's wife and their daughter. He saw Junior handle all manner of annoying work problems, soda dispensers that didn't dispense, parking lots riddled with potholes, the everyday problems of the fast-food business. Lou Junior was on the scene, sleeves up, ready to figure out a solution. But Ryan saw his boss off duty, too, and there Ryan saw Lou Junior as a man with an immense appetite for card playing, golf-course gambling, drinking, and strip clubs. He wasn't making a judgment. Not at all. Ryan's life was pretty much Junior's life. If Ryan's two years at Lansing Community had prepared him for anything, it was working for Junior. *Work hard, play hard* was an axiom they both knew.

They played golf across Michigan, in East Lansing, Flint, Battle Creek, all over Detroit. They took golf trips to Jacksonville, Pebble Beach, Phoenix, and (of course) Las Vegas. They played in and around Denver when the parent company held its annual conference at the Brown Palace Hotel downtown. There were days that started with store visits, followed by golf games, cards, steak-house dinners, and finally visits to strip clubs, unless they were going to Trumpps in Detroit, a restaurant and strip club in one. Ryan couldn't stand that combination, red meat on his plate and naked dancers in his sight line, but Junior was the boss, and Ryan was along for the ride. There was a lot of slack time. A lot of video blackjack, a lot of storytelling in rooms with no windows and no clocks.

How 'bout that time when Tiger was playing the Buick Open and he goes into the Miller Road store and orders like two bags of food, and Tom's like, "On us." And I'm like, "Tom, why would you give Tiger Woods free food? He's a fucking millionaire!"

Tom was the Miller Road manager. Ryan was his boss. Lou Junior was in the room. *Fuck* and its variants were part of the lingua franca.

That is, in the presence of Lou Junior. Not around Lou Senior. Senior was a model of discipline and comportment. Lou Junior was Lou Junior. One morning during the yearly conference at the Brown Palace, Lou Senior was in the lobby at seven a.m., in his coat and tie, ready for the day's first meeting, as per usual. Ryan, not feeling or looking great, was there, too, right on time. Junior was nowhere to be seen. Senior was steaming.

He went to the front desk and asked for a key for his son's room.
I'm sorry, sir—
I'm paying for that room. A key, please.
He got his key. He was Lou Senior.

Senior and Ryan went to Junior's room. Senior told Ryan to open the door. Junior was out so cold he looked dead. Senior made a U-turn for the elevator. Ryan got Junior up and out. "Alcohol," Ryan later observed, "brings people together."

Golf does, too. Golf and drinking were the shaky foundation of Ryan's relationship with Junior, their various high times paid for by their ability to sell Qdoba's chicken burritos and beef tacos to the large and growing population of rushed, white middle-class people in Michigan who wanted Mexican food that was fast, cheap, and reasonably fresh. They were sitting on a gold mine.

Ryan was making money. He had a high salary, regular bonuses, a company vehicle, and all the fast-food Mexican chow he could want, plus loads of free travel and free time. In other words, lots of time for golf.

Typically, Junior and Ryan would take on all comers. If there were losses, Junior paid the debts. If there were winnings, Ryan got 20 percent of the haul. In theory, but only in theory, Ryan could play loose because he could only make money. But that's not how it went. The games were tense. The games were fun because they were *not* fun. The tension made Ryan feel alive. There was so much action—closeouts, greenies, automatics—the matches needed an accountant to keep track of it all. Enter Junior. He had a gift for numbers. On a good day, Junior, who could shoot in the 70s, might win fifteen hundred dollars, which meant Ryan got 20 percent of that, or three hundred dollars. The matches were decided by the terms negotiated on the first tee, how hungover the various participants were, and who did what late in the back nine.

There was a match in Jacksonville, Florida, that was particularly intense, Ryan and Junior against two guys with deep pockets and a serious demeanor. Late in the round, Ryan was out of a hole—his score was too high to matter. But he was away (farthest from the hole) and putted anyhow. One of the opponents was pissed, because a meaningless putt can sometimes give a partner meaningful information. Also, the opponent stroked his putt just as Ryan putted, causing him to be distracted.

"What the fuck are you doing?" the other guy said.

"Oh my God, I'm so sorry," Ryan said.

"He was away, he can putt," Junior said.

"He was out of the hole, he shoulda picked up," the first guy said.

You could make the case either way. When you're out of a hole, you do often pick up. But you don't have to. Walking off the green, Junior said to Ryan, "What the fuck are you apologizing for?"

. . .

Eventually, the pandemic subsided in Nepal, and Pratima's parents seemed to be okay. At least, Pratima felt she could leave her parents without being overwhelmed with worry. She flew to Los Angeles and continued her American education at Cal State L.A. She was on the school's golf team and was one of its better players. She liked her coach, her teammates, her apartment, her borrowed Prius, her hand-me-down clothing from Sophia.

In the fall of 2022, Pratima was a fifth-year senior. She had one tournament in September and two in October. Shortly after Thanksgiving, with her spring graduation on the horizon, Pratima Sherpa turned twenty-three. A friend in her dorm surprised her with balloons and a cake. She visited the Montano family at their home in Ventura County and drove back for a group business-management project she was working on, its due date looming. I called the next day.

"I can't believe I'm a senior, and I can't believe I'm twenty-three," she said. Her voice was filled with energy. She was on the dean's list. Her parents would be coming to Los Angeles for her graduation in the spring. Her father still didn't have a birth certificate, but he had a passport. The power of persistence.

Pratima told me she had been working on her posture, trying to stand taller to the ball, with her shoulders higher. She was practicing with a towel underneath her right arm and against her torso. "One of my older friends at Royal Nepal looked at my swing and said, 'Your swing does not look good,'" Pratima said. "And that made me take a long look at it." She was trying to make a swing that depended more on body rotation and less on wrist lag. She said she hoped to represent Nepal in women's golf at an Olympics someday. She said she knew of two other young female golfers in Nepal who could break 80. The game was growing in Nepal, modestly. She looked forward to returning to Nepal after graduation and upon completing an internship with an American company in Los Angeles. She looked forward to a life in golf. There were mornings when she'd wake up with a swing thought. Every swing changes, over time.

On the day Pratima watched me hit balls at a driving range, my swing was lousy. No speed, no rhythm, no consistency. Earlier in the year, I had been playing and swinging half-decently, but whatever I had then was gone, at least on this day. In a delightfully direct but also positive way, Pratima saw something in my swing that made no sense—my lead (left) shoulder was lower than my right at impact. Yikes! I must have looked like I was chopping wood. The fix was pretty easy: Keep your left shoulder higher than your right. Pratima said she'd always wanted to teach golf. Not as a profession but just to help people start in the game or enjoy it more.

On another occasion, we watched a video of Lee Trevino at the same time. It was a clip from that winter-day session in Florida, at the Father-Son, when Trevino was giving a driving-range clinic to Tiger Woods and Charlie.

"It's so simple, what he says," Pratima said. "It all makes sense. It makes you want to try it. I love how humble Tiger is. Tiger knows his swing, of course, but he's still listening to Trevino and trying to do whatever Trevino says. Because he respects him. It's how my parents raised me, to respect older people. You can see how much Trevino loves golf. You can see that golf is everything to him." Pratima is Tiger, in those sentences. But she's Trevino, too.

On her last visit to Nepal, Pratima saw her parents in their new house. A well-to-do Royal Nepal member had helped arrange for them to move into a small, modern apartment. Another family, a mother and father and their two young children, had moved into the maintenance shed. The new residents were friends of Pratima's parents.

"Whenever I dream, I am always in my golf house," Pratima told me. "Every day when I was in Kathmandu, I visited the house. I would go to the range at Royal Nepal, and the new family would invite me to come by. I'd come by at two o'clock, and we would have tea and biscuits. I would say, 'I know every inch of this house. This house is like my friend. This is my lucky house.' I told the mom and dad, 'You may think that your kids cannot play golf. But they can!'"

The house no longer smelled of her mother's cooking and spices.

But she could still smell the petrol and see in her mind's eye her father filling the gas tanks of the club's workhorse lawn mowers. The lingering power of childhood smells and childhood sights. It all came flooding back to her.

• • •

The game became more important to Sammy in his Army years. Making the five-man golf team at Fort Jackson had something to do with it, particularly because the other four guys had all played college golf in major programs across the South. For two years, Sammy was playing with servicemen of every color and stripe and officers of every color and stripe. He was assigned to drive the base commander at Fort Jackson, General Normando Costello, to Augusta, two hours away, for the Masters in 1957 and again the following year. In 1945, as an Army colonel, Costello had overseen the peaceful surrender of Weimar. To the people of Weimar, and to his men in uniform there, Costello was a legend. To Sammy, Costello was an Army lifer and a golfer. Many of the officers were.

At a private club in Columbia that was ten miles from Fort Jackson, Sammy met a man who changed the course of his life: Melvin Hemphill, a golf pro at the Forest Lake Club. Hemphill was a noted teacher, and he taught Sammy the fundamentals he held dear. For the right-handed golfer: Cock your head to the right on the takeaway; bring the clubhead straight back for the first foot; kick the right knee into the ball on the backswing; get the left knee behind the ball at the top of the swing; make the longest backswing you can; finish with your hands high. No, Hemphill didn't drill all these ideas into Sammy in one lesson. But they were the fundamentals Hemphill believed in, and in time he delivered them all. He knew that once certain principles took root, you could spend the rest of your golfing life trying to master them.

Sammy was all in on Hemphill the teacher and Hemphill the man. There was something musical about him in his walk, in his swing, even in his penmanship. He was liked by the club's members and caddies and everyone else. He'd have a drink at the end of the day, or more than one. He kept the sorrows of his life to himself, in the manner of his time and place. He treated Sammy as the son he never had.

Hemphill told Sammy that he could play at a much higher level than he was playing. Many teachers will say something like that, and sometimes they mean it. Hemphill meant it. Over his two years in the Army, all of it at Fort Jackson, Sammy got better, and golf was becoming more important to him. (The graph of a person's interest in golf is never a straight line up.) He would sometimes play with visiting generals, one of whom tried to recruit Sammy to Paris, which sounded good, except that Betsy was still at Duke, and Sammy's courtship was going strong. Golf was giving Sammy Reeves opportunities. Better living through golf.

On a Saturday night in April 1958, Elizabeth Ann Webb and Samuel Thomas Reeves were married in a white-tie wedding at the First Presbyterian Church in Asheville. In August, Sammy was discharged from the Army. His father knew William "Buck" Dunavant in Memphis, a well-established cotton merchant with deep ties in the Southern cotton trade. The elder Sam Reeves called Buck Dunavant, and the younger Sam Reeves went to work for him. To his mother and father and sister, he was still Sammy. But in business and in golf, he was now Sam Reeves.

Sam and Betsy Reeves moved to Memphis, and Sam began a career in the only industry he knew anything about, cotton. The cotton industry in the South, to be more precise. In early January 1960, Betsy and Sam had their first child, a daughter, Liz. The family joined the Colonial Country Club in Memphis, the first time Sam had joined a golf club on his own. The Memphis Open was played there each year, and in 1960 Tommy Bolt won it, beating Ben Hogan and Gene Littler in a playoff. Colonial was the hangout for the good players in Memphis. Memphis Country Club, founded in 1905, was the place to practice social niceties. Sam was on the list to get in there, too, but that took time. The Reeves family was settling in.

Sam was working beside Billy Dunavant, Buck's son. Billy was two years older than Sam. Two young men who had grown up with cotton oil in their blood, pretty much. They were a good match.

In the summer of 1960, after only two years of working with the Dunavants, Sam had an opportunity to become a partner in the firm. He bought 15 percent of the company for sixty-five thousand dollars. He used fifteen thousand dollars of his own money, virtually everything he had saved from the age of nine until that summer, including his returns on different stock investments. The rest was a gift from his father. Sam was twenty-six.

Nobody would have guessed then that Billy's father, Buck, would die just months later, in January 1961, at age fifty-two, but that's what happened. Billy, all of twenty-nine, took over the family-owned business. Sam was right beside him. They were ready, or they felt they were. They had come of age in a confident decade. The prosperity of America in the 1950s was spilling into the new decade.

Sam would go to the office every day. The secretaries would flip their calendars every month. Life marched on, and 1961 turned into 1962. Liz now had an infant sister, Annesley. Sam had a bold idea to grow the business, though it would take Sam and Betsy and their girls away from their considerable Memphis comfort. It was a risky move, as all bold moves are, but Sam was not afraid of risk.

●　●　●

When Ryan and Junior took on all comers on the golf course, the tension was like a low-grade fever. When they played cards, it was different. There was more drinking, which lowered inhibitions, and more arguing. But those arguments were like pop-up fires. Tempers would flare, someone would storm off and pour a fresh one, then return to the table. The drinking got them up and got them down.

Their preferred game was euchre, a popular card game across the Midwest. Euchre is a short-deck team card game that combines elements of bridge and gin. The stakes—fifty dollars a point and one hundred a euchre—sound high, but they're really not, because euchre wins are seldom lopsided. On the days when Junior and Ryan had been winners on the course, like the day Ryan shot 68 at Warwick Hills and he and his boss won every way you could win, Junior made sure Ryan paid his own euchre losses, if there were any.

Many days, in between whatever fires at work needed to be doused, the order of events was golf, cards, dinner, all of which was accompanied by drinking, followed by visits to strip clubs, where there was more drinking. So a lot of drinking. But don't get the wrong idea. The ordering of their events was not that regimented. Cards could come before golf or after dinner, according to mood and weather.

Many mornings, Ryan woke up on a sofa in an unexpected place, his phone filled with texts from Margot that were never read. He'd find himself in Junior's house or at a golf resort or in a four-star hotel. Ryan and Junior and some confederates once awoke in a sprawling luxury rental house in Scottsdale and quickly realized that their credit cards and rings and watches were gone. The fellas had brought in paid entertainment for the previous night. The entertainers got the last laugh.

This may sound like Ryan did nothing but play, but he worked hard, and Junior did, too. Junior made decisions about where to build stores (as the Qdoba locations were sometimes called), and

Ryan made sure Junior's wishes were executed. They were almost like brothers. If Ryan handed Junior a profit-and-loss statement that Junior didn't like, Junior would throw it back in Ryan's face. Ryan didn't take offense. It was a macho culture. Ryan oversaw hiring and made sure employees who weren't born in the United States had credible documentation. He inspected bathrooms and parking lots and removed gum from under tabletops.

Ryan wore a Qdoba shirt and thick-soled black shoes and would help at the counter if the lunch line got long. He hired carefully and fired reluctantly and once had to let a battered husband go not because of his body odor, which wasn't helping his job performance, but because his wife was calling the store a dozen or two dozen times a day. For a while Ryan made his rounds in a Qdoba panel van with no side windows and a gigantic burrito depicted on its sides. The back of the van was typically empty, save for his golf bag and golf shoes, fresh shorts, a golf shirt—and various Qdoba wrappers.

This was Ryan French from age twenty-three to thirty. Yes, he was married. No, there was no way his marriage could survive this manner of living, nor could his job. Ryan thought he was having the time of his life. He wasn't fooling everybody. Ryan was dating a company employee while his wife, a nurse with a demanding job, was home alone as often as not. Or, viewed another way, every single night. Lou Senior, the picture of propriety, was not pleased. His instinct was to fire Ryan, but because he liked Ryan and because Ryan was good at his job, he only suspended him. The affair continued, and Ryan quit before the suspension turned into a firing. There was a long afternoon in Junior's office when he and Ryan wept, fought, hugged, and said goodbye.

Margot had started divorce proceedings. At least there were no children, no custody issues, except for their two dogs. Ryan started seeing a stripper.

He liked Las Vegas and had the money to go there. The stripper liked Las Vegas and wanted someone to pay her way there, which Ryan was more than willing to do. He liked to drink. She liked to drink. He liked the idea of walking through a hotel lobby with a stunning woman on his arm. She was more than qualified and willing to be that woman.

They flew to Las Vegas from Detroit and checked in to the Sahara, a vast glass-walled high-rise hotel on the Strip. They went to their room. It had been recently remodeled. They went to the hotel's various bars, blackjack and poker tables, the different pools. Then back to the room, back to the bars, back to the gambling tables, back to the pools. Their room had a wet bar, a king-size bed, a view from on high. What more did they need? They were both hammered pretty much all day, every day. Twenty-four-hour party people.

On one of their Las Vegas days, Ryan found himself alone in their hotel room. His lady friend was poolside. Ryan had been drinking and ruminating. Job, gone. Lou Junior and Senior, out of his life. Marriage, over. Ryan's mind was a high and raging river.

What am I doing here? Showing off for Junior? That makes no fucking sense.

Yeah? Wait till he sees the photos of me with my hot date. He's gonna want me back.

What, you're gonna text him photos from Vegas? You must be out of your fucking mind.

The war, the war, the war.

By that point in his life, Ryan at thirty could barely remember Ryan at twelve, going to the curb to get the *Free Press* and study the golf results. He had buried those long, tedious Alpena years when he needed the world to spin faster but it refused to do so. Everything was long and slow then. All those five-dollars-a-side gambling games on the city course with his father and his father's friends? *How boring.* All those chicken-wing dinners as the steak entrées just sat there on the menu, waiting for some special occasion

that might not ever come? *How pathetic.* The hunting trips. Please.
You want me to get up when?

Ryan French, living large in Las Vegas, had a message for all
those old men in Alpena who had spent years urging the man-boy
to get out of town: *I'm out of your shit town! I'm out and I eat steak
every night!*

He had spent more than a decade reinventing himself. Becoming the life of the party. The person who could tell the stories, laugh
at the jokes, get the drinks, hole the putts, pull the right cards, the
guy who could have sex whenever the urge visited, selling all that
I'm-the-man bullshit with such conviction. *I know how my life looks.
Pretty damn hot!*

On some level, in a place he could not usually reach, he knew
the whole thing was a lie. He knew that he loathed the person he
had become. On that day, alone in that Las Vegas hotel room, the lie
was screaming at him as it never had before. He was trapped, stuck
in skin he couldn't shed. He was everything to everybody (except to
Margot). He was so good at his job, even with all his extracurricular
activities, that corporate had asked him to address a conference of
hundreds of fast-food executives and franchise owner-operators on
the critical subject of operational improvements. He could do that
and did. People were applauding for him, and it was easy. He could
be that person all day long. And when his workday was over, Ryan
got his just rewards. The golf, the cards, the dinners, the strippers,
all that free booze. Free everything.

Could life be easier?

Could life be harder?

Ryan stood in his room at the Sahara, on its carpeted floor,
Jack Daniel's in his bloodstream, and reduced the whole thing to
a single sentence that rattled in his head like a tall truck in a short
tunnel.

How can I keep this whole fucking thing going?

And then somebody fired a starter's pistol, a sudden piercing blast from a long-ago track meet he never ran. Ryan took several giant steps to the window of his pathetic and luxurious hotel room, wanting nothing more than to jump out of it to his certain death on the pavement below.

But the window could not be opened, and it could not be smashed. It was designed to prevent suicide.

Goddamn building regs.

Ryan started calling people, everybody and anybody, but reaching nobody. He wanted to die and couldn't figure out a way to do it. The despair and the helplessness was like nothing he had ever felt. The last person Ryan wanted to call was his mother. He knew if he called his mother, the whole thing would be up. He called his mother. She and Howard were in Chicago, visiting Ryan's sister. Ginny could hear the manic hysteria in her son's voice. She became hysterical. Howard came rushing in. Dallas came rushing in. Ginny's training as a therapist kicked in. She kept Ryan on the phone. She used another phone to call 911 in Las Vegas.

I came of golf age in the 1970s. I got there with the help of Dave Anderson in *The New York Times*, the paper's sports section spread out on our kitchen table; the RCA Trinitron TV in the living room; the public course on Bellport Bay five miles to our east; the golf team at Patchogue-Medford High School; and every last person I played with, caddied for, bought clubs from, and the rest. Arnold Palmer was in contention (sort of) at the first U.S. Open I followed, in 1974 at Winged Foot, and the next year, Tom Watson won the British Open in an eighteen-hole playoff on a bleak-looking course (Carnoustie) on a dank Sunday in faraway Scotland. Watson had a shaggy head of reddish hair that his little plaid cap could not contain, a beautiful Jewish wife hugging him in victory, and a manful handshake for the man he beat by a shot, "Australia's Jack Newton," as he was described in print and on TV.

By then I was bewitched by the game, and when I played two balls at Bellport, I was both Watson and Big Jack. There was a six-pane window on a wall of our backyard garage, and I would practice in front of it, keeping my head in one windowpane while getting my hands at the top of the backswing in a higher one, taking my swing cues from Watson. I put a doormat on the grass where my swing bottomed out and felt a certain satisfaction every time I clipped it just so. The doormat had a little plastic sunflower sticking out of a corner. It was the Seventies.

Our family—mother, father, older brother, plus our wandering mutt—was drawn to the great outdoors, as my father referred to any place with sun exposure. That was also the name of a sporting-goods store on South Ocean Avenue where we bought tennis rackets, camping equipment, skis, badminton shuttlecocks, balls for Ping-Pong, baseball, and basketball, among other sports, though not golf. The Great Outdoors didn't sell golf equipment, and I was the only person in the house who needed it anyhow. You could buy "water balls" in the Bellport pro shop for a quarter each, which was more than chump change for me. (Our poker games were a nickel a hand.) I never bought a golf glove. My preference was to save up for Maxfli Blue Max golf balls or, better yet, Royals with dimples that were not circles but hexagons.

I started playing with a set of clubs I borrowed from my dentist's wife. My own first set was assembled by my mother, who sifted through the sporting-goods corner of Patchogue's Salvation Army to find them. Some of the clubs had metal shafts that were painted brown, to make them look like wood, in case the whole steel-shaft thing turned out to be a fad. The 5-iron was stamped with the signature of a man named Leo Diegel, a star golfer (I later learned) from the 1920s. I bought my first matched set of irons with lawn-mowing money from an old European woman who lived two blocks away and sold ripe tomatoes and bright flowers that she grew in her large, sunny yard. One day, and why I don't know, she was selling her son's Northwesterns in a ridiculously big brown golf bag. I took out seventy-five dollars from my savings account and bought them. By then I was already playing at Bellport, where the green fee was five dollars for juniors on weekday afternoons. I once paid with change. A junior membership was fifty dollars a year. All you had to do was fill out the form at Bellport's village hall and pay. I asked my parents if we could go fifty-fifty on it in the first year of my infatuation, and my father said, "Let's see how you feel about golf a year from now." My trumpet career had been short and was confined to the basement.

Bellport was a public course owned by the village but had once been, before the Depression, a private club, and it had a foot in both worlds. To get there, I biked with my clubs over my shoulder to the old Bee Hive, a Main Street department store with Patchogue's only escalator, and locked my bike to a post in front. From there, I took a public bus right to the course. Once, after I boarded the bus, the driver told me, "You need a cover on that bag. If one of those clubs goes flying out and hits somebody, I'm responsible." After that, I put a paper grocery bag over the clubs, which was deemed good enough. On the bus, I would regularly see the same man, seated almost behind the driver. He had a significant overbite, which I tried not to stare at, and large metal-framed glasses. He often wore out-of-date suits, one of which was powder blue, and had an attaché case sitting on his lap. He was on when I boarded and he was still on when I got off, right in front of the course, vaguely looking in its direction. I never forgot his forlorn face.

The first time I broke 100, I was playing at Bellport with the man who owned the bus line, Louis A. Fuoco. That is, the senior Mr. Fuoco, a well-known businessman and the head of a prominent Patchogue–East Patchogue–Bellport family. I was playing by myself when Mr. Fuoco invited me to join him on the fifteenth hole. I put my clubs on the back of his cart. That is, *his* cart. Nobody else at Bellport owned a golf cart, not that I knew. I must have told him what I needed on the last four holes to shoot my first two-digit score, because he congratulated me when I holed out on the last for 99.

On another occasion, I played with George Vineyard, a physicist and the director of Brookhaven National Lab, where my father was an engineer. Another time, I played with Lenny Silverman, owner of a lumberyard and the father of a friend I knew from nursery school and Hebrew school and actually every school Lori Silverman and I ever attended. In terms of ethnicity and income level, Bellport golfers were a mishmash. A mishmash of white people, I should say.

But the dominant culture at Bellport was Italian American and male. The head pro was a former ballroom dancer named Nick Petrillo, who was built like a middleweight boxer. His name was sometimes in *The New York Times* and more often in *Newsday*, when the papers published results from club-pro events and Nick had played well. Nick liked to stand on the drooping little porch outside his shop and say nonsensical things like: "On the tee, here's Larry Lodi from Patchogue. Larry-Larry-Larry Low-*die*." Larry and I played a lot together, and his mother, Helen Scotto, was an active Ladies' Day golfer at Bellport. Nick's assistant was a former Bellport caddie named Don Stephani, dapper and dignified. His wife was a Fuoco. Larry and I went to school with various Stephanis. Bellport's bar and restaurant was run by Charlie Greco. Mr. Greco had family members working all over the dining room and in the halfway house, an actual house that stood beyond the eighth green. The longtime greenkeeper at Bellport was Joseph Satornino, who went by Joe Mag. Bernie Garruppo was an outstanding junior golfer at Bellport, and his father, Gene, worked in the locker room, where penny-a-point gin games were a regular thing. Before Gene, the locker room was run by Tony Orsino, who had a fantastic head of hair, which he combed constantly. Tony's nephew was his weekend assistant and a classmate of mine. I bought my first good pair of golf shoes from him and didn't care that they were secondhand. You might see Mr. Fuoco's son Buddy or Mr. Fuccillo or Mr. Chiuchiolo in the locker room or on the putting green, especially during the Lions or Kiwanis outings, or during the golf day sponsored by the Fuoco family. The Fuocos ran an annual fundraiser for Camp Pa-Qua-Tuck, a summer camp for people with special needs.

Larry (Larry-Larry-Larry Low-*die*) was a natural athlete and a good golfer. He had a strong grip and a slow backswing, and his downswing was a blur. He was an excellent hotdog skier at our little local ski hill, the Bald Hill Ski Bowl. He was good at pond hockey and played baseball and softball on the various village fields down by the bay. Patchogue was a baseball town and a ferry town, with service to Fire Island and its ocean beaches. Larry could get anything out of the bay and onto shore or the deck of his boat, a seventeen-foot SportCraft with a balky sixty-five-horsepower Mercury engine. There were summer days when we would dig clams from early morning through midafternoon, sell them to the wholesale buyers on the Patchogue River dock, and play golf at Bellport after a quick and early dinner, Larry at his house and I at mine. We were as brown as chestnuts. For our evening games, Larry was allowed to use his mother's Buick LeSabre. It had electric windows and an FM radio that played a steady stream of hits by Steely Dan and the Atlanta Rhythm Section, and Larry sometimes played in a T-shirt that depicted Peter Frampton in his *Frampton Comes Alive!* period. In one after-supper game at Bellport, Larry was one under through sixteen. By that point, we were playing by moonlight. I went ahead on seventeen and eighteen to find his shots by golf-course sonar, and Larry went bogey-par without losing a ball for 71, a round of even par.

Larry and I played fast and always for money, enough to make matters more than interesting. Our putting-green game was a quarter a hole, with carryovers, winner calls the hole. And then the killer: One-putt wins paid double. So if you halved the first three holes, the fourth hole was worth a dollar, with the carryovers. And if you won that hole by making your first putt, you collected not one dollar but two. It was hard to change momentum and an expensive way to learn how to putt. I lost more than I won.

On the course, Larry knew I rushed the short ones if he stood close to the hole, flagstick in hand. So he stood close to the hole, flagstick in hand, his body language practically screaming: *Just miss it already.* But when we played high school matches together, he'd say, "Don't worry about the pin, I got it." He'd practically stand on the flagstick so nobody else could pick it up.

Patchogue-Medford High School was a three-year school, tenth grade through twelfth, and Larry was one year ahead of me. We got a kick out of our golf coach, a math teacher with a crooked nose and a dry wit named John Sifaneck. Coach Sif was a diabetic and always had hard butterscotch candies or soft caramels in a pocket of his windbreaker. He also had bursitis, which stunted his backswing, but he hit driver in play hole after hole. Coach Sif was in his late thirties and could do arithmetic in his head like he was signing his name. He coached the bowling team, and it was through bowling that Larry first met him. Sifaneck had a tidy VW Squareback with a decal from a national math fraternity on the rear window. He packed two or three of us in his car and drove us from school to our home course, a public course called Spring Lake. Several more rode in the bed of Bill Sweeney's tin-can pickup truck, getting bounced around as it went up and down the hills of Granny Road through Gordon Heights, a semi-rural hamlet where nearly all the residents were Black. Gordon Heights had small wood-frame houses on big lots crowded with scrub oaks and scrub pines, a tiny cemetery, an AME church, and a deli, Weir's, that was nothing like the Italian ones in Patchogue and East Patchogue. In an act of rookie indoctrination, some team elders sent me into the deli to buy a jar of pickled pigs' feet, which Weir's carried, along with off-brand sodas.

At night, after matches and practice, I cleaned my clubs in my mother's pink bathtub with a soapy nail brush. In the basement, I had attached a heavy monkey wrench to one end of a four-foot rope and knotted the other end to a broom handle at its midpoint. I would hold the broom handle even with my shoulders and twirl it to raise and lower the monkey wrench, in the name of bigger forearms. Tom Watson's were drumsticks. Mine were scorecard pencils, and that's where they remained.

I was some package, walking down school corridors in late March wearing a plaid flannel shirt and carrying my boxy plaid golf bag. You can imagine the envy.

Coach Sif would sometimes talk about the caddying he did at the Salem Country Club outside Boston in his high school and college years. This golfiest of jobs appealed to me in every possible way, starting with the chance to make money while being around golf. There was no formal caddie program at Bellport in the 1970s, but I managed to get work carrying for my high school principal, Frank Juzwiak, and his regular partner, Hugh MacLeod, who was the principal of the school where my mother taught. Joe Mag the greenkeeper was in this game, too. They often played as three, first group off. Mr. Juzwiak lived near us and would pick me up in his Cadillac as the sun was rising. My main responsibilities were to keep up and hold Mr. Juzwiak's pipe when he played his shots. Mr. MacLeod, as my mother noted more than once, was a dashing man, and he had the smooth and confident manner of somebody who had grown up in country club comfort. Mr. MacLeod was a good golfer, and he knew some of the top clubs on Long Island, including Garden City Men's Club, well west of Bellport, and Shinnecock Hills, thirty miles to Bellport's east.

In the summer of '77, the Walker Cup, the Ryder Cup of amateur golf, was played at Shinnecock Hills. I didn't go, but I did do a drive-by and saw its low, wood-shingled clubhouse on the top of a gentle hill. You could see huge swaths of the course from several public roads, enough to know that it was part of another world. Later, I caddied a few times at Shinnecock Hills and its neighbor, the National Golf Links of America, which had a grand and imposing stone clubhouse. It sat at the top of a sudden hill like an unreachable crown.

At Shinnecock, I caddied for a woman who had more woolen headcovers than I could keep straight. Somewhere on the back nine, I figured out that the number of stripes on the neck of the headcover was supposed to match the clubhead it protected. (Her 5-wood headcover had five stripes.) I offered unsolicited advice only once. At National, I caddied for two silver-haired gents who oozed propriety without saying much. My experiences at these two golf clubs settled deep within me. Part of it was the greatness of the playing fields. The quietude these courses offered. Their firm fairways. The coarse beach sand in the bunkers. The magic-carpet greens that looked like they could take flight. As for the members and their guests, I didn't know who they were, but they didn't live in Patchogue, and they weren't playing at Bellport.

It wasn't like I knew nothing about Long Island's summer people. We were members of a rustic cold-shower club in Westhampton Beach called Rogers Beach Club. There was an old rambling mansion in the dunes nearby, and once, after a game of running bases on the beach, I was invited to its oceanfront deck, where I saw an *outdoor phone*. That was a first for me. But my brother and I were raised not to worship money or things, nor people with money or things. Patchogue (this surely oversimplifies it) had working-class families, middle-class families like mine, and upper-class families, where you'd find a doctor in the house or a business owner or a lawyer. There was income disparity, of course, but it wasn't (again, too easy) immense. Going to National Golf Links was like going to a foreign country for which no travel guide existed. I was eighteen, with my nose in a hedge, standing on my toes but seeing nothing, making reckless, fantastical guesses about life on the other side of that green border wall.

During spring break in my senior year of high school, my friend Stuart Feldman, from East Patchogue and Bellport High, and I took an overnight bus from the Port Authority in New York City to Williamsburg, Virginia, where we stayed in a hotel, ate steaks for breakfast, and played the Golden Horseshoe course again and again, in a cart. Between rounds, we drove our buggy on Williamsburg's quaint streets (crazily illegal), parked it like a car, and ate lunch. We were fascinated by the man running the cart barn, an old Black gent named Kitchens, who knew the course and town in every dimension. Neither of us had ever met anybody like him. Stuart's father, Bernard O. Feldman, was a well-liked and humorous orthodontist who played golf at Bellport and not well. Stuart inherited his father's sense of humor and his Ginty clubs, laminated fairway woods with lead keels meant to be played, tellingly, from the rough. They had failed Bernie O. and were now in Williamsburg with Stuart. "Nick has advice for me," Dr. Feldman would sometimes say. Nick Petrillo, the Bellport pro. "Take two weeks off, then quit altogether." Stuart was better than his father, but not way better. I would say that what I lost to Larry Lodi, I made from Stuart. Stuart said of me on that trip, "You went listening to Simon and Garfunkel and came back listening to Hot Tuna."

In Williamsburg, Stuart and I got paired with two good ol' boys, and Stuart raised the name Lynyrd Skynyrd, rising stars of southern rock, with them. "Heard he *died*," one of the fellas said. We were in semi-rural Virginia five months after the band had been in a plane crash that killed three Lynyrd Skynyrd bandmates. *Heard he died* was a tragic non sequitur to our ears, but it did provide us with a running bit for the long bus ride home.

The PMHS golf season started a couple of days later. Our first session was on the field behind the school when there was still snow and ice on it. Coach Sifaneck had us hit three shots each, one golfer at a time. In other words, everybody watching. He had me go first. I took a deep breath, lightened my grip pressure, and caught three on the face. Coach said something about my spring-training trip.

Later in that same senior-year golf season, there was a story in the Patchogue weekly, *The Long Island Advance*, about the golf team under John Sifaneck. Here's how it began:

> *After six seasons of misery, Coach John Sifaneck of Patchogue-Medford High School was about to pack his clubs in; not one of his previous teams had even a .500 record. He decided to stick it out for one more year, a lucky seventh. Everyone but the opposition is glad he did. The Patchogue-Medford golf team is posting its best season ever. With 17 of the 20 scheduled matches played, the team is sporting a very solid 9-7-1 record.*

You can probably guess the byline that appeared above that crazy-long lede.

I graduated from high school in 1978, and that summer I caddied in the Bellport club championship final. My parents came out to watch, and I quickly realized that my father was aiming his Konica lens not at the two finalists on the course but at the lone *caddie*. I said to my mother, "Get him the fuck off this golf course *now*." My father snapped a photo capturing that exact moment. I'm certain that's the only time I used that word in front of my mother, and I regretted it almost immediately. But at that moment I was steaming. I knew somebody had to be thinking, *Is that your dad?* For a second there, I would have run him off the course myself, had I had the chance. The heat of the moment.

This might not sound believable, but my father and I were always close.

In the next few college summers, Larry Lodi and I played at Bellport occasionally, sometimes with Coach Sifaneck and his friend Ray Fell, a good golfer who had been one of our gym teachers. (Mr. Fell later became the superintendent of the Patchogue-Medford school system and was my mother's ultimate boss. Later yet, he became the mayor of Bellport.) In 1981 the United States Golf Association announced that the U.S. Open would be played at Shinnecock Hills in 1986, returning there for the national championship after a ninety-year absence.

Coach Sifaneck would have been at that Open, for sure. He would have loved it. But he died nine months before it was played. His diabetes had taken a toll on him, and he had a fatal heart attack in a hospital while awaiting leg amputation surgery.

Coach Sifaneck's love of golf was infectious. Larry played golf in college, another teammate started a small chain of golf stores, and the lone girl on our roster became a teaching pro. Shortly before he died, Coach Sifaneck made a hole in one, his first and only ace, with a fairway wood on the old sixth at Bellport, a long par-3 near the bay. His ashes were scattered there, and a large boulder was placed just off the tee in his memory. A plaque on the boulder honored John Sifaneck's life and times and forty-four years. It didn't mention his late-life ace. Everybody who knew him knew about that hole-in-one. Way more than that, we knew what the man had done, and how he had shaped most anybody who had walked fairways with him.

Wherever I lived in my student years at the University of Pennsylvania, I always had my clubs nearby, and a few times, I took the Market Frankford Line train to its western terminus, near the Cobbs Creek golf course, in West Philadelphia. One round began with an eagle. A smarter golfer would have walked in then and there. I went to a single preseason meeting of the Penn golf team. Everybody could break 80 regularly, and many of the candidates played at name-brand country-club courses, while I was an 85-shooter on a short, flat, easy public course. I slipped out. Even then, golf for me was not about the score. One of the team's top players invited me to play with him at a public course near Valley Forge National Park. He had a working car, a floppy bucket hat, and a superb short game, but I felt no envy for him—or not much. I didn't have a fantasy about becoming a scratch golfer. But I could already imagine golf always being in my life.

My main college hobby was reading old bound volumes of *The New Yorker* in the open stacks of the main library, Van Pelt. I would pull out a volume, open to a random page, and go wherever it took me. I read Talk pieces and tried to guess the writer. (White? Ross? Thurber?) I stumbled upon a Herbert Warren Wind road-trip piece called "North to the Links of Dornoch" in an issue dated June 6, 1964. In that same issue, Anne Sexton, John Cheever, and William Maxwell all had bylines. The joy of turning pages. I majored in English and wrote for *The Daily Pennsylvanian*. (Some of the best editors I've ever had were there.) But I could sit in a dream state with those heavy bound *New Yorker* volumes for hours, staying right through the midnight closing in Van Pelt's expanded hours as finals loomed. (I liked the university term *Reading Days*.) I was in the library late one December night when another student suddenly stood on a reading table and announced in a trembling voice that John Lennon had been shot. Most of us filed out of the library and gathered in front, some students holding up lighters into the dank, awful night. The broadcaster Howard Cosell broke the news during a *Monday Night Football* game telecast.

When I came out of college, my only ambition was to be a newspaper reporter. That is, a news reporter. I had a strong attachment to a word still in circulation then, though its use was already (and appropriately) in decline: *newspaperman*. In the winter of senior year, I sent letters and clips to virtually every daily paper in New England and one weekly, the *Vineyard Gazette*, on Martha's Vineyard. I didn't know you had to take a ferry to get there when I wrote to the paper, but I saved up enough busboy money (La Terrasse, RIP) to rent a car with cash, buy a car-and-passenger Steamship Authority ticket, and interview at the *Gazette* during spring break. That was the one job offer I got. I brought my clubs to the island and a tackle box, from my fishing days in Patchogue. Soon after moving to the Vineyard, I bought a small fiberglass sailboat with busboy savings and graduation-gift money. Also, for far less money, a rusty sky-blue Chevy Malibu from an up-island man named Mr. Howell. It was an island car, Mr. Howell explained. In other words, not a car you take off-island. She died off-island. I offered the car to a mechanic in Southborough, Massachusetts, for fifty dollars. He said for fifty dollars, he'd take it off my hands.

The *Gazette* was owned by James B. (Scotty) Reston and his wife, Sally. In the 1920s and the early '30s, as a high school student in Dayton and as an undergraduate at the University of Illinois, Scotty had been an outstanding golfer with dreams of turning pro, as other Scottish émigrés had done. But his mother had grander ambitions for her son, and Scotty became a newspaper reporter, in time a celebrated one. When I got to the Vineyard, he was an old but active columnist at *The New York Times*. Dick Reston, one of Scotty's three sons, was the editor of the *Gazette*. Dick knew his father's history in golf like he knew his own in baseball. In a complicated case of like father, like son, Dick ended up behind a typewriter, too.

When I arrived at the *Gazette* in 1982, everything we wrote came off upright, circa 1955 Royals. They were noisy beasts. The type bars, snapping to attention. The ringing bells. The song of rolling ribbons, as yellow copy paper was pulled out with ten eager fingers. As I think about it, two of the great, formative sounds of my life have been the clicking tap dance from a manual typewriter and the rhythmic clacking of a golfer in spikes on a brick walkway. I might add to that the hushed voices of public libraries. The Vineyard had six, each a unique oasis. The Edgartown Library in winter was a particular joy for me.

Dick used to chide me for my "sneak time" on the course, but not in a venomous way. There were four reporters at the paper, and three of us had played golf through high school and college: Andy Shanley, Jim Kelly, and me. We were close. Jim and I had one memorable fall day when we played golf in the morning and, after losing many balls, went sailing. We capsized. You're never supposed to leave your boat in those situations, but the current was offshore, and drifting farther out to sea didn't seem like a good bet. (One of Kelly's many bits involved the theme song from *Gilligan's Island*.) We swam for shore and our lives in 55-degree water and celebrated our survival with dinner at the Beeftender, one of the few year-round restaurants on the island in those days.

I had good company in my sneak time. Harvey Ewing, a legend of Vineyard newspapering and the chief of the two-person *Cape Cod Times* Vineyard bureau, logged a lot of cool-weather rounds on the Edgartown links, an unadorned and charming nine-hole course that, like Bellport, had the benefit of brackishness and age. In season, the Edgartown course was private, but by late September, you could find your way on. In other words, the Edgartown Golf Club was everything and nothing like the National Golf Links of America in Southampton, Long Island. The course in Edgartown, even though it was private, was still part of the town of Edgartown. In 1949, Henry Beetle Hough, the editor of the *Gazette*, wrote a detailed history of golf on the Vineyard. He cited ten courses, most of them little informal ones, and the word *private* doesn't appear once. Mr. Hough—who took over the paper in 1920 and was still its main editorial writer when I got there in '82—was not a golfer, but he walked every day and believed in the value of open, preserved spaces. I never talked to him about the game but was lucky enough to know him at least a little, and a few times, in bad weather, I was sent to his house to pick up his weekly editorials. He lived in Edgartown, not far from the *Gazette* office and not too far from the course, which was almost in town. I could walk to the course from my little house in the woods, down a narrow dirt road and to its eighth tee, in five minutes. When I slipped on, nobody seemed to mind, except maybe the many rabbits.

In 1985, I caddied in the U.S. Open, the British Open, and the PGA Championship. During the Masters, I caddied in an opposite-field event called the Magnolia Classic, in Hattiesburg, Mississippi. I caddied at the Dutch Open in Holland; the Met Open in northern New Jersey; and the BC Open in upstate New York. I was seeing golf as I had never seen it and gathering string for my first book, about life on "the pro golf tour," as it was called then. I caddied in a one-day thirty-six-hole U.S. Open qualifier (nope) and a two-day thirty-six-hole British Open qualifier (yep). My guy, a young pro from New Jersey, qualified on his honeymoon. Jamie and Dawn Howell. Nice people.

That qualifier was played at a course on the English Channel called Royal Cinque Ports, next door to Royal St. George's, where the Open would be played. Bellport was linksy in places. Shinnecock Hills and National Golf Links even more so. Edgartown was, too. But I had never seen a golf course like Royal Cinque Ports. The "Deal course," as the British golf writer Bernard Darwin referred to it, for the town where it was located. (I couldn't read enough golf then.) The course seemed to come out of the sea. Its turf looked like a pale green version of the ocean floor. It was the first linksland I had ever seen. I was mesmerized.

Even though the course was flat and about a yard above sea

level, you almost never had an even lie, and the wind often howled. (If you wanted to know the direction of the wind, you'd point your nose in its general direction, and when you felt the wind evenly on both ears, you had your true north.) The clubhouse was a necessary respite from all that windblown madness, a white fortress that anybody could enter that week, even caddies. The club was private, but townspeople were free to walk their dogs on the course, and they did. The head pro, Mr. Andy Reynolds, could not have been more welcoming or engaging or stylish, in that distinctly British way. Everything just so but somehow loose, too.

I stayed for a few nights in a glorified motel right on the Cinque Ports course called the Chequers Inn. There was a restaurant and pub beside it, and Jack Nicklaus and his people were there one night. Nobody made a fuss about him. Yes, he was Nicklaus, and the Open was in town. But he was also just another guy carrying glasses of beer to his table in his meaty hands.

There was another night when I slipped onto the golf course and played a few holes. I recognized two other caddies who were doing the same. I didn't know them, but they were real caddies (I was a tourist) who worked on the European Tour, probably just a few years older than I was (I was twenty-five). Both were blond and light on their feet. One was tall and lanky, and the other was built like a lightweight college wrestler. We nodded hello.

What made it memorable for me was the loveliness of the night, in all its unexpected stillness, the purity of the course, the scent of the nearby farms and sea and grass, and, more than anything, the joy emanating from my two fellow golfers. You could sense from ten yards away the pleasure they were taking from the course, their company, and their match. Ever since, that night has been a kind of inspiration for me, a reminder to breathe deep and feel the turf under my feet.

Later, I got to know one of the two, Dave McNeilly, who has had a long and sometimes comical career as a prominent touring caddie in Europe and the United States, working many majors and Ryder Cups. Through it all, he has been a model of fitness and good humor. I have visited with Dave dozens of times over the years and once had tea in his sunny kitchen at his home in Belfast. His tall and lanky compatriot was Lorne Duncan. Lorne, too, was a celebrated caddie, but his career, unlike Dave's, didn't go on and on. He never worked much in the United States. He preferred the tours in Africa, Asia, Australia, Europe, and his native Canada. Duncan had long, flowing hair, he towered over his players, and he caddied in sandals. (Bad feet.) The only time I ever saw Lorne in person was that July night in 1985 at Royal Cinque Ports.

Thirty-five years later, I began an email correspondence with him and was surprised to learn that he had deposited the evening in his memory bank, too. Lorne remembered the night's stillness and how he and Dave played the same three holes again and again. They were there for the Open. Dave was working for Nick Faldo, and Lorne had Mark McCumber, a leading American player. The Irish Ryder Cupper Eamonn Darcy had given them a lift, after a practice round, from Royal St. George's back to their camper, their digs for that week and many others. Their camper was parked in a field near the Chequers Inn. On the way home (as it were), while on a rural back road, Darcy stopped the car to admire a cow with an especially large head. The veteran pro then dropped off Dave and Lorne at the caravan park. From it, the Deal links beckoned. Dave and Lorne hopped a stone wall and played a course that was nearly empty. Eventually, well past ten, they ran out of light, retired to the Chequers pub, hoisted pint glasses, emptied them, and called it a night. One night among their hundreds. Lorne remembered it in living color.

A year or so later, I resumed my interrupted life. In a stroke of good luck, I got a job covering high school and suburban sports for

The Philadelphia Inquirer. I can't imagine the paper's editor, Gene Roberts, read a word of my typing before I came aboard, but he told somebody, "I like the way he got around the country on the cheap, doing that caddying thing." Roberts was a legend.

Another reporter had the golf beat, but I did write some golf stories, including a piece about six brothers who had turned their dairy farm into a public course and its milking station into a pro shop. I also fell in with a small group of editors and reporters who liked to play, and I joined their time-warp Monday-outing group called the Philadelphia Newspapermen's Golf Association. The PNGA had improbably high standards. For instance, even when the host club permitted shorts, PNGA rules required its members to wear trousers. No, there were no women PNGA members. My little gang had a winking tolerance for the whole setup, but we were still happy to pay our dues. We were half viewed as wild-eyed liberals, but cheap golf on good courses carried the day for us, or at least for me. Bob Warner, a political reporter on the *Philadelphia Daily News* and a PNGA golfer, paved the way for me to join the Philadelphia Cricket Club, with its lovely tree-lined A. W. Tillinghast course. I was single and not yet thirty, and that put me in a category where I could afford it, or close enough.

It was a gentle club. The prize for a pre-Thanksgiving members' golf event was a free turkey. I played a lot of afternoon golf with another member in my category, Burt McHugh. I had met Burt's mother and sister while caddying for Brad Faxon at the Hartford Open. Gigi, the daughter, was a Princeton grad, a former child actor, and a five-tool player, of a kind. She was a fledgling golf writer and wanted to interview Brad. She surely didn't need my help, but her mother asked me for it anyhow. Later, they introduced me to Burt, and later yet, I became the godfather (one of two) to Burt's namesake son. Burt's waggle was so good it improved your own. He was close to scratch and in our game he gave me half a shot a hole. Any hole where we made the same gross score was a win for me. It was amazing how often our matches were settled on the last two holes. Our regular game was for a dollar. We took our inspiration from the wager that moves the plot of *Trading Places*.

My first workstation at the paper was in a small suburban newsroom where I sat next to Kit Seelye, who covered Main Line politics for the *Inquirer* (and, later, national politics for *The New York Times*). Kit logged a lot of miles on her bike and one day got caught in a driving rain far from her home and out by the Cricket Club course. The ladies there invited her to come in and dry off. The world as it should be.

Kit and I both knew a man named Fred Anton, who had several preoccupations, two of which were golf and politics. Fred was the president of a large insurance company. He was also a kingmaker in Pennsylvania politics, so Kit had ample reason to talk to him and he to Kit. Early on, she wisely said to him, "Think of me as Bob Warner in a skirt."

Over time, Fred and I became unlikely friends. He was twenty-six years older than I, and if you were tracking differences, that would be merely a starting point. But we shared golf in a meaningful way. He had caddied in the 1950 U.S. Open at Merion and, in person, watched Ben Hogan win the event's Sunday eighteen-hole playoff.

Fred and I were once at one of his clubs—he belonged to four or five—looking at a portrait on a clubhouse wall. The subject was Fred's lawyer and the founder of the club. Fred knew the man well. I mean, he had spent his adult life plotting with him and playing golf with him across the United States and in the British Isles. Fred stared at the painting for a full second and said, "Eyes are to a portrait what greens are to a golf course!" He blurted out those words (many of his sentences ended in exclamation marks) as he blurted out many of his insights. He had a deep, intuitive understanding of golf, people, politics, and the politics of relationships. The starting point of our connection was caddying. His own eyes were blue, sad, and observant.

While at the *Inquirer*, I started dating a New Yorker (by way of California) with an adventurous spirit named Christine. (Green-eyed and lively!) We had our first date in New York City some hours after I interviewed Arnold Palmer for the first time, at a golf tournament in suburban Philadelphia. At the paper, after starting in sports, I went to news (which I considered my real home), but was traded back to sports in 1990, when the *Inquirer* needed a beat writer to cover the Phillies. Two months into the baseball season, Christine and I got engaged. (Yep! As Tug McGraw used to say, You gotta believe.) That was several hours before a Phillies-Cubs matinee at Wrigley. Chicago, just then, was getting ready for a U.S. Open. Chicago, like New York and Philadelphia, was an entrenched capital of both golf and baseball. Also (free advice if you're looking) an excellent place to get engaged.

There's a lot of overlap, in baseball and golf. I had one round with the Phillies manager, Nick Leyva; his bench coach, Hal Lanier; and Hal's friend Blaine McCallister, a PGA Tour player. I played multiple rounds with David Montgomery, a Phillies executive and a singularly fine man, and with his boss, Bill Giles, the team president. Also with the Phillies leadoff hitter and center fielder, Lenny Dysktra, who had been mauling National League pitchers that year. Lenny was a model of athletic arrogance on the tee and in the batter's box. His stakes were too steep for me (I kept my distance after escaping my brush with them), and the idea that he could lose on the course never seemed to occur to him. He was a good putter from ten feet and in, but Burt got way into his wallet. Lenny wouldn't take shots from Burt, though he needed them, got a lubricating 7 and 7 at the turn, then doubled down on the terms without success. As the saying goes, golf undresses a man.

In mid-June, the U.S. Open was played at Medinah. I watched chunks of its first four rounds in the manager's office at Veterans Stadium in Philadelphia. Hale Irwin and Mike Donald were tied for the lead through four rounds and met in an eighteen-hole Monday playoff, an off day for the Phillies. I knew Mike, so I had a serious fan interest. (He later became one of my closest friends.) Even if I hadn't known Mike, I would have been rooting for him. Hale Irwin was already in the golf pantheon and a megatalent, and Mike was making a living at the thing he loved most. After eighteen holes, Mike and Hale were still tied. From there, the U.S. Open went to sudden death for the first time. Hale made a birdie putt to win on the tournament's ninety-first hole. As Irwin celebrated his victory (it was brief and appropriate), Mike had the presence to retrieve Irwin's ball from the hole and return it to the man who had used it so efficiently. What class.

The Cincinnati Reds and the Oakland A's met in the World Series four months later. The paper had three writers covering it, and I sat next to a columnist I'd grown up reading, the *Times*man Dave Anderson. Had the series gone seven games, it would have wrapped up on October 24. Christine's and my wedding date was October 28, on Shelter Island, New York. (One friend took four ferries to get there.) But the Reds won the series in four games, and that gave me time to gather a small group for a golfing get-together at the Cricket Club. We played for a goofy little golf trophy I had found in a glorified junk shop near the Oakland Zoo. I named the trophy for Shivas Irons, the mystic teaching pro from *Golf in the Kingdom* by one of my heroes, Michael Murphy. I don't know a golf book with a better epigraph: "The game was invented a billion years ago—don't you remember?"

Christine and I were married on a wooden deck overlooking a secluded cove. Annie Warner—daughter of Bob Warner and his wife, Jeannie Hemphill—was our flower girl. Four months later,

Christine and I left for Europe. She had resigned from the advertising agency in New York where she worked, and I had taken a leave from the *Inquirer*. My hope was to catch on as a caddie on the European Tour. I had a small photocopied European Tour schedule folded in my wallet, showing the tour's stops in France, Spain, Portugal, Italy, Belgium, Monaco, and across the British Isles. My friend Jim Finegan in Philadelphia, the age of my parents and an expert on golf in the British Isles, pointed me to Scottish golf courses with unfamiliar, musical names: Machrie, Elie, Golspie, Nairn. Christine and I had two one-way tickets on Pan Am to Nice, France. I had a job lined up for the first week, caddying at the Mediterranean Open in Saint-Raphael, in the South of France, for an American golfer named Peter Teravainen, who had been eking out a living on the European Tour. (Good driver, mediocre putter.) As far as an actual plan, that's as far as it went. Christine was all in and then some but could not have fully understood how insecure employment was for any touring caddie, let alone one fresh out of a low-ceilinged newsroom.

We left Christine's apartment on East Eighty-Fourth Street on a cold Sunday in February, got in a New York City yellow cab, and asked the driver to take us to JFK. We were both thirty. I could smell Christine's perfume (a hint of Coco Chanel) on her sweater. The Chris Isaak hit "Wicked Game" was playing on the radio. My clubs were in the trunk. Why I was bringing them, I couldn't really say. I had no idea when I'd be able to play. I had no idea how our lives would play out in Europe. I had no idea how our lives would play out, period.

TURNING

This act is called Love and Marriage.

—Stage Manager, *Our Town*

Ginny French called 911 in Las Vegas, told a dispatcher that her son was in a hotel room, in a hysterical state, and had been talking about ending his life. Emergency responders went to Ryan's room, tranquilized him, and rushed him to a hospital. Howard and Ginny drove straight to O'Hare, got on the next flight to Las Vegas, and went directly to the hospital. Even with the sun down, the summer heat was oppressive. They never saw any sign of Ryan's companion or heard anything about her. Ryan was so sedated, he was unable to speak. After several interminable days, Howard and Ginny brought Ryan to Alpena. He was thirty, unemployed, soon to be divorced. It was not the homecoming anybody would have expected or wanted. But he was home.

When Ginny Eustis was growing up in Alpena in the 1950s and '60s, one of her closest friends was Debbie Isackson, whose father, Isadore, was a prominent lawyer in Alpena. Mr. Isackson got around town on one natural leg and one wooden one, which he would unscrew whenever Debbie wanted to show it to her squeamish friends, like Ginny. The Isackson family had a stately home in town and a beach cottage on the lake. Ginny had her own seat at their Friday-night Shabbat dinners.

Years later, Debbie married a psychiatrist in Southern California named Stephen Groban, and Stephen and Debbie, by then a social worker, came to Alpena every summer to stay in the beach cottage and, later, its replacement. They loved it there, and Stephen and Debbie and Howard and Ginny had a long series of engaging dinners at the beach and elsewhere.

After the Las Vegas episode, one of Ginny's first calls was to Stephen, who was in Alpena at the time. He was not licensed to practice psychiatry in Michigan, but he could talk to Ryan. Over time, in bits and pieces, Stephen helped Ryan think about his life in new ways. Another psychiatrist figured out which antidepressant would work best for Ryan. A medical diagnosis proved elusive. The working theory was bipolar disorder, but that typically comes with multiple events where a life spirals into chaos. Ryan had only one episode, the one in Las Vegas, which meant his parents were on constant guard for the next one. The persistent worry was exhausting but better than the alternative.

Ryan and Dr. Groban—Ryan was addressing him as a medical professional—talked about how Ryan could reconstitute his life. Golf came up in their sessions. The game had been a positive for Ryan, when you weighed it all out. Golf was something he could do while he was in Alpena. It would get him out of bed, out of the house, outdoors, in front of other people. Dr. Groban told Ryan what he told Ginny and Howard: "Let's get through this."

Golf had changed for Ryan in the dozen or so years since he had graduated from Alpena High. At Lansing Community College, golf came with the adrenaline rush of playing matches and being on a team. Golf with Lou Junior came with drinking and gambling and a different sort of adrenaline rush. For Ryan, golf with his father at Alpena this second time through was boring. His game was south of rusty and terrible. He didn't want to talk to anybody. He went from the car to the first tee without stopping in the pro shop. His high school coach worked on the course as a ranger, and it was hard for Ryan to even say hi. He was embarrassed. Growing up, he had been told he had the stuff to get out of town, to put Alpena in his rearview mirror, and here he was, back in Alpena for all the wrong reasons.

All the while, Ryan knew Alpena was saving him. Dr. Groban and other medical professionals were in his life. His parents were there every single day, with their familiar surroundings, patterns, smells. The photos on the bookshelves, the food in the fridge. The isolation of Alpena and its natural splendor, its hard-earned simplicity, its lack of temptation.

Dr. Groban helped Ryan understand his addiction to adrenaline and how it masked other pain in his life. Ryan came to understand that the bigger his life became—more Qdoba stores to manage, higher gambling stakes, more drinking, better strippers—the more adrenaline he needed to fuel the life that had become his identity. Bigger and better was his motto, until that day in the Las Vegas hotel room.

There were days when he felt like he was in high school again, playing golf with his father on the short, flat city course in Alpena, as per usual, but with less future. There were more days when he felt like a man in his early thirties who had been fitted finally for glasses that allowed him to actually see. He had insights into himself and his father that he'd never had before. Ryan could hear his father berate himself—*You are such a fuckup!*—and see for the first time what it was: his father's own depression, his own fear, his own loathing. And seeing those things in his father helped him see them in himself.

As for Howard, he had Ryan right where he wanted him: unable to escape his this-is-life commentaries. *You know, son, all that drinking, all the Las Vegas shit that nearly killed ya? That's not life. That's some fucking fantasy. This is life. Now let's see you make this goddamn putt.*

There were things about being home that Ryan liked. His mother's low-heat, no-spice cooking. His father's predictable comments during dinner and on the golf course. It was all kind of boring, on this second pass, and it was all kind of okay. Ryan was working his way through his own depression. With counselors, there was a lot of discussion about his drinking. When he was drinking heavily in his Qdoba heyday, he could easily have ten or more drinks in a night. But in Alpena, he was finding that one drink did not trigger a compulsive desire for more. Most days, he didn't have any alcohol, and didn't want any.

He was weaning himself from his desire to chase the burn, the moment of delicious pins-and-needles anxiety when the putt is rolling toward the hole, when the card is sliding toward your stack, when the stripper is heading in your direction. His needs had become more basic. The episode in the Las Vegas hotel came because he hated the person he was pretending to be. His depression in Alpena was relatively mild. He missed the burn. He missed the bars, missed being the life of the party. But on the positive side of the ledger, he was alive. He was rewiring himself. He was starting over.

• • •

By the summer of '62, Sam and Betsy Reeves had been married for four years. Sam was twenty-seven and Betsy twenty-six. They had two young daughters. They had a lovely home in a lovely section of Memphis called Hedgemoor. Sam worked downtown in a busy office with chalkboards crowded with fractions, ringing phones, and clacking typewriters. The office was near the Memphis Cotton Exchange, the epicenter of Southern cotton. Sam's company was now called Dunavant Enterprises, and he was one of its four partners. His family was well positioned in every way in Memphis.

And it was into all this good-life comfort that Sam dropped a ten-pound monkey wrench. He packed the family up and moved the clan to Fresno, California, where neither Sam nor Betsy knew a soul. They had no church there, no bank, no club, not a single relative or friend. But Sam (in concert with Billy Dunavant) had a belief and a hunch about the future of the cotton business and its California future. Right alongside that, Sam had an almost compulsive need to see what he could do with his life, his business life and his *life* life.

Sam believed that the greatest cotton in the world was already being grown in the San Joaquin Valley in central California, better than any cotton you could find in his native American South or Egypt or Peru or anywhere else. His hunch was that California cotton was undervalued and underappreciated and that there would be growing national and especially international demand for it. He felt that production of high-quality California cotton could increase, significantly.

To buy massive quantities of California cotton and sell it to the world would require two main things: deep relationships with the California cotton farmers and deep lines of credit from California banks. Dunavant Enterprises had neither. Fresno was the unofficial capital of the San Joaquin Valley. Enter Sam, flying the Dunavant flag, his family in tow, after a three-day drive.

On the family's first day in Fresno, Sam ran all over town. To a furniture store, a car dealership, a bank. Multiple trips to the modest apartment on Van Ness Avenue where the family would be living while searching for a house. In the late afternoon, Sam found a Fresno County Yellow Pages and looked up *Golf Courses, Public*. And in that section, he saw a daily-fee course called Fig Garden Golf Club. He drove over to take a look. It was on the outskirts of town, in the vicinity of the San Joaquin River. Sam parked his right-off-the-lot Ford and walked his new-in-town self into the pro shop. (His Southern drawl, a rarity in Fresno, might have been one tell.) There he was welcomed by a man named Gordon Knott. Mr. Knott, Sam quickly learned, watered his own greens, manned his own shop, and ran his own golf course. Like a child on his first day at a new school, Sam had made a new friend, and he had a new playground, too. A few days later, Sam discovered Hank's Swank, a lighted driving range with late hours where you could hit off plastic mats or real grass. Now Sam had a place to hit after-work balls. He was settling in. A couple of hours away, at Pebble Beach, the Crosby Pro-Am was played. During their first year in Fresno, Sam and Betsy drove over to take a look. Sam saw Pebble Beach for the first time. He saw Cypress Point. Windblown golf and crashing surf. Two of his favorite things.

Right around then, a young Jack Nicklaus (in his early twenties) was making a heavy-footed entrance into professional golf, and an old Ben Hogan (in his early fifties) was making an Irish exit. But Sam was like a million other golf fans. He was an Arnold guy. He was captivated by Palmer's vitality, by his vibrant play, by the yellows and pinks he wore so well, by the charisma and warmth he brought to his golf and to all of golf. What Arnold was doing on the course matched what Sam was trying to do in business. Sam had sworn off brown and, years earlier, made yellow his primary color. His many yellow sweaters and ties were a perfect match for the California sunshine that had become central to his life. He went looking for people who radiated vitality, regardless of their station in life. He liked his new home.

Sam started making regular trips abroad, to Brazil, British Hong Kong, India, Singapore, South Korea, Pakistan, Japan, Africa, eventually China. He was trying to open markets for American cotton in general and California cotton in particular. He could imagine shiploads of cotton made under the Dunavant name heading to growing countries that both needed it and could pay for it, or would be able to in the future, under better economic conditions. He was traveling for business, assessing the quality of national highway systems, warehouse capacities, the strength of domestic currencies. Fortunes have been built on less intelligence. Sometimes the roads were so bad, he got around on a motorized scooter. Sam welcomed it all. He was assessing potential like a baseball scout looking at promising players on bumpy fields in the Dominican Republic, in Panama, in Venezuela. In Cuba, if you could get in. All the while, on these overseas trips, Sam would note the vitality of the country's people. Developing countries with a vibrant citizenry, Sam believed, would eventually reject the status quo. The people in those countries would want more. The more his passport was stamped, the more Sam realized that wanting more was good for business. He rejected greed. He embraced the idea of people raising their standard of living.

Home was home. President Kennedy was assassinated in 1963, and Cliff Harrington, the gifted Army golfer Sam admired, was killed in South Vietnam in 1965. Both deaths filled Sam with sorrow. As someone who went to church not dutifully but out of actual faith, he was taken aback by a 1966 *Time* magazine cover that carried these words: *Is God Dead?* By 1967, Sam was certain the Vietnam War was unwinnable and a colossal American mistake. In 1968, Martin Luther King Jr. was assassinated on the second-floor walkway of the two-story Lorraine Motel on Mulberry Street in Memphis, not even a mile from the Cotton Exchange building. As a sentient and aware human being, Sam was startled by the violence, the antiwar protests on college campuses, the demise of civic norms on city streets, the malaise that seemingly had settled on the Lower Forty-eight like a heavy fog. As a citizen, a husband, and a father, he was pained to the core by the divisions. How could he not be?

But those accumulated horrors did not diminish his faith in mankind, nor in the global community. He was fluent in the ways and mores of the American country club, and he appreciated its comforts, but Sam had become a student of discomfort, his own and other people's. He was learning from it. He *liked* being in countries where he stood out as a minority, where he would need several languages (and interpreters) to go from one border to another, countries where there was no plush anything, where he had no privilege. In such places, he could learn something. He liked being in countries that were rich only in promise. In his travels, Sam saw knockoff Rolex watches, imitation Lacoste shirts, Japanese versions of Caterpillar tractors. It made him realize that other countries wanted what the United States already had. That was obvious. But it also made him realize that, with enough capital, those countries could make whatever America was making, possibly at a higher quality. The United States was good at banking, manufacturing, transportation, distribution. But it didn't *own* these systems. At the end of every trip, Sam returned to Fresno bullish on the world.

Travel opened his eyes in every way. By the time he'd left Thomaston for Chapel Hill at eighteen, he knew a lot about the Lehman and Goldman families, financiers of the American cotton trade. Now he was reading about the Hardoons and the Sassoons, two of the great Eastern dynastic textile and banking families. Along the way, he was learning about the difference between Sephardic Jews (the Hardoons and Sassoons, with their Eastern roots) and Ashkenazi Jews (the Lehmans and the Goldmans, with their European roots). He would meet with foreign ambassadors and diplomats who would help him read political tea leaves. He wanted to know political trends before they appeared on the front pages of *The New York Times* and *The Wall Street Journal*. Sam started making regular trips to East Asia in 1962. He and Billy Dunavant anticipated that China would open to U.S. trade long before Richard Nixon made his historic trip in February 1972. Nine months after that visit, Dunavant Enterprises became the first American cotton merchant to do business in China. There was no precedent for the company's scale of business that year. Sam and Billy had secured the services of David Hardoon as a high-end interpreter to the mysteries of China's politics, cotton trade, and social customs. Hardoon had earned knowledge, a century in the making. It paid dividends.

Sam's humanity grew with his travels. Walking out of a hotel in India, he saw a group of four young boys, nine or ten years old, as close to the entrance as they could get, dressed in little more than rags. One boy had a patch over one eye. Sam asked why. He learned that the boy's eye had been "harvested," excised by hoodlums and sold on the black market for fresh organs. Sam gave each boy an American quarter. The next day, eight kids were waiting for Sam as he came out of the hotel. Sam asked the new kids how they had found their way there. Each of the four first-day boys had told a friend about the tall American handing out quarters, Sam was told. The kids were looking out for one another. That was Sam's take. He could see that the kids were bright but malnourished. He imagined what they could do if they could eat as he ate, growing up in Thomaston, if they had his access to protein. He noted chicken production, cost, and availability wherever he went. He could see a connection between the demand for cotton and the availability of chicken. He could see a connection between growing economies and vibrant populations. He could see connections, period. He came to realize that *everything is connected*. For Sam, those three words were almost like a mantra. He picked up the word itself on his travels. He pronounced it almost as *MEN-trah*, as many Indians do.

In Thomaston, in Memphis, in Fresno, nobody was talking about China. Sam played China close to his yellow vest. When he and Billy Dunavant talked about China by phone, in their Fresno-to-Memphis conversations, Sam made sure nobody else could hear him.

Wherever he went, Sam made inquiries about the golf scene and would play sometimes with borrowed clubs, typically on primitive courses with old British Empire roots, with greens slower than the fairways back home. He wondered how long it would take for a golf craze to sweep Africa or Asia or China. He wondered about a lot of things.

•　•　•

Howard French had an idea. He and Ryan could revive one of their old father-son activities and take a caddie trip. They would identify a professional event on one of golf's smaller tours, drive to the tournament several days before its start, find a pro who needed a caddie, pitch a tent at a campsite, work the event, drive home. They had done it before. They could do it again.

Howard mentioned a tournament on the Canadian Tour being played near Toronto. This was unsaid: *It could be good for you, son.* Ryan would be up and out early in the morning, in the web of golf again, the game that had connected father and son almost forever. Ryan said yes.

Ryan called the caddie master at the course where the event would be played. The tournament, it turned out, was desperate for help. The Canadian Tour didn't typically require players to have caddies, but Golf Channel was shooting a feature, so caddies were encouraged, to make the event look more professional. For the players in the top twenty on the weekend, in the third and fourth rounds, caddies would be required. An APB went out for caddies across Toronto, with a promised per diem of fifty dollars Canadian. Unemployment was high in Toronto, and the caddie master was getting some calls, but chiefly from people who didn't know a 6-iron from a 9.

"Have you played golf?" the caddie master asked.

Ryan said he had. "Loads of golf. Me and my father."

"Good," the caddie master said.

That seemed to be the main prerequisite, to have played a round of golf.

"We have a meeting before the tournament where we go over caddie dos and don'ts," the caddie master said.

"Like what?" Ryan asked.

"Where to stand, appropriate attire, things like that."

Ryan said he and his father knew where to stand, that he had played on a college team and his father had caddied for him in hometown tournaments.

The caddie master asked Ryan for his phone number.

A couple of days later, Ryan and his father made the eight-hour drive to Toronto with camping equipment in the trunk of the car. They found a campsite near the golf course and pitched their tent. The aluminum-tube framing, the heavy steel stakes, the braided nylon guylines; the Coleman stove, the Igloo ice chest, the Kmart sleeping bags: It was all coming back to Ryan. The tent, bought used, was big enough to accommodate all five French family members, but on this trip, there were just two. The familiar musty smell of the tent's canvas walls unlocked memories of long-ago family camping trips for Ryan. They crawled into sleeping bags bigger than the cots that supported them. There was a tarp beneath them that was meant to keep the tent floor dry, not that it did.

The campsite was near an active train line, although they didn't realize how close it was until their first night. "Those goddamn trains sounded like they were coming right through the tent," Howard said. He made his morning coffee on their portable stove, green (of course) and semi-reliable.

127

The campsite had a communal restroom with several sinks and showers with warmish water. One morning, Ryan was brushing his teeth when a young man—almost a kid, really, maybe a decade younger than Ryan—came in wearing pressed pants and a fresh golf shirt. He had the at-attention manner that is common among pro golfers. He was playing in the tournament and staying in his camper, parked at the same campsite.

On other caddie trips, Ryan had seen plenty of young pros able to shoot 66 on any given day, players so good you could barely tell the difference between them and the boldface names you saw on CBS golf telecasts, Jim Nantz presiding. This kid was most likely another one, another rising talent on his way to the tour. As if it were that easy. Ryan talked for a minute with the young touring pro. He was a member of the Canadian Tour, and his camper was his home that week, as it had been at the previous event, and as it would be for the next one. Ryan stood there looking at the golfer, and a phrase came to him: The kid was chasing it. Chasing after his ball, swing improvements, lower scores, a tour he could call home. He was chasing the Friday-night cutline and the Sunday-night pay-outs. Fueling it all were the daily act of trying and the nightly act of dreaming. It was suddenly clear to Ryan. The kid's life was so simple. He was chasing it.

The phrase and the concept behind it were about as old as golf. Lee Trevino could tell you all about the chase, how fun it is, how exhilarating, how consuming. Golf promises you nothing and loads you up with problems you largely manage yourself. Yes, you might have an encouraging playing partner, a helpful caddie, a teacher who actually knows something about the swing. But over that ball, you're alone on an irregular playing field, in fickle winds, making your way to greens that are difficult to read. As is the state of your mind while it deals with athletic insecurity, physical limitation, various and sundry vulnerabilities. And still the golfer stays at it, up early, wearing a polyester costume that says *I know what I'm doing*. All that bravado and aren't-I-special self-talk. That kid in his camper was not one in a million, he was one among a million, every last one of them getting themselves to the course, to the range, to the practice green. Every last one of them saying the right things while hiding their interior lives, lest they look weak. Every last one of them, by ancient tradition, carrying themselves with a certain gentility while fighting a war within. It's not a natural thing, but it has been a way of life in professional golf for a hundred years.

Ryan and his father drove to the golf course and pulled into caddie parking. They both had bags for the week. With their qualifications? As the caddie master told Ryan, they'd be getting players with a chance. These things are hard to predict. Ryan's player missed the cut, but Ryan still made it to the weekend. He picked up another player, a young Canadian named Ryan Yip. On Thursday morning, Yip, his bag on his shoulder, was one of the 156 players in the field. By Saturday morning, he was in the top twenty and required to take a caddie. He was chasing it. Ryan was beside him, helping this new Ryan while chasing his own thing.

• • •

Sunnyside, Fresno's most prominent country club, is aptly named. The San Joaquin Valley gets about 260 sunny days per year. As soon as he could, and that was within a year or so after moving west, Sam, with his family, joined Sunnyside. Sam had never walked on such springy fairways and had never putted such smooth greens. He got into a regular game with two men, accomplished amateur golfers and former teammates at Stanford, Dick Giddings and Charley Seaver, both about twenty-five years older than Sam. They could all shoot scores in the mid- and low-70s on a regular basis and were capable of breaking 70 on any given day. They played even up (no handicap strokes) for low stakes, and if you lost two dollars, either you had played poorly or somebody else had played well. Charley had no interest in gambling. His family, growing up in Los Angeles in the 1920s, had been rich, with a tennis court and a three-hole course in the backyard. He prepped for Stanford at the Hun School, a boarding school in Princeton, New Jersey. The Depression wiped the family out financially and shaped the path of Charley Seaver's life. What he made, he kept. He was a conservative man.

Dick, a successful mortgage banker, was looser. He belonged to a half dozen clubs and had homes in Fresno, Palm Springs, and Pebble Beach. There was a lot of overlap between his golf life and his business life, but in the end, golf always won. Like Sam, he always wanted to play for something, it didn't matter what. Golf was like oxygen to Dick Giddings. When his clubs were closed on Mondays, as private clubs often are, he would play at public courses. He played in the Sunnyside club championship every year, the Fresno city and county championships, the various Northern California amateur golf events, USGA qualifiers. He always encouraged Sam to join him in these events, and Sam did, when he could. They had a golf friendship, an intimate one.

Charley had played at a national level as a young man, but his golf in adulthood was limited to weekends and holidays. He had a Monday-through-Friday job as an executive at Bonner Packing, a dried-fruit packaging company. (Bonner packed raisins by the ton, and Charley once told his bosses that cereal manufacturers should put a scoop or two of raisins in their boxes of bran flakes.) On Saturday mornings, for years and decades, Charley played with Dick and Sam. The three of them, with different fourths, played hundreds of rounds together. On Sundays, Charley and his wife, Betty, often played with Sam and Betsy. Those games sometimes came after Saturday nights at the Seaver home, a modern one-story, three-bedroom ranch house about a half mile from the Sunnyside

clubhouse and a few blocks from where the Reeves family had settled. Charley and Betty had a large lot that was lined with neat rows
of pomegranate, orange, and lemon trees. Charley tended to them
faithfully, sometimes with the help of his two sons and two daughters. They were all sturdy, attractive, and independent, with can-do
energy. They all knew their way around an extension ladder.

Sam's golf season mirrored the pro season but only by coinci-
dence. He started playing again each April, a week or so before the
Masters. He stopped playing around Labor Day, a few weeks after
the PGA Championship. In the fall and winter, cotton in the San
Joaquin Valley was harvested, ginned, baled, and shipped, and Sam
was in on every bit of it. Being a cotton merchant in central California was not a desk job. The starting point was good relationships
with the growers. Also a cadre of bankers, truck drivers, merchant
marines, mechanics, and an army of others who collectively turned
raw cotton into towels and T-shirts and powder-room rugs in numbers too big to count accurately. Sam would often say, "People need
food, and people need fiber." He was all over the fiber part of it.
During the harvest, especially from early October through the end
of February, many cotton workers Sam knew, at every level, didn't
take a day off, except maybe Christmas. Get behind, they would say,
and you would never catch up.

In Sam's business life, he was around a lot of men. But women
influenced Sam's *life* life immeasurably. In his Thomaston years,
little Sammy grew up with four women in the house: his sister and
their mother, their grandmother, and their nanny, Miss Mag. Years
later, in Fresno, a woman named Char kept order in Sam's life, for
life. Betsy and Sam brought their two young girls, Liz and Annesley, to California, and in Fresno, at St. Agnes Hospital, they had
two more, Sandy, born in 1965, and Virginia, in 1971. Sam became
active in medical philanthropy through a remarkable executive at
the hospital, Sister Ruth Marie, who was devoted, as Sam was, to

the health of both the spirit and the body. At the height of his powers at home, Sam was the executive vice president of Reeves Enterprises. Everybody reported to Betsy Reeves. With their mother's
encouragement, the four Reeves girls were active in their church,
high achievers in their schools, and dedicated to their various sports.
They swam and skied, they played golf and tennis.

Sam was in charge of overseas travel. Starting in the late 1960s,
whenever he went abroad, he brought along at least one of his
daughters. Sam wanted to make sure each girl, through her own
eyes, saw how people lived in other parts of the world, and over the
years, through multiple trips, each did. They visited hospitals and
orphanages and temples, led there by road signs that even locals
struggled to decipher. For Sam and his four daughters, the trips
were raw, emotional, eye-opening, bonding. The girls returned
to their home, their country club, and their public school with a
heightened sense of appreciation. Sam believed he and Betsy were
raising children who were both curious and empathetic. For years,
he wrote a letter to each daughter, sharing his observations of their
growth and thoughts, big and small, about the world in which they
lived.

Sam's business life, family life, and golf life were all booming.
Golf and business were largely on different tracks for him. When
Sam played with Charley and Dick on Saturdays or in tournaments,
or went to Hank's Swank for after-work range sessions, that time
was *his* time. Golf was a mini-vacation for him, a break from the
rest of his demanding life. He loved playing with Dick and Charley.
He loved standing on a range, even in intense heat, and watching
the flight of his ball, one shot after another. In his business life, Sam
thought big. Golf allowed him to narrow his focus. On the floor
above his office in Fresno, he had a second "office," this one with a
plastic-grass putting green, gym equipment, and a net he hit balls
into. He was always trying to get better.

Dick and Charley were both modest by nature, Charley especially so. Over the years, in bits and pieces, Sam learned about Charley. He found out that Charley had played several times with Bobby Jones, Sam's childhood hero. That in the 1930s, Charley played golf at Stanford, on the same team as Lawson Little, later a U.S. Open champion. That Charley had played on the American Walker Cup team in 1932 at The Country Club, on a team captained by Francis Ouimet. That Charley had played dozens of times in the Crosby Clambake at Pebble Beach and knew Bing Crosby well.

Charley was responsible for one musical footnote himself. He and Betty were married in '32, and on their honeymoon in Phoenix, they heard a piano man in a hotel lounge play a song they liked so much they asked the gent to write down the lyrics. More than twenty years later, a musical Stanford student named Dave Guard came by the Seaver home in Fresno to call on one of the four Seaver kids, Katie, who also went to Stanford, where she played volleyball. But Katie wasn't home, so Charley and Betty entertained him with their honeymoon song.

Scotch and soda, mud in your eye,
Baby, do I feel high,
Oh me, oh my,
Do I feel high.

Dave Guard liked the song so much that *he* wrote down its lyrics. A few years later, the Kingston Trio, a group Guard founded with two friends, recorded it. They tried to find the name of the original composer of "Scotch and Soda" but never could.

Betty and Charley had another, younger daughter named Carol. She was a natural athlete, too, and studied physical education at UCLA. Later, she lived in Africa with her husband, a doctor and

Peace Corps supervisor. Betty and Charley's older son, Charles Jr., was tall and rangy, and he swam at the University of California, Berkeley. He later became a writer, social worker, and sculptor who lived in Greece and New York City, among other places. He was as liberal as his father was not. The youngest of the four Seaver children, Tommy, was a promising pitcher, first at Fresno High, later at Fresno City College, and then, briefly, at the University of Southern California.

While Tommy was at USC, there was a lot of back-and-forth between the Seaver family and the office of the commissioner of Major League Baseball over Tommy's amateur status. There were stories about it in *The Fresno Bee*. People were talking about it all over town. But Tommy's path from USC to the New York Mets barely made a dent in Charley's golf-course conversation, even after the Miracle Mets won the 1969 World Series.

Tom Seaver won the Cy Young Award in 1969, '73, and '75 as a dominating righthander for the Mets. In the Reeves home, when *Game of the Week* featured the Mets, the TV was on. Sam was part of Charley Seaver's life in those years. As a father of four himself, Sam noted how Charley treated his four children equally. When they were home, they all picked backyard oranges, lemons, and pomegranates. They were grounded. Charley Seaver had grown up in a Jazz Age palace in Los Angeles with a backyard three-hole golf course, but things had changed. In Fresno, a full house meant six Seavers at home, two in each bedroom. All that left an impression on Sam, too.

• • •

For the next two years, as Ryan tried to find his way back to sunlight, he and his father continued to take their caddie trips. It never became routine. The opposite.

They traveled by car and only once stayed in a hotel, in rural North Florida, and even there, three hundred dollars for the week didn't get two people much except a room with a heavy metal key and a carpeted floor that made you want to keep your socks on. They worked events on tours named for Canada, the Dakotas, and Hooters, where the waitresses wear short shorts the color of a new basketball. They waited out rain delays where caddies huddled in maintenance sheds and played cards, smoked cigarettes, debated betting lines, and continued domestic squabbles by phone. In their golf duds, Ryan and Howard waded into a Deep South workingman's diner where (in Howard's frequent retelling) the music stopped as they slid into their booth. They spent hours and hours together in the car, sometimes ten at a stretch, Howard monitoring the fuel gauge on its way to empty on one big-log drive after another.

But it was all good. Father and son, sharing campsites and caddie yards. Not close to perfect, but certainly better than Ryan and Lou Junior on their road trips, or Ryan and Coach Blake, when Lansing Community College was playing away. At the end of one windblown Saturday during a Hooters event in Conover, North Carolina, Howard and Ryan returned to their campsite to find their tent in a tree. They laughed. A day in the life.

Ryan was caddying that week for a young player from Miami named Michael Buttacavoli, who was contending through two rounds. Sometimes a player and caddie connect, and Ryan and Michael did. Their first-round 71 and second-round 68 only helped. During a wait on a crowded tee, the two other players in the threesome started talking about the prospect of college athletes getting paid. One of them made a racist remark. Ryan and Michael, disgusted, walked off the tee in protest. That connected them, too.

Then came the third round, played on that windy Saturday, the day the French tent was uprooted and deposited in a tree. Michael shot 86. One day after his 68, he needed one more stroke per hole.

"You think they're gonna cut me from the tournament?" Michael asked Ryan, who was older and more experienced in these matters. The golfer knew something about the 86 Rule, which existed at Hooters events and on other tours. Shoot 86 or higher, you're out of the tournament.

But Ryan knew that the rule applied only to the first round. "Nah, dude—we're gonna be fine," he said. *We.*

The winner of that Hooters event was a huge talent named Willy Wilcox. Wilcox's caddie carried his big tour bag by the handle, as if it were a piece of luggage, and while wearing a NASCAR T-shirt. No caddie would get away with that at a Canadian Tour event, with its requirements for appropriate attire, but this was a Hooters stop in North Carolina, in the heart of stock-car country, at an event named for and sponsored by a nearby Ford dealership.

At night, wherever they had pitched their tent, Howard and Ryan would compare notes about what they had seen and heard. The player who had every shot a golfer might need, except the first shot on each hole. The player who refused to wear a hat in the blazing sun, not even the next day, when his face was crispy and red. The player who holed out from the fairway for an eagle on a par-5 and showed no reaction at all, and the player who holed out for an eagle on a par-3—that is, a hole in one—and started dancing like James Brown. The player who was so slow they called him the human rain delay. The player who cried after a bad Thursday, saying he was ready to quit, then came back the next day, went low, made the cut, and extended his life as a touring professional by at least a week.

Howard caddied at a tournament for Mario Tiziani, a son of the Midwest and the brother-in-law of Steve Stricker, the PGA Tour veteran. All through the Sunday round, Tiziani kept asking Howard for the time. Howard finally asked why. "I've been on the road for six weeks," Tiziani told him. "I gotta get that last flight out tonight. I need to get home, see my wife, see my kids."

Howard and Ryan were seeing life in action. Ryan was seeing how slow and wrenching life actually is.

Howard caddied for a golfer named Parker LaBarge, who was spending more than he was making. Howard asked how long he would stay at it. LaBarge said, "As long as I can honestly say I'm getting better, I'll stay at it. If I can honestly say I'm not, I'll quit. The hard part is being honest."

At another tournament, Howard worked for an Australian pro named Mitch Tasker. They were standing on the first tee, before the first round, preparing to go off.

"Good luck," Howard said.

"I don't need luck, I need to play well," Tasker said, not harshly. "You can say, 'Play well.'"

"Play well," Howard said. He was happy to learn something.

For years to come, Howard shared these little stories, with their life-lesson punch line quotes, with anybody he thought might appreciate them. That was most people.

Don't say good luck, say play well.

A year after their first caddie-trip event in Toronto, Howard and Ryan returned to the same campsite and the same tournament, and this time Ryan had Ryan Yip, the young Canadian golfer, not just for the weekend but for the whole tournament. After seventy-two holes, Yip was in a three-man sudden-death playoff. Howard came out to watch.

On the third playoff hole, a par-5 reachable in two, Yip's tee shot was heading for a fairway bunker. It missed. Howard gave the shot the baseball safe signal. Yip figured that meant he had a decent lie in the rough. He walked up to his ball. It was nestled down in the rough. "What the fuck is your dad talking about?" Yip said to Ryan. The heat of the moment.

Yip slugged his second shot from the rough and got his third on and his fourth in. With his birdie, he won the tournament. The first-place check was for twenty thousand dollars, and he made an extra five thousand for being the low Canadian. A fortune. The tournament director gave Yip a large cardboard check, suitable for photography but not for deposit.

Ryan asked Yip what he would do to celebrate. Eat at McDonald's, Yip said, and then make the drive from Toronto to Montreal for the next event. He put the cardboard check in the backseat and told Ryan he would mail him a check for the caddie's cut of the winner's haul. Two practice rounds, four tournament days, lots of encouragement along the way. Caddying is interesting work. You get to see people in stressful situations play a difficult sport at close range. You get to help. Ryan wasn't doing it for the money, but he wasn't turning down money, either.

Howard and Ryan drove back to Alpena. Soon after, the check from Yip arrived, for five hundred dollars, along with a note. Ryan could have made more in one afternoon playing golf and cards with Lou Junior. But this was better. Ryan framed the note and hung it on a wall. It read like a nice thank-you note. Ryan took it for more than that. It was about Ryan's fight to stay in the game. Ryan French *and* Ryan Yip.

• • •

The 1972 U.S. Amateur at the Charlotte Country Club had been on Sam's mind for a year or more. The course was one Sam played first as a student at the University of North Carolina, three hours from campus by car. He was a teenager then. Sam turned thirty-eight in the summer of '72. He and Betsy had four children. He was running (with Billy Dunavant) a global cotton business from an office in Fresno. He was working compulsively on a deal with China the likes of which most cotton people never could have imagined.

But always, with Sam, there was golf. He had his regular weekend games at Sunnyside and a spot practically reserved for him on the Sunnyside driving range. When he couldn't get there, he had Hank's Swank. (He always had clubs in the trunk of his car.) Through the years, Dick Giddings had encouraged Sam to play in the qualifiers for the U.S. Amateur, and Sam had tried a handful of times without ever making it. The window was closing. The U.S. Amateur was dominated by golfers in their twenties and early thirties. Arnold Palmer won the 1954 U.S. Amateur at age twenty-four. In 1955 and '56, Sam's Chapel Hill years, the Amateur was won by E. Harvie Ward, a debonair life-of-the-party North Carolina alum in his early thirties. The event was won later by top college players, including Jack Nicklaus from Ohio State and Bob Murphy from the University of Florida. In the summer of '72, if you followed amateur golf in the United States, you knew the name Ben Crenshaw. Crenshaw, a star golfer at the University of Texas, was the headliner going into the Amateur in Charlotte, at least to the small number of fans who followed an obscure offshoot of a niche sport. Thirty-eight wasn't old. But it was getting there.

DICK: *You're playing good golf.*
SAM: *Be fun to finally get in one, make it a sort of homecoming.*
DICK: *You play your regular golf, and that should be enough.*

Dick was talking about the thirty-six-hole qualifying events that served as the gatekeeper to the Am, as the players call it.

Across the country, there were thirty-nine qualifying events and 2,295 golfers playing for 143 available spots in the '72 Amateur, contested not in its traditional match-play format but (getting toward the end of an experiment) as a four-round stroke-play event, no different than the weekly PGA Tour tournaments. Sam signed up for a qualifier at the Silverado Country Club, part of a sprawling resort in Napa Valley, a straight-shot four-hour drive north on California

99, through Modesto and Stockton. At Silverado, forty-nine play-ers would compete for three spots and a no-expenses-paid trip to Charlotte.

Sam could never contend with the Ben Crenshaws of American golf, not over multiple rounds, but just to get in the same field as that crowd in a national event would be a remarkable achievement for a thirty-eight-year-old weekend golfer with a family and a job. The pursuit of status is a motivator in every walk of life, but Sam's drive seemed to be more inward. He liked the test. He liked finding out what he could do, identifying what he could not, and trying to get better at it. In his own way, Sam was like James Gatz, with his "general resolves." (*Read one improving book or magazine per week. Save $3.00 per week. Be better to parents.*) Sam was always trying to get better at golf. He tinkered with new equipment, tried to make his practice sessions more effective, sought ways to streamline his swing thoughts. Years earlier, he had figured out that he retained only about 1 percent of what he heard and maybe 5 percent of what he saw. (He had been compensating for nearsightedness all his life.) But what he *experienced*, he found, settled in his core. And that was part of golf's intense appeal for Sam. Golf was an experience.

You and your playing partners and opponents. You and the course. You and your clubs. You and the elements. You and your own self. Sam believed that any round of golf was a real-life *some-thing*, with the capacity to be transformative, just as a book or a lecture or a sermon might be, but way more fun and way more invigorating, what with the wind, the passing (you hope!) showers, the sunshine, the camaraderie. The big field and the little ball and the distant hole. Sam found that every round of golf taught him something, and competitive golf taught him even more. The higher the level at which he played, the more intense the experience be-came. That might not sound like a good time to you, but it was for Sam. He could feel the joy of it in his bones.

Any USGA championship event is, by definition, a national event. Qualifiers are regional, but the main-stage shows are national affairs. Arnold Palmer liked to call the U.S. Open the *National* Open, borrowing the phrase from his father. Playing in a U.S. Open was not realistic for Sam. Even the last guy in an Open played at a far higher level. But a spot in the National Amateur was feasible, and just the idea kept Sam up at night. Sam had grown up on Teddy Roosevelt's man-in-the-arena credo. He had been close to getting in before. He could imagine the first-tee exhilaration that would come with having your name announced by a blue-blazered USGA official. He welcomed the chance to go mano a mano with his nerves. He liked that success or failure rested on a number on a scorecard for which he alone was responsible.

He brought a caddie with him to Silverado, a young man from Fresno named Mick Gromis. Sam knew Mick from their church in Fresno, First Presbyterian. Mick was in medical school. He didn't know much about golf, and Sam didn't need him to. What Sam needed was a caddie who could keep calm and keep up, and Mick could do that. They drove to Silverado the day before the qualifier and spent the night at the resort.

For the qualifier, Sam was in a group with a significant figure in American golf, a San Francisco lawyer named Sandy Tatum. Tatum at fifty-two still played good golf. He was a formidable presence: tall and strong, with thick, white hair and a magnificent vocabulary. (He loved the word *appropriate*.) Sandy had grown up on the country club side of the tracks in Los Angeles and, as a kid, had watched Charley Seaver and Bobby Jones play. (Also, from a greater distance and with a different kind of zeal, Katharine Hepburn with Howard Hughes.) Tatum played at Stanford a decade after Charley Seaver. He was on the USGA's executive committee, bound for its presidency, and persuaded its members to bring the U.S. Open to Pebble Beach, where it had been played two months earlier. That 1972 U.S. Open was the first one held at Pebble Beach, and the ABC telecast showed Pebble in all her ocean-sprayed majesty. It was the first U.S. Open held at a public course, and it was won by golf's most dominating player, Jack Nicklaus. Though the course was short, the scores were high—the week showed the USGA at its stern-father best. Nicklaus shot rounds of 71, 73, 72, and 74. Arnold Palmer shot himself out of any chance to win with a fourth-round 76; Lee Trevino did, too, with a closing 78. The event was glorious, and some of its glory illuminated Tatum by way of bounced light. Tatum's status got a bump.

And there Tatum was on the first tee at Silverado, pipe in mouth, shaking hands with Sam Reeves. They had never met. Giddings and others had advised Sam to be careful to do *everything* by the book, because Sandy Tatum would be watching, and Sandy Tatum knew all. If you were going to hit a provisional for a possible lost ball, announce it, because the rule book requires you to do so. Like all true golfers, Sam believed the rules were the foundation for tournament golf. But he also believed that USGA officials sometimes went out of their way to catch players breaking rules inadvertently, that they played *gotcha!* and enjoyed it, and Sam despised that. If you investigate at all, you'll find that every rule is steeped in logic, but you'll run out of air trying to convince nonbelievers of that.

Sam had prepared for the qualifier the only way he knew how, which was exhaustively. He called his old teacher from the Forest Lake Club in Columbia, Melvin Hemphill, and they talked about the importance of Sam beginning his swing with his chin making a gentle nod in the direction of his right shoulder, and the right shoulder rotating from twelve o'clock to one o'clock. (Golfers use the faces of clocks, whiskey barrels, panes of glass, heavy ropes, buckets of water, and other images lying around in an effort to manage their swings. Sam was a golf-swing obsessive, so all these items were rattling around in his head.) Every golf swing reflects the personality of its owner-operator; every swing blends the tried and true with personal bits. All swings share some traits—they start and finish— and all swings are unique. Sam's swing was long and upright and fast. Sandy Tatum, on his backswing, came to a complete stop, like his swing was going to take a little nap before heading on down. Sam had never seen anything like it.

The golfers and their swings were off and on their way. As every swing is the same and different, every round of golf is the same and different, too. You head out, make the turn, head home. By the time you're done, you're never exactly the same. Chaucer would have loved golf, and Updike did. Sam was making pars. His walk had a rhythm and his swing did, too. He was getting the messages from his head to his hands without interference. He was making good swings.

Sam's threesome made the turn. In stroke play, there are no fresh starts. The tenth hole makes way for the eleventh, but the tenth is on your card forever. You go step by step until you pick your ball out of the eighteenth hole. Sam signed for a first-round 72. His day was halfway done, and he was in it. He ate a quick lunch and was off again. Sometimes it's night and day, two rounds in one day, but Sam kept it going on this day and went out in 36, even par. With nine holes to go, he was in good shape, but the challenge in golf, always, is getting to the house.

Like a million golfers before him, Sam was talking to himself:

Two hands on the wheel.
Don't make a double.
Doesn't have to be great, just good enough.
Two-putt here and call it a day.

His *here* was the home green. He two-putted there for an afternoon 76. He was at 148 for the two rounds. (Tatum had shot 75 and

79 for 154.) Now all Sam could do was wait and see what the rest of the day would bring. He would not be the medalist, the old Scottish term for the day's lowest score (from the modest medal awarded for monthly competitions at many Scottish clubs). Bruce Robertson, a Stanford golfer, had shot 146 and was the leader in the house. But Sam knew he had a shot at advancing to Charlotte. All he could do was fidget and wait. There's no defense in golf.

The day's highest scores were upsetting to see. The USGA had put together two older and decorated players and sent them off as a twosome: a noted California golfer and bartender named Verne Callison and his friend E. Harvie Ward, fifteen years past his prime but eager to try to get back to North Carolina, his home state, for this U.S. Amateur. The day before the qualifier, Ward told a sportswriter from the *San Francisco Examiner* that his job would be to "hit the ball, drag Verne," riffing on Callison's slow playing pace. Sportswriters loved E. Harvie, and some knew the story of his 1956 match, in which Harvie and Ken Venturi, then another hotshot amateur, played Ben Hogan and Byron Nelson at Cypress Point in a birdie-fest better-ball match. Harvie was a popular figure in the game, one who logged many long nights in various taprooms. Leading up to that qualifier at Silverado, he had stopped his evening habits and worked on his game for months. But the word at the qualifier was that he had succumbed to the lure of the lounge the night before, alongside Verne. Callison shot 91 in the morning and 83 in the afternoon. The only score higher belonged to Harvie, 82 and 93. That hit-and-drag bit no longer seemed amusing.

The day's low score turned out to be the 146 shot by Robertson, which meant that another Stanford golfer was going to the Amateur in a long list of them, as Tatum had done in his day and Seaver in his. Mark Lye, a member of the San Jose State golf team, was in at 148, the same score as Sam's. Those were the low three scores for most of the afternoon, until twenty-year-old Bill Malley came in at 147. That meant Robertson and Malley were in, and Lye and Sam would be in a playoff for the third spot. But that situation didn't last long.

Shortly after Malley signed his scorecard, a tournament official told him that he had been disqualified. Earlier in the summer, Malley had tried to qualify for another USGA event, one for amateur golfers who didn't belong to private clubs, called the U.S. Amateur Public Links Championship, an event that Verne Callison had won twice. The USGA had a rule by which you could attempt to qualify for only one or the other, the Publinx (as it was known) or the Am. Malley didn't realize that *attempting* to qualify for the Publinx—he had not made it—left him ineligible for the Am. There's a lot of fine print in every USGA competition. Pages of rules, regulations, and requirements. Malley was out. Harsh but fair, and Malley accepted his fate without complaint. The USGA ruled with an iron fist in that era, and the golfers were happy to have it as an authority figure in their lives, to tell them what to do and keep a sense of order and decorum. Mark Lye and Bruce Robertson went out for dinner. Sam and his caddie, Mick, drove back to Fresno, Mick with a wad of fresh cash in his wallet. Golf turns on happenstance, luck, all manner of events, fortunate and otherwise. But doesn't everything?

●　　●　　●

Ryan was home, and nobody knew for how long. Ginny and Howard—and now Ryan—were living out in the country, seventeen miles from downtown Alpena, down a long driveway, in a house built by Ginny's parents, by then long gone. Over time, Ryan was helping more in the house and on the property. Clearing snow, raking leaves, getting the mail, painting and plumbing and the rest. There was a lot to do.

"If Ryan winds up living with us for the rest of our lives, are you okay with that?" Ginny asked Howard.

Ryan had turned thirty-one on their watch, and then thirty-two.

"It's not what we ever would have expected," Howard said.

"But would you be okay with it?"

"Of course."

They were half expecting that to be the case, so they were startled when Ryan told them he was ready to be on his own again. He wanted to move to Chicago. This was in the dog days of summer in 2010. Ginny and Howard's fear that another psychotic episode could come had never abated.

"I'm going to prove to you I can do this," Ryan said.

Ryan was not ready for his mother's response. She thanked him.

"For what?"

"For letting me be your mother again," she said.

Without a moving truck or any sort of grand farewell, Ryan made his way to Chicago, six hours by car from Alpena. A first step toward resuming his adult life. He had a job lined up with Qdoba corporate, nothing to do with Lou. Ryan's sister lived in Chicago. Ryan had a friend in Chicago named Jacob, the manager of the Qdoba store at the corner of LaSalle and Washington. Jacob had invited Ryan to live with him. Ryan could stay as long as he wished while he figured out his life.

Jacob had a Halloween party at his apartment in Boystown, a historic gay neighborhood. Jacob invited a friend from college, Stephanie, a young nurse. She once was engaged, but her fiancé had died. Jacob introduced Stephanie to his new roommate, Ryan French. Jacob was gay, and Stephanie figured Jacob and Ryan were a couple, but they weren't. Just friends.

In the following weeks, Stephanie came over to the apartment and hung out with Jacob and Ryan and Jacob's pals. One night the whole gang went to a drag bar near Jacob's apartment. A performer, a man wearing blue lipstick and a dress, approached Ryan.

"I know you're straight," the drag queen said.

"I am!" Ryan said.

"Then why are you here?" the performer asked before planting a blue kiss on Ryan's cheek.

Ryan laughed. Stephanie found that endearing. Her late fiancé would not have responded like that. Nor her father. Nor any other man she had ever known. They were all so worried about their image. Ryan was different. Like Ryan, Stephanie was unplanned. She was born ten years after her father had undergone a vasectomy that apparently didn't work. Stephanie was looking for people who were open, welcoming, and accepting. That's how she was, and she could see Ryan was, too.

By the time they had their first table-for-two date, Christmas was in the air. Stephanie had played cello all her life as Ryan had played golf. They debated which pursuit had higher snob appeal. Cello playing won once Stephanie came to understand Ryan's Alpena course was nothing like Judge Smails's Bushwood Country Club.

Stephanie was twenty-five, and Ryan had turned thirty-three. They were both in Chicago to start over. Stephanie had grown up in Traverse City, on the other side of the Michigan mitten. Her parents were as reticent as Ryan's were open. Her exposure to golf was limited to a single round in high school when she was trying to get a boy to notice her. Her fiancé had died of a massive heart attack in the middle of the night, in a bed they shared in a house in Grand Rapids. The fiancé's mother blamed Stephanie for not saving her son's life. *You call yourself a nurse?* After the death, Stephanie's father drove from Traverse City to Grand Rapids. He said to her, "Well, these things happen." Stephanie couldn't get out of Grand Rapids fast enough.

And now she and Ryan were on their first date, at the Rock Bottom Brewery, near the Navy Pier, in the vicinity of so many apparently happy and demonstrably shiny people, walking through Chicago's downtown, and their lives, in some kind of contented daze, frothy coffee drinks in hand. Ryan and Stephanie were barely aware of them. Later, Stephanie had the date of their engagement tattooed on her left foot. Yes, she was drunk. Still, she had no next-day regrets.

Who can explain chemistry between two people? This wasn't caddie-player chemistry, even when jump-started by rounds of 71 and 68, although it had elements of that. It wasn't let's-see-where-it-goes chemistry. It was off-and-running chemistry. Fifteen months after they met, Ryan and Stephanie were married in Key West, Florida. They stayed at the Southernmost Inn. They were married on a beach by Ginny's addiction-prone sister in one of her semi-sober periods, ordained for the occasion. Aunt Helen was a gay woman and briefly a train conductor. Everybody at the wedding knew the story about when she and a nun broke out of rehab, sledded down a giant hill on flattened cardboard boxes, climbed a fence, and resumed their drinking lives at a trucker bar they found after crossing a freeway.

Aunt Helen was on her game that day, spectacularly so: "This is a happy occasion, as Ryan and Stephanie stand before us to declare and celebrate their love and their marriage. Their path has not been easy. Perhaps because of this, they value their commitment and their happiness, and indeed this wedding, much more so than had it been otherwise. They know they can never take their relationship for granted. They know that they have found in each other that unique, mysterious quality whereby they know they were meant for each other. They know, too, with the poet, that 'true love comes but once.' Love, in human life, is acknowledged by all, but it eludes all defining and explanation. Only the poets dare comment."

Stephanie and Ryan wrote their own vows. Ryan promised Stephanie "to grow old with you and to stay young with you." Stephanie promised Ryan "to always see the good in you."

They wrapped up the public portion of their wedding night at a strip club in Key West. The groom was still wearing his pink Loud-mouth pants from the John Daly collection. The bride was still in her traditional white dress, accented by a pink ribbon and with deep pockets sewn into it to hold her waterproof insulin pump. The wa-terproof part is noteworthy because on their first morning as a newly married couple, back in their wedding-day finery and at the request of their hilarious wedding photographer, they jumped off a dock and into a Key West bay. Stephanie's dress was suddenly swarming her head, and for a while there, she flailed around amid all that wet linen and chiffon, desperate for air. Privacy concerns were nonexis-tent for a few long and frightening moments. Ryan later imagined a *Miami Herald* headline: BRIDE DROWNS IN KEY WEST AFTER STUPID STUNT FOR PHOTOGRAPHER. They dried off and returned to Chicago.

In the early months of their marriage, Stephanie and Ryan lived with Jacob. Ryan could say about his life with Stephanie what she could say about hers with Ryan: Each had never been happier. Each could be open with the other. There was no posturing. Stephanie had their wedding date tattooed on her right foot, a complement to the tattoo on her left, with the words *Love Conquers All*. She was not drunk.

When her father died, Stephanie asked Ryan, "Is it wrong that I'm not more upset?" She had a husband and a partner she could actually share things with.

Ryan was working in the food business, sixty and seventy hours a week. Stephanie was working as an emergency room nurse. They were a busy couple. But they were together, and it was good.

• • •

Sam's father was ill. He was being treated for lung and throat cancer at the Mayo Clinic in Rochester, Minnesota. Like a lot of the people of his generation, especially in small southern towns, the elder Sam Reeves was a smoker. Sam had been visiting him there for months.

When Sam was at Silverado, playing in the U.S. Amateur qualifier, Betsy and the girls were in Europe. Overseas travel was always a high priority for the Reeves family, and they didn't travel with steamer trunks. Sam would have joined them had he not qualified for the Amateur. But he did, and that changed his end-of-summer plans. His first stop on his way to Charlotte was to check in on his father, at Mayo. Sam saw immediately that his father's health had deteriorated since his last visit. That confrontation with the inevitability of death is always startling, especially when it comes at arm's length or closer.

"Should I still go to Charlotte?" Sam asked.

"Absolutely," his father said. "Just do your best."

Sam wasn't so sure, but he went.

He flew first to Columbia, South Carolina, to see Melvin Hemphill, and they worked together at Forest Lake on a Sunday, a day Melvin normally took off. Sam played practice rounds at the Charlotte Country Club on Monday and Tuesday. The first round was scheduled for Wednesday, the second for Thursday. If you made the two-day cut, you played on Friday and Saturday. Sam stayed with a college friend who lived in Charlotte.

A heavy rain delayed first-round play, and instead of going off at his scheduled time, close to noon, Sam and his two playing partners went off shortly after four p.m. They finished in the gloaming. Sam shot an 81, with three double bogeys. The next day, Sam shot a 77, with a double bogey on the eighth, just as he had done in the first round. Four over on one hole, and he missed the cut by four shots. It's easy to slice off four shots in your mind, but four shots is a chasm, really. Mark Lye missed the cut, too. Bruce Robertson was one shot off the lead through two rounds.

Sam won just by getting there. He was able to prove to himself that he was good enough to make it into the tournament. If he had played his best, maybe he could have made the cut, but that's golf. You can't just summon your best every time. Nobody ever has. Up and down the range and in the locker room were players Sam could beat two times in ten, if that. Joel Hirsch, an insurance executive from Chicago. Mark Hayes, a star golfer at Oklahoma State. Vinny Giles, a lawyer from Richmond. Ben Crenshaw. They were all in the same tournament, but they played a different game, in a different league. Sam had tried his best. He had no question about that. He had followed his father's imperative.

• • •

Ryan and Stephanie had their first child, Annie, fifteen months after their wedding. On the day of her birth, Ryan thanked his parents for the two-plus years he'd spent in Alpena discovering himself and reclaiming life. His list was long: Dr. Groban and other counselors; golf games with his father; their caddie trips; the many, many meals with his parents; and all that everyday conversation about Michigan football, Michigan State basketball, Detroit Tigers baseball, and who did what at this major golf event and that one. "If that window in Las Vegas had opened, I wouldn't be here," Ryan told his mother.

Yes, Ginny thought. *And if you hadn't met Steph, we all wouldn't be here.*

Two years later, Stephanie gave birth to a boy. Annie had a kid brother. The parents had a large baby. Jack arrived a month early and weighed in at ten pounds, six ounces.

When he was little more than a month old, he started projectile-vomiting every day, even though he had no obvious signs of illness. In the middle of the night, he would often shriek in pain, but he had no fever, no congestion, no digestive issues. Ryan and Stephanie were mystified and terrified.

One doctor said Jack was being overfed, and another said he was being underfed. There was a revolving door of doctors' appointments and MRIs. Jack's first two-word sentence was *No masks*. When he saw the mask, he knew it meant he was going under for another bone-rattling MRI. The months turned into a year and most of a second. Nobody could explain Jack's vomiting, his nighttime pain, his poor balance. His cerebral development was fine. Better than fine. But the quality of his life was severely compromised by his mysterious pains.

After one MRI, Ryan and Stephanie were in a waiting room when Jack's report, somehow routed the wrong way, was brought directly to them. On the report, Ryan and Stephanie could see, plain as day, two words listed under the possible diagnosis: *Chiari malformation*. Even with all of her nursing education and hospital experience, Stephanie was unfamiliar with the term. In that moment, a Google search box is not your friend. *A condition in which brain tissue extends into the spinal canal.*

Jack's second birthday was approaching. Annie would soon turn four. Stephanie and Ryan, functioning day after day on little sleep, found their way to a pediatric neurosurgeon in Chicago named John Ruge. Dr. Ruge had experience with Chiari (*KEE-are-ee*). In Jack's case, and to put it crudely, the interior of his skull (nothing anyone could detect from the outside) was too small. That is, the actual volume of space, which meant his brain tissue did not have the space it required. Seeking more space, his brain matter was forcing itself down into the northern reaches of his spinal canal, the vertical tunnel that houses the spinal cord. In these crowded conditions, the part of the brain that triggers vomiting can be stimulated. It's an odd and rare disease.

The surgical fix was one Dr. Ruge had performed before. Yes, it was brain surgery, and as Dr. Ruge explained to Steph and Ryan, all brain surgery is a ten on the one-to-ten this-is-serious scale. One goal of the surgery, in the interest of creating more space for Jack's brain, was to stretch and score the dura, the protective cushion around the brain. That is, pull it tightly in all directions while making tiny incisions in it, to promote elasticity. Another goal was to scrape bone matter from the bottom of the skull, again in the name of creating space. Those two objectives only begin to describe the intricate, complex nature of the surgery that Dr. Ruge would be performing and Jack would be enduring.

The young patient, a month short of two, was in the operating room for ten hours. At the end of a long, stressful day, Steph and Ryan huddled in a quiet corner of a waiting room in a hospital in Oak Park, Illinois. Dr. Ruge entered and walked toward them. The parents were terrified. Dr. Ruge's face was impassive. Steph and Ryan could read nothing in it. The walk might have taken half a minute, but it seemed like half an hour. Ryan began to prepare himself for the worst news possible, but his mind wouldn't go there. Dr. Ruge's mouth began to move in slow motion.

Everything went as planned. No complications. It all went well.

Stephanie had never felt a greater sense of relief. Jack's pain was her pain, and it had been lifted. She looked at Ryan, thinking she should try to keep her composure for his benefit. She couldn't. He couldn't, either. At that moment, they realized, your doctor becomes your god, no matter how agnostic you might be.

After the surgery, Jack's violent vomiting ceased. So did the middle-of-the-night fluid buildup and the incapacitating pain it wrought. Jack's balance remained poor. His capacity for problem-solving remained high. There were some quirks. He was shy and quiet. (His sister compensated in those areas.) When he started drawing and writing, Jack used his right hand for the right side of the paper and his left hand for the left. Or maybe that, too, was another sign of superior intelligence, along with his early reading? Football was put on Jack's prohibited list. As were boxing and lacrosse. Other sports were fine. They weren't likely to be easy for him, but Jack could try as much as he liked. He could hunt.

Great, just what I need, Ryan thought. A hunter.

That summer, the summer of '17, young Jack French was recovering from his surgery. He had turned two. His sister had turned four. Ryan had turned forty and was working seventy-hour weeks for McAlister's, a national chain of delis. Stephanie continued to work as a nurse but had left the emergency room for the operating room. They had a large mortgage on a small home in the village of Lombard, in suburban Chicago, and costly medical bills. These bills were coming from everywhere, it seemed, and for Ryan and Stephanie, it was overwhelming. They negotiated the bills as best they could, in accordance with the semi-accepted parameters of the modern health-care industry, but the grand total was still over fifteen thousand dollars, which would have wiped out their savings. Ryan and Stephanie got on a monthly plan to pay off the bills. Their legal obligation was one thing, their psychic debt to the Chicago medical community something more. Dr. John Ruge, along with the residents, nurses, technicians, orderlies, and all the other people around him, had saved their son's life.

Ryan's work-life balance was nonexistent. Playing golf was out of the question, but he followed professional golf as he always had, as an early-morning hobby, plus golf telecasts on the weekend. With the internet, it had never been easier to keep up with who was doing what. If a pro was cashing a tournament check somewhere—on the PGA Tour, the Korn Ferry Tour, the European Tour, on tours in Asia and Latin America and the Dakotas—chances were good that Ryan had seen the name and the number. That was his connection to golf.

With Stephanie working a forty-hour week and Ryan working far more than that, they needed a full-time nanny. For most of the previous two years, they'd had one, Paulina, a student at Elmhurst University with good instincts, a playful manner, and a desire to teach Annie and Jack her native language, Polish. But she graduated from college, got a job in her chosen field (finance), and moved on. Steph and Ryan struggled to find a replacement.

In came Jordan, by way of a website. She was twenty and disarmingly attractive. She would arrive at the French house in the western suburbs of Chicago in little more than a sports bra and sweatpants, and that didn't help. It quickly became apparent that for wit, musical ability, and some other things, Jordan was never going to be the Maria of Chicagoland governesses.

The beginning of her end started on her first day, and it concluded for good one afternoon when Ryan and Stephanie were moving their two car seats from Jordan's car to the French family Dodge Grand Caravan. The car seats reeked of freshly smoked pot. Not that the Caravan smelled like a fresh daisy on its best day. In a previous life, it had been used for soup delivery, and when Stephanie and Ryan came into it, the first thing they had to do was strip its sides of stickers depicting giant bowls of chicken potpie. Yes, it was another work van. But spilled soup was one thing. Spent weed was another. Jordan was out. Stephanie had a replacement in mind.

"You hate working at McAlister's," Stephanie told Ryan. "Between your job and mine, it's like we're leading separate lives. We're spending a fortune on nannies, and we can't find a good one. Why don't you just quit and be at home with Annie and Jack?"

That little speech changed everything. It didn't make sense—they were already broke—but it did change everything.

· · ·

Vinny Giles, the Richmond lawyer, won the 1972 Amateur on the Saturday of Labor Day weekend. Bruce Robertson finished sixth, which qualified him for the 1973 Masters. Sam was back in his father's room at the Mayo Clinic by then. He told his father about the event, but they didn't dwell on it. He knew his father was getting near his end. Sam could see it and hear it.

"The doctors are keeping me alive, but they don't know the pain I'm in," his father said.

Sam knew then that he'd be staying until his father died. They talked a little, about golf, family, the cotton business, Thomaston. Not much about God or the hereafter. The elder Sam Reeves wasn't built for that and had never been a big talker under the best of circumstances. Father told son, "I hope your children turn out as well as you and Martha did."

His funeral was in Thomaston two weeks later. Thomas Fambro (Sam) Reeves was sixty-eight. His obituary noted that he was a member of the United Methodist Church, the American Cotton Shippers Association, and the Thomaston Country Club. Sam delivered the eulogy. He said, "My prayer must be that I can be as good a father to my girls as he was to me."

Two months later, Sam received this letter from Melvin Hemphill, written in artistic cursive on Forest Lake Club stationery:

Dear Sammy,

I hadn't known about your father's death until I received your letter. I know how close the two of you were and what he meant to you, but it was a blessing. He had suffered so much.

Under the conditions, I didn't expect you to play well in the National Amateur. In fact, you played better than I expected.

It did my heart good for you to compare me with your father.
Give my regards to Betsy and family,
Melvin

Regarding *under the conditions*, Melvin Hemphill wasn't referring to the long, wet course in Charlotte, Sam was sure of that. Melvin meant Sam's state of mind, the distraction of knowing his father was in a hospital room in Rochester, Minnesota, in pain, far from his family, preparing for the inevitable. In a peculiar sort of way, the 148 that Sam shot at Silverado was a final and unexpected gift from son to father, but also from father to son. Little Sammy had started on a nine-hole course in Thomaston where his father played and had made his way to the National Amateur.

• • •

The French family experiment, with Ryan as a stay-at-home dad, started in the summer of 2017, after Jack's surgery. It continued into the fall, when Annie began preschool. The family was still living in the same house, in Lombard, twenty miles west of downtown Chicago. The family paid its bills, and the mortgage, on what Stephanie earned as a nurse. At least they tried to. Ryan took jobs as needed. He was a server for a while, then a bartender. He stocked shelves at a supermarket, the Jewel-Osco on Main Street in Lombard, working the eleven p.m. to seven a.m. shift. He would come home, and Stephanie would leave for the hospital. That arrangement didn't last long.

Ryan was looking for ways to be productive. Every day, he looked up golf scores across the internet, a modern version of what he used to do as a kid in the sports section of the *Detroit Free Press*. He still had more interest in the bottom of the list than the top.

The internet was a bottomless mine of golf results—if you knew where to find them. Ryan did, but it was work. He would check the websites for the Canadian Tour and the Dakotas Tour. *Do they go from Minot to Fargo, or Fargo to Minot?* He followed the qualifying tournaments that determined eligibility for the PGA Tour. He followed the Tour's Monday qualifiers, where one hundred or more dreamers would attempt to play their way into Tour events. He had a morbid curiosity in the pre-qualifiers for these Monday qualifiers. Basically, he was interested in the path that golfers took, or tried to take, to get to the show, the PGA Tour. Ryan was almost consumed by it, and he imagined there had to be other fans who were, too. He wondered: Could there be a hundred other people who had his level of interest? Sure. A thousand? No way.

As a public service, and for the fun of it, Ryan tried to create an electronic repository of this arcane information. The results, he imagined, could be distributed on Twitter, although he knew almost nothing about Twitter. His first task, he discovered, would be to give his new account a name. This was about a year after Jack's surgery. He was about to turn three and doing much better.

Ryan liked a *Seinfeld* bit called "a case of the Mondays." He tried to play off it with a nod to his interest in Monday qualifiers. It was rejected by way of an automated response. Ryan tried some variants. Twitter, with robotic efficiency, suggested this unclaimed handle instead: *acaseofthegolf1*. Ryan thought, *How stupid does that sound?* But he took it anyhow, for the benefit of his hundred hypothetical followers.

Most golf websites lead with the famous and go to the obscure reluctantly. Ryan was doing the opposite. His golfers were the players he saw on the caddie trips he took with his father. The young pro in the restroom at the campsite in Toronto and a thousand others like him. Within a month or two, Ryan had seven hundred followers. Tiger Woods, at that point, had more than six million. Still, seven hundred was about six hundred more than Ryan thought he would ever have.

He named the account (a broader heading than the handle) Monday Q Info. When he talked about it with Stephanie and his golf friends, he referred to it as *the account*. When he told his father about the account, Howard said, "Can you print it out?" *Well, you can, but that's not how it works.* His father was not the target audience. Howard checked his email weekly.

Monday Q Info gave Ryan something more purposeful to do than watch cartoons with Jack on TV. He worked on the account while sitting at a small desk in the dining room.

Ryan knew weird things about golf's struggling class. He was drawn to those players. He knew the names of well over a thousand professional golfers who were, as he liked to say, chasing it. He knew the name of every player who had ever Monday qualified into a PGA Tour event and then won that event. Kenny Knox, for instance, Monday qualified for the 1986 Honda Classic, then won it. Years later, Ryan named a black Lab for Kenny. When Corey Conners won the Valero Texas Open as a Monday qualifier in 2019, that was like a gift to Ryan and, as he would say, the account. Ryan knew the circuitous route Ted Potter Jr. took from the Hooters Tour, where he won often, to the PGA Tour, where he once missed twenty-four consecutive cuts. Ryan knew how Jonathan Byrd, a five-time winner on the PGA Tour, was pushing his own cart at Monday qualifiers, trying to play his way back to the show and saving money while doing it. You don't have to take a caddie at the Monday qualifiers. You do have to pay to play in these PGA Tour qualifiers. Ryan wrote about those entry fees with righteous indignation. It was a natural stance for him to take, to stand up for the little guy. On any given day (pretty much), Ryan could tell you where Kent Jones was playing, and how he was doing. After that encounter at the Bob Evans in Flint, during the Buick Open? Kent Jones had a fan for life.

What Ryan didn't know, when he started the account, was how much interest there was in the lives *behind* the Monday Q names. Ryan started to figure that out when he did a simple, short question-and-answer interview with a golfer named Kyle Thompson. Thompson had won five times on the Web.com Tour but could not bring that game to the PGA Tour. He answered Ryan's questions in a plaintive way—he missed his family on the road; professional golf for him meant constant financial pressure—and the interview took off. At forty-one, Ryan was a cub reporter, and he loved it. A little-known golfer named Cliff Kresge told Ryan what it was like to try to beat Tiger Woods. Gold! Everybody was telling Tiger's story. Nobody was telling Kresge's. Before long, Ryan had fifteen thousand Monday Q followers.

The followers came from unexpected places. An NBA beat writer told Ryan he was going to start covering twelfth men and ten-day contracts like Ryan covered golf's underclass. Followers donated to a junior-golf charity Ryan had started. They donated a wide range of sums—three dollars, fifteen hundred, twenty thousand—to the various hard-luck golf cases Ryan wrote about. They invited Ryan to speak to their golf groups about his beat. He was chronicling the intersection of the golf gene and the grit gene.

Readers suggested stories on pros trying to make it from unlikely places, from plastic-mat driving ranges, from overseas tours that even Ryan didn't know existed. Players asked Ryan if he would caddie for them. This was all, taken together, a new kind of thrill for him, a distant cousin to the adrenaline rush he used to get from the card games and golf games in his Qdoba days. Except that what he was doing now was *good* for him. But there was also a major problem, as Ryan saw it. He was working on the account maybe forty or fifty hours a week, and it wasn't making the French family a dime.

"I need to give it up and find a job," Ryan told Stephanie.

"Don't you dare," she said.

But Ryan knew better.

He told various friends that he'd be giving up the account. One of his confidants worked for the PGA Tour's website. The Tour liked what Ryan was doing. The friend told Ryan not to do anything rash. He soon came back to Ryan with an offer he couldn't refuse: one piece a week at two hundred dollars a story. The account lived.

Under the arrangement, Ryan was able to keep the account going under his name, but he was also, in a manner of speaking, working for the PGA Tour. He was a golf outsider under the umbrella of professional golf's ultimate establishment organization. With the marketing might of the PGA Tour behind him, the number of people following Ryan continued to grow, which was good. But the growth came with costs and annoyances. Ryan had to bill the Tour for every story he wrote, and the Tour's payment schedule was haphazard at best. When players described some of the grimier aspects of professional golf to Ryan, those parts were sometimes edited out. The Tour's social media staff seemed happy with his work, but Ryan was less than sure. Near the start of the 2021 golf year, Ryan was invited to meet with some of the staff at the Monday qualifier for the Phoenix Open. That is, the Waste Management Open.

Ryan detailed for them the ins and outs of what he did and how he did it. Reading the tea leaves of the Phoenix Monday qualifier, Ryan suggested that a camera operator stay with a young golfer named Nick Hardy late in his round. There were 143 players playing for three spots. You couldn't follow anything like all of them. Ryan's instinct was uncanny. Hardy holed a bomb on his last hole to get the last spot. His fist pumps, captured by a PGA Tour camera operator, were out of the Tiger Woods highlight reel. The Tour posted the twenty-four-second clip on its various social media platforms, and well over a hundred thousand people clicked on it. For the Tour, all this fit under a marketing category called Fan Engagement, a phrase that meant nothing to Ryan. He was fascinated by the grit and the dream and where that could take a golfer. After the Monday qualifier, Nick Hardy made the cut at the tournament, finished near the bottom of the field, and earned almost thirty thousand dollars. Careers and lives can turn on a week like that.

Soon after, the PGA Tour offered Ryan a job, doing what he was already doing, but now with the Tour's stamp on it and the Tour riding herd on all he did. He was offered a starting salary of thirty-two thousand dollars. Ryan turned it down. From the PGA Tour, which had millions sitting around in jars, he thought that figure was a joke. For that meager amount, the Tour thought it was going to buy Ryan's independence? No way.

Ryan soon learned he had fans in other places, most notably at a new golf-media company based in California called the Fire Pit Collective. The founder, Matt Ginella, and his wingman, Alan Shipnuck, offered Ryan a starting salary of eighty thousand a year, with full health benefits and this directive: Write what you want to write, without fear or favor. He leaped at it. It was Ryan's first full-time job since before Jack's surgery. Early on, his beat was given a name: Dreamers. It almost didn't seem possible. Ryan had created a life in which his job was to write about golf's dreamers, and he was one himself. The offer came in a Zoom conversation that Stephanie could hear. Ryan clicked off, and Steph started bawling.

Around that same time, *Golf Digest* published a piece by Ryan about his experiences as the Monday Q guy. Really, the piece was more by the editors than by Ryan, but it ran in the actual magazine, under the headline CASE OF THE MONDAYS, and the magazine paid Ryan five thousand dollars for his stories and insights. *Five thousand dollars!* Howard French was beside himself with joy. He showed the magazine to all his golf buddies. He and Ginny drove from Alpena to Chicago to take Steph and Ryan out for a celebratory dinner. His son was forty-four, married, with two children, and a promising new career in golf, the sport he had shared with his father pretty much all his life. His son was the Monday Q guy, with seventy-five thousand followers on Twitter.

Howard and Ginny were in their mid-seventies. They were grandparents, long retired, slowing down. Their walks through the corridors of Alpena High and across the Michigan State campus and under the moonlight on the golf course in their backyard had all happened a long time ago. On that eight-hour trip to Chicago, Ginny did all the driving. Two years earlier, Howard had had a stroke, and now it was he who was riding shotgun anywhere he went. On the drive to Chicago, Howard said to Ginny something like: "Isn't that just so great, that Ryan got that article in *Golf Digest*, and can you believe what they paid him for it?" A few days later, he said nearly the identical thing. *Yes, dear, it is.* Ginny knew what Howard did not, that something was going on.

. . .

On the Monday before the 1973 Masters, the USGA stripped Bruce Robertson of his amateur status for the crime of selling a "substantial amount" of golf equipment and golf balls, in violation of the *Rules of Golf*. Because Robertson was in the Masters as an amateur, he withdrew from the tournament so the lords at Augusta would not have to do it for him. Robertson also lost his place on the Stanford golf team. "What bullshit," Sam told Dick Giddings and Charley Seaver, back home in Fresno. *Kid with no money selling some clubs. Doesn't the USGA have better things to do? They should be encouraging people to play.*

Ben Crenshaw, in the tournament by way of his second-place finish in the Am in Charlotte, stayed in the attic dorm room in the clubhouse with the other amateurs at that Masters. He met Gene

Sarazen and was interviewed in Butler Cabin at the end of play. He was the low am. The club gave him a silver cup and many slaps on the back. Crenshaw was both a mega-talent and a golden boy, and his life in golf was off and running. Bruce Robertson, as a national golf figure, was never heard from again.

• • •

Ryan followed the NFL closely and the league's Midwestern teams with particular interest. He'd grown up with the big three: the Lions (Detroit), the Bears (Chicago), and the Packers (Green Bay). Ryan knew the names of all the assistant coaches on those teams, the punters, the GMs and their proclivities. He could go through the rosters of the Minnesota Vikings and the Cleveland Browns, too. He was a son of the Midwest. Of course he knew that Joey Harrington, the onetime Lions quarterback, was distantly related to Pádraig Harrington, the Irish golfer who won the 2008 PGA Championship at Oakland Hills in suburban Detroit. Ryan read the *Free Press*. How could he *not* know?

Ryan viewed Twitter as a two-way street, and through his account, he heard about a high school in rural Westville, Indiana, that was trying to keep its golf team afloat. He wanted to do what he could to help it. He mentioned the team's plight in a tweet. Soon after, Ryan received a direct message from Aaron Rodgers, the Packers' quarterback. They had never met or interacted. Rodgers wrote, *I'm here for the quiet support of golfers as well. If there is a fund set up or an anonymous giving opportunity, please pass along the info to me if you would. Absolute golf nut over here, love your posts.*

Rodgers had started his path to the NFL at a community college. Nobody ever predicted he'd be a world-beater. What Ryan was doing with the account, shining a light on players with more talent than opportunity, was in Rodgers's sweet spot. Rodgers and

Ryan began trading messages. Whatever cause Ryan got behind, Rodgers was in, too, generously and anonymously.

One of Ryan's closest friends in golf was a journeyman chaser named Mark Baldwin, a tall, slender, bespectacled Notre Dame grad. When Aaron Rodgers was playing college football, Mark Baldwin was playing college golf, not that they ever crossed paths. Ryan met Mark through the Monday Q account and started documenting his golf exploits. Their relationship went from virtual to actual. Ryan caddied for Mark in some of his tournaments and documented their adventures on the account. With Ryan on the bag, Mark made the cut in 2022 at one of the PGA Tour's best-known events, the AT&T Pebble Beach Pro-Am, the tournament Bing Crosby started. Rodgers wore out his exclamation key in direct messages to Ryan. After more than fifteen years of playing tournament golf, and in his late thirties, Mark was playing in the fourth PGA Tour event of his career. Pebble Beach. A player with a never-quit backstory and an unlikely caddie who doubled as his Boswell. Aaron Rodgers couldn't get enough of that story or any like it.

Mark was like a lot of the golfers Ryan wrote about. He was good enough to dream. Ryan caddied for Mark at a Monday qualifier for a Tour event in Reno. Seventy-one players, four spots. Mark shot 65, as did a golfer from Australia. Three guys shot better, so now Baldwin and the Australian golfer were in a two-for-one playoff. The Aussie missed from eighteen inches on the first playoff hole, and Mark was in. A brutal example of every shot makes somebody happy.

The next day, Mark played part of a practice round for the actual PGA Tour event with Bill Haas, a veteran player who had been on three Presidents Cup teams. Mark flushed a series of shots, and Haas said to Ryan, "Who *is* this guy?" You can't buy speed, and you can't buy flush. Mark made the cut in that Reno tournament, but golf will expose your weaknesses over time like few things will. The line between playing on TV in PGA Tour events and appearing in Ryan French's Monday Q Info Twitter feed was razor-thin. Everybody who had seen golf's major and minor leagues up close, Aaron Rodgers among them, knew that.

Rodgers knew the struggle, internal and external, to make it in golf because he had faced the same struggle in football, though his time line was far more consolidated. Rodgers had an innate grasp of the underbelly of the PGA Tour because every professional league has a seamy side, the NFL particularly. His attachment to Ryan's working-class golfers was both emotional and intellectual. Rodgers had played golf with former NFL quarterback Tony Romo, an outstanding golfer who played in a Tour event and shot 72-76, missing the cut by eight shots. Rodgers had played with Phil Mickelson. He had played with golfers whose games were much closer to Mickelson's than Romo's. But those golfers would never be Mickelson, and Romo would never be those golfers. There are layers and layers and layers in golf, and Rodgers knew it.

In football, you can be outstanding in one narrow area—kicking!—and become a legend. A golfer has to do it all. A golfer has to change speeds constantly. It's almost comical to call it a game because golf is ruthlessly unforgiving. As Lee Trevino has said forever, golfers have to play their foul balls. The elite play a game that ordinary golfers both know and can't even imagine. When the guy sitting next to you on the plane says he's an 80-shooter, it's usually a study in delusion. Add ten and go from there.

Ryan, once an undistinguished community-college golfer, played a PGA Tour course from the back tees with Mark and shot 86. Mark casually broke 70. Ryan mentioned his score on the account, and Rodgers saw it. Rodgers knew that to shoot 86 from the back tees on a good course, everything in the hole, you have to be a pretty legit golfer. On any given day, he'd be looking to do about the same.

Soon after, they met in person, and Rodgers said to Ryan, "Good score, dude!"

And Ryan wondered: How could that have even happened? How did he get his life into such a place where he was standing on a driving range with an NFL god who knew what he had shot in a meaningless round? It was bizarre, but it did happen.

Rodgers was playing in a celebrity tournament near Lake Tahoe. Mark and Ryan were there. By previous arrangement, Rodgers, Ryan, and Mark met on the practice tee. A TV crew was there, too. Rodgers played the role that his public life demanded he play. He was aware of the cameras and fans and his obligation to sign autographs. But with Mark and Ryan, Rodgers let his guard down. They talked about the state of Mark's game and where he could play next. They talked about the dreamers Ryan was writing about and the golfers and golf programs he was trying to help.

There was something about Ryan. You could breathe around him. He accepted you as you were and figured you'd do the same. He was a dreamer and a grinder, and those two things don't often go hand in hand. He worked at a difficult craft and was trying to get better at it. All that was true for Mark Baldwin, too. They knew where they stood. They were two middle-aged guys, closer to the shoulder than the main road, who had become friends. Each was trying to make it, whatever that might mean. Each was defining the phrase for himself. Ben Hogan once said, "I am the sole judge of my own standards." Ryan and Mark would have said the same.

And Rodgers was just *there*, getting the camera off him by focusing his attention elsewhere. He stood on that practice tee and hit balls and looked at swings. He offered this and that to Ryan and Mark. He listened more. He was doing what he could to keep his feet on the ground. You could tell. *Hold on to sixteen as long as you can.* How efficient can one songwriter from Indiana (or anywhere else) be? Here was the kid on tippy-toes, imagining life on the other side of the wall. That was the starting point to Ryan's beat. Forget that and you're cooked.

. . .

For a decade, starting in 1976, the year he turned forty-two, Sam stopped playing golf. He didn't have the time. He had been traveling abroad for work for years, but after 1974, with China now open to U.S. trade, those trips became more regular and more intense. Dunavant Enterprises was by then the largest seller of cotton in the world, and Sam owned 25 percent of it. Dunavant was one of the largest privately owned companies in the United States, with dozens of operations around the country and around the world. Sam was forever on the move, and not just for work. As his income went from good to significant to vast, he bought a ranch, a beach house, a series of ever bigger airplanes. It was a big life, frequently with his wife and one or two or three or four daughters in tow.

But the most significant development in Sam's life was internal. People who thought they knew him well through golf or business were seeing only slivers of him. Starting in the mid-1970s, Sam became more active at the family's Fresno church, First Presbyterian. He didn't have a light bulb moment. He had a desire to raise his daughters as his parents had raised him, with a sense of gratitude. Sam's travels got him (and those with him) to places where he could see and experience, at close range, the extreme disparity of wealth but also how connected the human race is. This is not a motto of Sam's, but it could be: read widely, travel deeply. He read as he traveled, to understand more. He knew that the starting point to understanding Nixon was to read Kissinger. For Carter, Rosalynn Carter. For Reagan, Milton Friedman and David Stockton, but also John Maynard Keynes and John Kenneth Galbraith.

The Reagan presidency was good for business, and Ronald Reagan reflected Sam's optimistic nature and big-picture view of the world. He rejected any political stance that isolated America. A significant pejorative for Sam was to call a person *narrow*. He despised the idea that the world began and ended at the borders of the United States. His own spiritual life, starting with his belief in Jesus Christ as the ultimate role model, was his own spiritual life. He wasn't pushing it on others. He believed that capitalism, as practiced in America, was the best and most viable economic system, but not the only viable one. A word that came up in his everyday conversation was *Sure. Shuu-errr*, in his drawling, relaxed baritone. The answer, whenever possible, was *Shuurrr*. Or *Yes*. Or *Let's give it a try*. He said it to himself, and he said it to others. He was open, to new people, new ideas, new experiences.

On that basis, Sam spent several days in a monastery in Northern California. (More silence than he could stand, but a good experience.) He spent nearly a week on an Israeli kibbutz, with its communal living and communal working. (An interesting way to live, but too much common space.) Sam and one of the Reeves girls stayed in an orphanage in Kenya for a week, there to work, not to watch. Sam and another daughter spent a week volunteering at a children's hospital in Pakistan. Other times, he and one daughter or another stayed on farms owned by working families in Brazil, Thailand, and China. In the immediate aftermath of the Kosovo War, Sam and his youngest daughter, Virginia, volunteered at a refugee camp in Albania. Later, Virginia lived in Albania for six months. Sam, along with other family members and a godson, made two other long trips to Albania, in a modest effort to help a worn-torn country heal. Sam and Virginia had stayed in that refugee camp, with a population in the thousands, for close to a month. Sam was mesmerized by the children there, by their play, by their willingness to share. He was awed to learn about the many births taking place in the camp's makeshift hospital. New life, amid all that death and destruction.

Sam made it a point to distinguish between the governed and their governments. In the Soviet Union, Sam saw hundreds of grounded airplanes rusting on tarmacs, waiting for mechanics who would probably never arrive. It made him dubious about the promise of the Soviet Union as a place to make a big investment, in time or money, as a market for American cotton. But those idle planes were a *government* failing, not a reflection of the Soviet people. When he traveled in China, he knew he was being watched by agents of the government, possibly recorded, that his belongings were being turned inside out when he left his hotel room. But Sam didn't hold that against the Chinese *people*.

The Reeves family was traveling way off the tourist trail. In Israel, all six family members were being driven on a desolate road when two Israeli soldiers stopped the car. The soldiers saw that the driver was Palestinian and demanded, at gunpoint, that he get out. They wanted to know why Sam had hired a Palestinian driver. They had a series of pointed questions for the driver. Their voices were loud, and the episode was frightening. It was also a lesson in the insidiousness of distrust and the power of a gun. The girls could see, maybe for the first time, that their father could not control everything, let alone fix the problem. Sam's charm, intelligence, and humanity were no match for a random roadside stop that was five thousand or so years in the making.

In Beijing, two of the girls were touring a zoo, accompanied by an interpreter, a young woman who did a lot of translation work for Sam. When the interpreter had the chance, in a furtive voice and while avoiding eye contact, she posed three questions: *How does divorce work? What do you know about Chiang Kai-shek? Who is Jesus Christ?* The girls noticed later, while driving by abandoned churches, that there were no crucifixes in the customary places. Their eyes were open. They were looking. Their father was there to point the way.

•   •   •

As a student of mini-tour life, Ryan knew about the Dakotas Tour, a well-funded, well-lubricated summertime circuit that took players on a nine-week golfing safari from Sioux Falls, South Dakota, to Fargo, North Dakota, among various other places ending in Dakota. If you know the life and times of Kevin Streelman, you probably have heard about the Dakotas Tour. Streelman grew up near Chicago and caddied as a kid. After he graduated from Duke, he packed up his mother's car, headed west, and got himself on the Dakotas Tour. That was his start in professional golf. Twelve years later, he was a runner-up to Tiger Woods at the Players Championship. As Woods used to say, it's a process.

One of the first caddie trips Ryan and his father made, after Ryan's return to Alpena in the aftermath of the Las Vegas incident, was to a Dakotas event. The tournament was in Yankton, South Dakota, on the Missouri River, almost in Nebraska. It took Howard and Ryan two days and fifteen driving hours to get there. They pitched their tent in a state park, their canvas dwelling dwarfed by the towering metal campers beside them. The tournament was a three-round event, two of which were pro-am rounds played at a crawling pace. (But as the saying goes, somebody's got to pay the bills around here. Enter the ams.) The course was flat, easy, and dull. Neither Howard's guy nor Ryan's played any good, and Ryan felt like half a prisoner all through the trip. He wasn't ready for that much Howard and was still in withdrawal from his cards-and-golf-and-drinking life. Yet even with all that, the week made a powerful and positive impression on him.

The winner shot rounds of 66, 70, and 67 for a one-shot victory. First place paid ten thousand dollars. Fifteenth paid about eight hundred, and no finisher south of that got paid at all. Everybody in the top ten could flat-out play. From that week on, Ryan started following the Dakota results. Kevin Streelman, he came to realize, was an outlier. You could be a legend on the Dakotas circuit—an Andre Metzger from Sioux Falls, a Tim Ailes from Delaware, Ohio—and never sniff *status* (common shorthand for playing privileges) on the PGA Tour. For Ryan, that added to the appeal of the tour. The Dakotas Tour was like its own little golfing ecosystem.

Eventually, Ryan kept seeing the name Brady Calkins in the Dakota results. He knew that Brady was from Chehalis, a small, isolated, working-class town in central Washington with a short public course. Ryan imagined Chehalis as another Alpena. Brady had turned pro at nineteen and started dominating in the Dakotas in his mid-twenties. He had won in Yankton and most everywhere else, and he'd closed down bars in Yankton and most everywhere else. Ryan noted Brady's wins on the account and interviewed him by phone. Ryan hadn't met him, but he knew what everybody knew, that Brady Calkins was a wild man and a great golf talent and had no problem keeping it real.

In 2022, Brady played in a two-round, one-day U.S. Open qualifier in Bend, Oregon. There were sixty-five players playing for three spots. Nobody shot lower than Brady Calkins. At twenty-seven, eight years after he had turned pro, Calkins was going to his first U.S. Open.

As was Ryan. He was going as a writer, a podcaster, and a tweeter for the Fire Pit Collective. For the first time in his life—twelve years after leaving Las Vegas, four years after cradling Jack in his arms at home after surgery and starting the account—Ryan would be at a major golf event with a media credential dangling from his neck.

That U.S. Open was held at The Country Club, in Brookline, near Boston. It was where Francis Ouimet, as a twenty-year-old club caddie, defeated two British golf stars in a playoff to win the 1913 U.S. Open. The Country Club is as old and as clubby as American golf gets. The narrow service steps in the yellow clubhouse, the towering sycamores on the course, the Sunday-morning gents on the first tee—everything there sort of creaks. The course rises and falls, and you play by ancient rocky outcroppings known as pudding stone. Time stops.

For the U.S. Open, the USGA repurposed the club's nine-court indoor tennis building and turned it into the tournament media center. Ryan sat near Jaime Diaz of Golf Channel, Andy Johnson of the Fried Egg, and his new Fire Pit Collective comrades, including Alan Shipnuck, author of a newly published bestseller about Phil Mickelson. I had recently joined the Fire Pit Collective and was spending time with Ryan. Alan, Ryan, and I did daily podcasts as a threesome, each of us holding a big black mic that looked like something Edward R. Murrow might have used while covering World War II.

Ryan marveled at the vast quantity of free food in the media center, and laughed at the widespread grumbling about it. Complaints about the sporadic internet connection hit closer to home for him. *You get better connection in Alpena.* When the first-day tee times were posted, Ryan saw that Brady Calkins would be playing in the day's last threesome, going off the tenth tee at 2:42 p.m. You couldn't have a worse time. A long and anxious wait. All that adrenaline with nowhere to go. Bumpy, crusty late-day greens. But Ryan also knew if anybody could handle such a lousy tee time, it would be Brady Calkins at his first U.S. Open. Brady's attitude about the afternoon Country Club greens would surely match right up with Ryan's attitude about the afternoon press-tent snacks. *You're at the U.S. Open.* The USGA was paying players ten thousand dollars for missing the cut. Brady Calkins was going to be ahead for the week no matter what. Ryan French was, too.

• • •

Cotton merchants sink or swim on their cotton classers, employees who judge incoming fiber as coarse, fine, or somewhere in between. That is, short or long or medium staple, and in fact many more gradations beyond that. Skillful cotton classers, working in large, quiet, smoke-free warehouses and under intense light, can see two dozen shades of white as they take stock of the raw fiber. They measure, with machine-like accuracy, the length of fiber strands by wrapping them around their knuckles, as average fiber length is how cotton is classified. The best can do this not only with astounding accuracy but also at an astonishing pace. You can always tell true working cotton merchants, as Sam was, by the calluses on their knuckles. The same was true for Billy Dunavant, Sam's partner, whom Sam regarded as the best judge of cotton he had ever known. If you want to make money in cotton, you have to be able to classify quickly and accurately. Otherwise, you might sell a thousand bales of medium-staple cotton at a short-staple price, and be late with it, too. You'll take a bath. Classify it correctly, and it's a path to a new fleet of trucks.

As a young executive in the cotton business, Sam became mesmerized by a cotton classifier he met from Clover, South Carolina, named Emanuel Pettus. Manuel, which is what he went by, was about a decade older than Sam and had grown up around cotton, working in cotton fields as a boy and alongside other Black field workers. He didn't get far in school. He had grown up in the South under Jim Crow laws, and every boss he ever had he called *Sir*. Sam was taken with Manuel's style, his speed and accuracy as a cotton classer, and his vitality.

In 1962, shortly after heading west, Sam tried to lure Manuel from a mill in North Carolina to the Dunavant operation in Fresno. Sam offered Manuel a big bump in salary and responsibilities. In Fresno, Manuel would have about a dozen people working under him, and although he would report directly to Sam, he wouldn't be calling him *Sir*.

Fresno did not have Jim Crow laws, but it was very much a segregated city, and it was no Eden for many of its Black residents, most of whom lived in cramped and dangerous neighborhoods near downtown. But Manuel's wife, Vera, was a schoolteacher, and they figured she would be able to find a teaching job in Fresno. They had no children, but knew that could change. They could see themselves saving up and buying a house in one of Fresno's newer developments on the safer outskirts of town. Stanley Mosk, California's attorney general in the early 1960s, had started a civil rights division that protected the rights of Black property buyers. (He also successfully sued the PGA of America over the organization's clause that restricted membership to Caucasians.) Sam didn't need to do much selling. Manuel and Vera were happy to go west.

And after a few years in Fresno, they bought their dream house. By then they were a family of three, with a daughter named Sonya, who quickly showed herself to be an outstanding student in the public schools she attended. Vera was teaching. Manuel was working for Dunavant, which was growing. The family had its house in order in every way.

Manuel was a slender man, a few inches under six feet, who went to work as he went to church, in well-shined shoes, narrow pressed pants, and a fresh shirt. Once he could afford it, he started driving Cadillacs. By then he was a vice president in Dunavant's Fresno operation and one of Sam's top deputies. Each man was fond of the other. They worked long hours, often side by side. Sam and Manuel would sometimes go out for lunch, either in Fresno or, though not often, at mom-and-pop cafés off the two-lane highways that connected the great farms of the San Joaquin Valley. When Sam forgot his wallet, which was more than occasionally, Manuel was happy to step in, giving Sam grief all the while. Manuel always had money in his wallet and a heavy billfold in his pocket.

"Why do you do that?" Sam asked, wondering why Manuel carried so much cash.

"I like to know I have it," Manuel said. He didn't always. Now he could buy the boss lunch.

To the California cotton farmers, these two Southern men were an unlikely pair, but Sam and Manuel spoke the same language. Sam grew up knowing the other side of the Jim Crow South, where, if you were born white and well-to-do, you were already on third base. In his adult life, he became aware of the unfair nature of the world. He was thrilled to see a Black manager prospering in the cotton business and happy he had played a role in it. The Pettus family in their new home was a living example of the American dream.

On a Thursday in early October 1980, Manuel put in his usual long hours in the vast Dunavant sorting room, with its cement floors dotted by thick rubber floor pads. After work that night, instead of going home, Manuel met a couple of friends at Warnors, Fresno's enormous Spanish Colonial Revival theater, to watch Larry Holmes and Muhammad Ali fight for the WBC heavyweight title. The fight was in Las Vegas and was being shown around the world on closed-circuit TV, including a second-floor auditorium at Warnors. Ali was thirty-eight and past his prime, and the bout was billed as "The Last Hurrah." Holmes was thirty and at the height of his powers. The fight was hard to watch. There were no knockdowns, but Holmes won the first ten rounds, decisively and by unanimous consent, before the bout was called. Ali was staggering.

Afterward, Manuel drove to the Hilton Hotel in downtown

Fresno, a mile from the theater, and had a drink by himself in its ninth-floor Skyroom Bar. He finished his drink and returned to his car around eleven-thirty, parked outside the hotel on Van Ness Avenue. Forty or thirty or even twenty years earlier, such an evening would have been unimaginable in Fresno. A Black man going to Warnors for a show and to a downtown hotel bar for a drink? There was no way. But now it was 1980.

At his car, Manuel was approached by two men who attempted to rob him. An altercation ensued, and Manuel was shot directly in the heart. Emanuel Pettus was found sprawled on the Van Ness Avenue sidewalk, clutching his wallet. In a pocket, he had about five hundred dollars secured by a money clip. He was pronounced dead at Fresno Community Hospital. He was fifty-three.

Within weeks, a man in his early twenties was charged with the murder and tried by a jury of his peers. The chief witness against the defendant was his cousin, who was granted immunity. The witness-cousin was described by *The Fresno Bee* as a pimp who was wanted for crimes in other states. At the trial, it was revealed that one of the two men had apparently dropped a brown shopping bag with tailored clothes in it while running away. In the trial, the prosecution established that the clothing in the bag fit the defendant perfectly. His conviction came quickly.

The Thursday-night murder was written up on the front page of the Saturday paper, and the article mentioned there would be a Monday-morning memorial service for Emanuel Pettus. That service was held at Fresno's leading Black funeral home, named for its founder, Jesse Cooley, who had Southern roots himself. Even though the family had been in Fresno for only fifteen years, the hall was packed. Sam delivered a eulogy. A long series of exultations, in a mesmerizing rhythm, bounced off the walls and in the direction of Mr. Pettus's coffin.

Hallelujah!

Preach it, brother!

Glory be to God!

The mourners were celebrating through their tears. Sam could feel a pain in his heart but a distinct warmth as well. He felt bathed and welcomed by the mourners. A pastor followed Sam at the pulpit and reminded the congregants that Manuel had been called home and was now in a better place. Manuel's body went home to Clover, South Carolina.

Sam stayed in touch with Manuel's widow, Vera. As a Black girl growing up in a small North Carolina town in the 1950s, she wasn't allowed to enter the public library, but she was allowed to pick cotton, and she did. As a woman in Fresno, she became the beloved principal of an integrated public elementary school. Her daughter and only child went to medical school at the University of California San Francisco and did her residency in anesthesiology at Stanford. After that, Dr. Sonya Pettus returned to Fresno to begin her medical career.

Whenever *The Fresno Bee* referred to the murder outside the Hilton on that October night in 1980, it used the phrase *attempted robbery*. There was no evidence that the two hoodlums had run off with any of Manuel Pettus's money. A hardworking man was killed that night for the crime of having a late-night drink at a downtown hotel after watching a heavyweight fight. But the gunshot to Manuel's heart could not kill the Pettus family's promise. Mother and daughter were wounded forever. But they carried on. Everybody in Fresno who knew them could see that.

• • •

Ryan flew to Boston courtesy of his new expense account. Ditto for his hotel and his meals, including a dinner at Bar 'Cino on Beacon Street in Brookline, where you could get a wood-fired pizza with "roasted Rhode Island mushrooms" (said the menu) and cut it yourself with scissors brought to you by your server. As an alumnus of Mark's Pizza in East Lansing, Ryan thought that was just hilarious. It was his considered opinion that pizza should be served (or boxed) sliced. Ryan's new people, the young Fire Pit Collective producers and editors at the table with him, were amused by his analysis. Everybody was getting to know one another's moves, quirks, and sweet spots. Ryan hadn't had coworkers since his McAlister's Deli days, and they smelled like chicken broth. Now he was in the company of *colleagues*. It was strange and different. It felt good.

Until that U.S. Open, Ryan had never ridden to a tournament in a media shuttle or had his backpack inspected upon arrival. He had never imagined that golf stars from yesteryear—a Curtis Strange, a Ben Crenshaw, an Andy North—would just show up at a tournament and wander around, saying hello to anybody who said hello first. (Shouldn't such gods be in bulletproof carts along the lines of the popemobile?) He had never been to a golf-tournament press conference, let alone one where he was standing fifteen feet from Phil Mickelson and next to Christine Brennan, the *USA Today* sports columnist and network sports commentator.

That press conference took place on the Monday morning of the tournament. (Ryan was not going to call it the *championship* just because that was the preferred term of the USGA.) It was Mickelson's first public appearance in the United States since he had joined a new by-invitation-only global golf league called LIV Golf, financed by a vast Saudi Arabian investment fund ultimately run by Mohammed bin Salman, aka MBS, the country's crown prince. The league's marketing line was *Golf, but louder*. People who liked their golf quiet were offended. The Mickelson press conference was stilted from the get-go. It seemed like everybody was coming in with an agenda. A USGA media official called on reporters and thereby served as a sort of stage manager, but you would need a mind like Shakespeare's to sift through all the politics, personal and global, lurking beneath the surface.

Question on the right.

"Phil, Christine Brennan. Hi there. As you know, you've been criticized by many people, as you referred to. In the *New York Post,* Brian Wacker reported that the 9/11 families sent you and others a letter alluding to Osama bin Laden and to the fifteen of the nineteen hijackers that the Saudis, of course, sent. And they say now you are a partner with them. And you appear to be pleased, in your business with them. Terry Strada is the person, of course, who wrote this letter. Her husband got on the plane in Boston that flew into the World Trade Center. They say the deaths of your fellow Americans . . ."

While Brennan spoke, Mickelson was handed a water bottle, took a long sip, put the cap back on, wiped his lower lip, and continued his listening tour until he no longer could. "No, I've read all that. Is there a question in there?"

He was standing on a small, raised stage in a small, packed tent with a floor covered by gray industrial carpet. He barely used his hands as he spoke, which was unusual for him. There was a scrim behind him, as you might see at a play, festooned with the USGA logo. It was all there: stage, protagonist, Greek chorus, the stage manager. The lighting was good. Mickelson wore no hat (also unusual), and his hair was wet or gelled.

"Yes, there is. How do you explain to them—not to us but to them—what you have decided to do?"

Mickelson took a full second or two to gather his thoughts. "I would say to the Strada family, I would say to everyone that has lost loved ones, lost friends, on 9/11, that I have deep, deep empathy for them. I can't emphasize that enough. I have the deepest sympathy and empathy for them."

The questions and answers went on like that for twenty-five

minutes until the session, mercifully, came to an end. Afterward, Ryan had two main thoughts:

That wasn't a press conference—that was a show.
I'm glad I cover the golfers I do.

He had one question for Mickelson, though he never asked, and it was decidedly practical and on brand: *The PGA Tour suspended you over the whole LIV thing, but could you play your way into tournaments through Monday qualifiers? Because I don't think they're run by the Tour—right?*

Later that day, Ryan found Brady Calkins while he was playing a practice round. Ryan said hi and was welcomed right in. The two walked down fairways together. That's not the player-reporter norm, not at a U.S. Open, but how would those two know? Ryan asked questions in his regular-guy way, and Brady answered them without a filter. Ryan told Brady he wanted to write up Brady for the Fire Pit Collective website and not sugarcoat anything. Brady said that was fine. They talked about the Dakotas Tour, how Brady was raised, his recipe for playing through hangovers. Brady talked about his drinking, his shaky finances, his mother's tough love. Ryan knew he was getting good stuff. Every reporter has had that moment when the questions are coming and so are the answers, when you're so lost in another person's life that your body is tingling. Talk about empathy. You need to be curious, but you can't be a good reporter without empathy.

Before he left, Ryan talked to Brady's friends and relatives who had accompanied him on this epic road trip. At that moment, Ryan felt as if he could see right into the meaning of it all. They had gone from nowhere to the bigs, Brady and his people. The whole thing might last only a week, but they had made it. Brady's journey was theirs, too, and nobody was taking anything for granted. They were at a U.S. Open at The Country Club. Ryan's job was to capture the moment truthfully and for posterity, for Brady, for Brady's people, and most significantly, for the Fire Pit Collective readers who would never meet Brady Calkins, never come to a U.S. Open, never know what it's like to play your way from Chehalis, Washington, into American golf's greatest championship.

The story was posted on the Fire Pit Collective website on Wednesday morning, the day before the tournament began, under the headline THE LEGEND OF BRADY CALKINS.

BROOKLINE, Mass.—*It's three a.m. in Yankton, S.D., and the Cockatoo Gentlemen's Club is rocking. The Dakotas Tour is in town for its annual stop, the final round is the next day, yet half the field is still in the house. Among the carousers is tournament leader Brady Calkins, whose tee time is a mere six hours away. A few hours later, looking for a caddie to help him get through the round, he would call a player who had missed the cut. "Get here," Calkins says. "I'm fucking shaking, I'm so hungover. I'll give you a thousand dollars if I win."*

A good lede makes you want to keep reading, right? On it went from there.

Nobody could have seen that story coming in the run-up to that U.S. Open. The stories were about Phil and LIV Golf, about the course and its setup, about the 1913 U.S. Open and the legacy of Francis Ouimet. Ryan got help with the writing from Alan Shipnuck and Mark Godich, a Fire Pit Collective editor. But Ryan had brought all the bricks and most of the sentences. He had written a *story*, on deadline, one that nobody else had, arguing with his editors to let Brady be Brady, even if some readers would be offended. It was all new territory for Ryan. On his Twitter account, he often commented on leaderboards and quoted from interviews he'd done. But he had never reported and written a piece anything like this fast profile. At fifteen hundred words, it wasn't a major opus, and it didn't need to be. People liked it for what it was. Reporting the piece and getting it published was a different kind of buzz for Ryan. In the media center, other reporters were congratulating him. So were readers. There was an audience for what he was doing. Even prior to the U.S. Open, Monday Q had more than a hundred thousand followers.

On Wednesday afternoon, the day before the start of the tournament, Brady played a final practice round. He was standing on the tenth tee when Ryan arrived. Brady approached Ryan. He was wearing wraparound sunglasses and a Titleist baseball cap low on his forehead, making it impossible to read the golfer's face or mood. Brady Calkins had a short review for Ryan French before he returned to the business at hand:

"Fuckin' *loved* it."

Stephanie French read her husband's story about Brady Calkins in the family's new temporary home on the far outskirts of Alpena. The home was actually a vacation house on Hubbard Lake that belonged to Ryan's brother, Scott, a former auto executive who, in his early fifties, had stopped working. He was the oldest of the three French children and had come up with the idea that Ryan and his family could move into the house, rent-free, for as long as they wished, to help their parents. Scott lived in the Detroit suburbs with his family. Dallas, who lived in Chicago with her family, liked the idea, too. Their father's recall and mental capacity had now been in decline for several years. The goal was to keep their father in his home and with their mother.

Ginny and Howard had been together for more than sixty years, well over twenty thousand days, most of them good ones. Now they had good days but, as time marched on, more trying ones. One of the issues was that Howard's libido was revisiting its glory days. Ginny could handle that. (That was always a thing for them. When Ryan was in middle school, a friend was at his house for a sleepover. Around midnight, the kid said, "Hey, Ryan. I think your house is falling down!") Howard's depression, temper, frustration, and, on rare occasions, physical outbursts, all elements of his dementia, were another matter. Alpena County had good services for the elderly, but having Ryan and Stephanie nearby could only help. They took Scott up on his offer to move into what he modestly called his cottage. The cottage had five bedrooms, four bathrooms, and a deck overlooking Hubbard Lake. Scott called his four-bedroom, beach-front penthouse condo in Florida an apartment.

Ryan and Stephanie sold their house in suburban Chicago, used the profit to pay off their medical debt, and packed their things. Stephanie was going to take a break from her work as a nurse to focus more on Annie and Jack. Scott's property had plenty of open land for the kids to wander and lead some version of the Eisenhower-era childhood that Ryan's parents had enjoyed in Alpena. But Ryan extracted a promise from Stephanie, too, that she would spend more time on herself. For Stephanie, living on an insulin pump, there were no easy days. Her energy level would rise and fall by the hour. To keep her sugar level where it needed to be, she self-medicated with cans of soda, drinking six or seven by day and sometimes having more during the night. After Jack's surgery, Stephanie had been the family's main breadwinner, but now Ryan could be, through his job with the Fire Pit Collective. Getting anywhere from Alpena is not easy, but Delta had a daily flight from Alpena to Detroit. From there, the country and the world opened up for Ryan.

They had made their move two weeks before the U.S. Open at The Country Club, Stephanie and the two kids in her old Hyundai with Illinois plates and Ryan in a U-Haul truck. Both vehicles were crowded with taped boxes, large plastic toys, bikes, golf clubs, and other artifacts of suburban living. They left Lombard, Illinois, early on a June morning and arrived at their new home a long half day later. They unpacked. Ginny and Scott helped. His face said it all: *Here come the Beverly Hillbillies.* Ginny was watching and laughing. A couple of weeks later, Scott's hayseed sportswriter brother, at age forty-five, ate his first scissor-sliced pizza—and covered his first U.S. Open.

Ginny read her son's story about Brady Calkins more than once. It stopped her cold. She could imagine the thousand people in Chehalis, Washington, who had put Brady on a pedestal because he was good at golf. She had seen a lot of that, growing up in Alpena. As a retired drug and alcohol counselor, she could see that Brady might be heading to a Las Vegas moment of his own. She could see that Ryan, as a reporter and a writer, had the ability her father had, to take a reader to a distant place. (A stream in rural Alpena County, a strip club in Yankton, South Dakota.) In the piece, Ginny sensed empathy from Ryan and no judgment. She was reminded of Ryan as a kid, growing up in Alpena. In his twenties and into his thirties, something had changed—his main interest was his own jollies, and to hell with everybody else. Then came Las Vegas and its aftermath. Dr. Groban. Stephanie. Annie and Jack. The account. The Fire Pit Collective and his colleagues there. A new profession, one he never could have imagined when he was scraping gum off the underside of Qdoba tables. Ginny read the Brady Calkins piece to her husband.

* * *

In the summer of 1984, Sam and Betsy organized a six-week overseas trip for forty-four college students. They gave this odyssey a name: the Seekers Tour. They launched it in conjunction with the

First Presbyterian Church of Fresno, among other churches. Sam and Betsy underwrote a lot of the expense, as did other benefactors, but each student had to pay something. The itinerary was rooted in religious education, even when it looked like *National Lampoon's European Vacation*, which was being shot then.

The Seekers flew to London and started their tour in Paris. They went to Geneva, Lucerne, and Munich. They went to Salzburg and Prague and Austria. They went to Venice, to Florence, to Athens.

But the trip wasn't the Griswold family, led by Chevy Chase, roaming Continental Europe. Not at all. The itinerary included Dachau. A refugee camp in Austria. The Vatican. The Seekers went from Europe to Kenya, then to Egypt, and finally, to Israel. In Kenya, they went to schools and hospitals. In Egypt, they visited museums and the pyramids. In Israel, they went to Jerusalem and Nazareth and Bethlehem. They did the traditional walk-with-Jesus tour, as innumerable Christian pilgrims before them had done.

All the while, Sam—often working out of cramped phone booths, his pockets weighed down by heavy piles of domestic change—tried to keep up with his business life. He tried to keep up with his on-the-move daughters, with the news of the world, with various sporting events. Sam was in Kenya when Seve Ballesteros won the British Open at the Old Course in St. Andrews. Sam didn't see a shot but was delighted to hear the news. Nobody played with more spirit than Seve, and St. Andrews was golf's Jerusalem. Sam could see it in his mind's eye.

By then it had been eight years since he had last played golf, but it wasn't like his interest in the game had vanished. About a month after Seve's win, Sam, home in Fresno, watched one of his golfing heroes, Lee Trevino, win the PGA Championship at age forty-four. The winner was still "the Merry Mex" on ABC, the network announcers clinging to some yesterday version of him that never existed. Trevino liked being called Mex by his friends but had no use for the word *merry*. Barry McDermott, on the scene for *Sports Illustrated*, saw the actual man. He described Trevino pulling taped notes off his locker and saying, "Nobody gave me nothing coming up. I don't need anything now." Sam knew about the public-private divide in Trevino's life. He didn't care about it. What drew Sam to Trevino was the way he stepped into his shot like there was one spot reserved for his left foot and another for his right. What drew Sam to Trevino was the golfer's commitment to his craft, and the vitality with which he played the game.

But in the end, Trevino's unexpected win was a footnote for Sam in the summer of '84. The discoveries he made alongside the Seekers were on a higher plane.

He had stood in front of the furnaces at Dachau and considered mankind's capacity for depravity. He met AIDS patients in Kenya, bound for a painful death, and the medical mystery of their condition gnawed at him. The trip was marked by pungent smells, searing heat, scarce water—a trip where you used all your senses, one that unsettled you and settled in you.

Sam had been to Israel twice before. But on this trip, he saw Israel differently. This time, he was walking on Jesus's path with his fellow Seekers, the college kids he had gathered. This time there were scholarly guides at every stop. *This is the Church of the Nativity, where Jesus was born. This is the Jordan River, where Jesus was baptized. This is Kfar Nahum, where Jesus healed St. Peter's mother.* Sam knew the drill: If you went to Israel looking for Jesus, you were going to find a lot of Jesus. But he made a discovery in Israel in the summer of '84, something he told people then, on his way home, and for years afterward: You don't go to Israel to see it from a Christian perspective, or a Jewish perspective, or a Muslim perspective. You go to Israel to *make* yourself part of the connection between ancient life and modern life. A trip to Israel, Sam realized, was the ultimate *secular* expedition. You go to Israel to see for yourself why the world is so foul and so beautiful, to understand mankind's capacity for horror and its capacity for coexistence. After all, despite the odds and the setbacks and challenges, Israel did exist.

Sam turned fifty during that trip. He felt closer to eighteen, fresh out of his small-town high school, ready to get out and see the world.

• • •

Almost every day, Ryan or Stephanie or both, sometimes with one or two children and Kenny Knox (the family dog) in tow, would make the thirty-mile, nothing-but-trees drive from Scott's lake house to Howard and Ginny's home, a mile down a gravel drive-way. The back of their property ended at the Thunder Bay River. The drive took forty minutes, and you wouldn't dare speed, not because of hiding state troopers but because of darting deer. The old O. B. Eustis property was remote and isolated, and the house was well constructed and simple. It was a beautiful wilderness, but nobody would say living there was easy.

Ginny and Howard, after decades of not owning a TV, now had one, and Ryan and Howard would watch golf on it. Ryan did most of the talking. He began many sentences with the same two words. *Remember when you caddied for me in the City Open? Remember when we went with Grandpa to watch the seniors in Traverse City? Remember when Mitch Tasker told you, "Don't say* good luck, *say* play well"?

These were good questions because Howard had done all of those things multiple times. There were many paths in.

Ryan showed his father photos to see what they might trigger. *Here we are in Traverse City. That's Nicklaus. Right? That's Arnold, of course. That's Lee Trevino. Remember what Grandpa said about him?* ("Who woulda ever thought a Mexican would make it so big in golf.") There were days when Howard did remember. There were days when Howard would respond as if he were a pull-string doll. And there were days when he had nothing at all.

Howard was still slender and fit, with well-barbered white hair and a neatly trimmed beard. He wore fresh clothing most days and, when the mornings were cool, a flannel shirt. Had his photo appeared in *The Alpena News*, readers would have recognized him. *Still looks like he could bury an open jumper.* But Ryan and the rest of the French family knew what was missing, the indignities mounting gradually, then suddenly. It pained Ryan to take his father to the driving range, see him flail at fifteen or twenty balls, and then see him erupt. Nobody had ever warned Howard French that you get the gift of eye-hand coordination on a loaner basis. It pained the family to see Howard sit in his favorite recliner and turn pages in a newspaper he could not read. He was trying to fake it, but he didn't realize nobody was fooled. It pained family members to have to tie Howard's shoes, but of course they did, without saying a thing. Howard preferred his slippers. They had no laces and were sturdy enough to wear on the back lawn, soft and damp though it often was because of the nearby river.

Mark Baldwin came to town. This was about six weeks after the U.S. Open at The Country Club. Mark had played in five PGA Tour events and made the cut in the last three of them, each time with Ryan as his caddie. Mark had come to Alpena to return the favor. Howard had caddied for Ryan close to twenty times in the Alpena City Open. Now Mark was going to carry the bag. Mark ate meals with Ryan's parents, and he stayed with Ryan, Stephanie, Annie, and Jack in Scott's cottage. He was getting the full experience.

For the first round, Mark forgot to bring a range finder, the essential tool of modern caddying, used to measure distances. He did remember to say to Ryan on the first tee what Ryan always said to him: "Let's have a day." He didn't say *good luck.* He didn't say *play well.* Golfers and their rituals.

Mark, a clear and tidy writer, filed a report about the two-day event for the Fire Pit Collective. One observation, among the many: *Skiba, our playing partner, throws fist pumps or clubs, depending on the outcome of the shot.* Mark was referring to Todd Skiba, a two-time winner of the event and a member of an Alpena clan that numbered more than fifty. There were Skiba lawyers, doctors in all the popular categories, insurance agents, contractors, a high school golf coach, and a painter of seascapes. Ryan grew up with a dozen or so Skibas of varying ages and, during his extended homecoming stay, discovered that many of them were still around. The whole scene, the magnetic pull of small-town living, was familiar to Mark. He'd grown up in rural Gilford, New Hampshire, population seven thousand or so, a town with a lot of deer, a big lake, and nearby golf that was good enough.

Homecoming II, with a wife and children and improving mental health, was a completely different experience for Ryan than the previous one, in the aftermath of the Vegas episode. Stephanie was picking up right where she'd left off, but under happier circumstances. She had grown up in rural northern Michigan in a home where nobody spoke about anything. Stephanie and Ryan had a field day with *everything*. On one of her first days in Alpena, she went to a supermarket with Ryan and the kids. Ryan was loading the Hyundai, with its out-of-state plates. An older woman began a conversation with Stephanie. *New in town? Know about the farmers' market on Saturdays? Cute kids, where are they in school? Well, welcome, and make sure you lock your car—lot more Blacks and Hispanics in town than there used to be.* The woman waved goodbye, and Ryan and Stephanie could see her gun in its holster. They revisited that episode now and again, under the heading *Welcome to Alpena*.

It took them half an hour to get anywhere. Annie and Jack were enrolled in the public elementary school nearest to Scott's house, and it was twenty-seven miles away. Socially, school wasn't easy for Jack. He was quiet, clumsy, whip-smart. But at home, Jack and Annie were getting a message from their parents that had worked for them: It's okay not to be okay. Stephanie and Ryan didn't want their children to have a marketing-driven expectation of the perfect childhood or the perfect life. *When I'm traveling for work, you might need to get Mom a soda in the middle of the night, because that's what she needs, and she can't get it herself, and we're all looking out for each other. Right?* Steph had Type 1. It affects life expectancy. They had lived enough to know not to take *anything* for granted.

This family dealt. Jack's brain matter had spilled its way into his spinal canal, but now he was about the brightest damn kid in his school. Annie was a natural athlete, wildly verbal and personable, but at nine, she struggled as a reader. Mother and daughter read a book together about a Black woman who pitched in the Negro League in the 1950s—and Annie enjoyed it. There was every reason to think she could make herself a reader. Her father had made himself a sportswriter, after all. He had created a beat out of nothing. Along the way, he had created a sui generis life for himself and, by extension, his family. The starting point for the family was honesty. That, and love. Stephanie got COVID, which, in conjunction with her diabetes, was especially worrisome. She was in bed, isolated, communicating by text. She wrote to Ryan, *When I met you, my life was suffocating me, and you let me catch my breath and figure out how to breathe on my own.*

Yes, the family was living in a vacation house, surrounded by forest, meadow, beach, and lake, all of it ripe for exploration. But nobody was pretending they were in a fantasyland. Life nipped at them, as life does. Howard's dementia didn't take a holiday. Jack's balance, Annie's reading, Stephanie's diabetes, Ryan's depression—you couldn't snap your fingers and make these things disappear. You enjoyed the good times and handled the rest. The future was the future, both a puzzle and a mystery. The day brought what the day brought. Kenny Knox had been chewing on his own furry coat all night and into the morning. The vet was a half hour away. The car might need gas. The beautiful mundanity of everyday life.

• • •

By the spring of 1986, Sam and Betsy's two oldest daughters had graduated college, the third was in college, and the fourth was in high school. Sam had a little breathing room. A friend invited him to the Masters, played every April at Augusta National. The tournament, started by Bobby Jones, is famously associated with blooming azaleas, and the tournament itself is golf's invitation to start fresh. A friend of Sam's, a member of the club, invited him to attend. It had now been ten years since Sam had played golf and over ten since he had been to a tournament. He didn't feel golf gnawing at him. But he was glad to be invited, and he went.

That 1986 Masters turned out to be one of the most memorable ever played. Jack Nicklaus, at age forty-six, with his son caddying for him, was trying to win a major for the first time in six years. The weather was glorious, cool and breezy at the start of the tournament and warm and still by the end. (All of April in a single week.) There were innumerable birdie and eagle roars through the weekend, for Nicklaus, for Greg Norman of Australia, for Bernhard Langer of Germany, for Nick Price of Zimbabwe, for Seve Ballesteros of Spain. The Masters is a global event, but there's something distinctly southern and provincial about it, too. It seemed like everybody was rooting for Nicklaus, the Ohio State legend who had already won the Masters five times. Sam wasn't moved. His man was Seve, the dazzling Spaniard.

For a while on Sunday, it seemed like Seve had the tournament in his tanned hands. After an eagle on thirteen, he had a three-shot lead. But then he hit a toe-hook 4-iron second shot on the short par-5 fifteenth hole and made a bogey, when a good shot most likely would have resulted in a two-putt birdie. That 4-iron haunted him for the rest of the day, and the rest of his life. As Seve stood on the sixteenth tee, his chances weren't over mathematically, only psychologically. Nicklaus won by a shot over Greg Norman and Tom Kite. Sam, off to see one of his daughters in Atlanta, was gone by then.

Seve finished two shots back. The event was a painful reminder for Sam about how unforgiving the game is. Unforgiving in the most exquisite way. Golf's a strange game and not for everyone. But it was part of Sam, and it remained so even during that long hiatus.

Sam got home to Fresno and started making regular trips again to his spot on the Sunnyside range. (He had never given up his membership.) At night, after work, he headed back to Hank's Swank, the driving range where he could hit balls under the lights. Charley Seaver had moved to Pebble Beach, but Dick Giddings was around, and he and Sam resumed their old ways, playing regularly. They picked right up where they had left off, two tall, slender men who had a similar appreciation for the game. Sam was struck by how good Dick still was. He was more than twenty years older than Sam but beat him more often than not. Melvin Hemphill had died, but Sam could still hear his old golf instructor in his head. Sam's game was still there, hibernating inside him, his old feelings for the game and the swing coming back to life like late-fire coals in a bellows' gust.

Dick was still qualifying, or attempting to qualify, for USGA competitions, now senior ones. He encouraged Sam to do the same. In 1989, Sam turned fifty-five, the minimum age for the U.S. Senior Amateur. He qualified. He didn't do anything once he got there, but he had qualified.

Dick and Sam started making regular trips from Fresno to the Monterey Peninsula, sometimes by car (three winding hours), more often on Sam's plane (one hour, no fuss). Dick was a member of

Cypress Point, with its quaint and charming pro shop and its aromatic back-to-back par-3 holes, numbers fifteen and sixteen, one a wedge shot over a bit of ocean, the other a driver over even more of it. Sometimes they would play the two courses at the Monterey Peninsula Country Club, where Dick was also a member. Now and again they would play Pebble Beach, the course that Sam loved more than any in the world, a course that anybody could play if you could manage the outrageous green fee and get a tee time. If there were tournaments or other things going on, or sometimes just for a change of pace, they would play the municipal course in Pacific Grove, with its modest, pay-at-the-counter green fee and its own views of the ocean. (Pacific Grove has a half dozen holes that offer as much coastal golf fun as anything you'll find in Scotland or Ireland.) In June 1992, the U.S. Open was held at Pebble Beach, and Sam and Betsy were there for it. Nicklaus, the winner of the 1972 U.S. Open at Pebble, was in the field. Tom Watson, the winner over Nicklaus in the 1982 Open at Pebble, played, too. Tom Kite won that '92 Open at Pebble on a Sunday when the course was so windblown that flagsticks were bending like old men in prayer.

Two years and a month later, in late July 1994, Sam and Betsy and the girls and their significant others gathered at a beach house Sam owned near Oceanside, in Southern California, to celebrate Sam's sixtieth birthday. All his life, Sam had been drawn to golf courses and oceans. In Oceanside, Sam could play golf, and he could get in the ocean. He loved bodysurfing, as did the whole family: the speed of the wave, the timing of the launch, the sunshine on your back, the salt water on your skin, the sense of letting your body go amid all that gravitational pull and heavy water.

There were days when it was a struggle to walk from the back deck of the Reeves house to the ocean because of all the rocks covering the beach, deposited there in the ocean's high tide. But there were also nights when those beach rocks would wash back out to sea and leave a wide swath of smooth sand. Sam could imagine the tumbling rocks, and the current that carried them, heading four hundred miles north to Pebble Beach. All that connection. One of Sam's running themes.

At sixty, Sam was starting to consider his life as coming in three parts. He thought of his first thirty years as Preparation. He called the next thirty Implementation. Now he was sixty, and he wondered what the next phase of his life might bring and what he might call it. Eventually, he settled on a word: Validation.

• • •

For the few American writers left on the golf beat, the U.S. Open in mid-June represents the height of the golf year. After the U.S. Open comes the British Open, the PGA Tour's FedEx Cup tournaments, and the U.S. Amateur, followed by (depending on the year) the Solheim Cup, the Ryder Cup, the Presidents Cup, and the Walker Cup. In 2022, for the first time, there was LIV Golf, the Saudi-backed series of golf tournaments. It lured players with massive guaranteed paydays and had signed name-brand players including Phil Mickelson, Dustin Johnson, Brooks Koepka, Bryson DeChambeau, and others with far less fame. Alan Shipnuck of the Fire Pit Collective was covering LIV Golf closely. So was Bob Harig from *Sports Illustrated*. But Ryan's beat kept him far from it, and that didn't bother him at all. He had his beat to himself.

Ryan wrote a piece about a young aspiring pro named Matt Moroz that became a sensation. The story came out of a pre-qualifier for the Korn Ferry Tour qualifying tournament. Yes, a qualifier for the qualifier. Few would have even known it existed. On the fifth hole of his third round, with his two playing partners conveniently out of view, Moroz claimed that a shot he had sculled, one that had almost no chance of reaching the green, went into the hole. Other incredible (not credible) nuttiness ensued before the round and the event were over. The story ran under the headline A Q SCHOOL DQ FOR THE AGES. Ryan's follow-up stories were even more bizarre. The audience for this odd cheating scandal was massive, and Ryan was a guest on various golf shows. But all the while, he wisely kept his eye on the prize: his job. Before the year was out, Ryan wrote, podcasted, and tweeted about the Dakotas Tour. About a dormant pro tour in Africa that suddenly and conveniently had captured the interest of LIV Golf. About his friendship with Mark Baldwin. Ryan wrote about a noted Alpena golf bum (*not* a pejorative) and the immense kindness he showed Howard on a golf-course visit. He podcasted about Willy Wilcox, a pro golfer who, in a Fire Pit Collective piece, talked about being a PGA Tour member with a drug addiction. Ryan had first seen Wilcox a decade or so earlier, at a Hooters event in Conover, North Carolina, where Wilcox won and made twenty-eight thousand dollars. That was the week when Ryan and Howard's tent was uprooted by the wind and ended up in a tree.

Firearm deer season begins in Michigan each year on November 15, and most schools in northern Michigan, including Jack and Annie's, close for it. Annie didn't show interest in hunting, but Jack did, so Ryan made sure that his son, at age seven, had taken an age-appropriate firearms safety course. On opening day, he put Jack in orange and camouflage, and they headed into the woods. As Bob French had taught Howard how to stalk and kill a deer, and as Howard had taught Ryan, Ryan was now teaching Jack. Ryan despised hunting. The only thing that drew him into the woods on opening day was Jack's interest in it, in autumn's first snow. They got a foot in a day.

Opening day for firearm deer season fell on the same day as the first round of an Asian Tour qualifying tournament being held in Sedona, Arizona. It was a tough day for Ryan to have no access to the internet. But hunting with Jack was always going to carry the day. Jack was beside his father when Ryan killed a deer. Ryan gutted the deer in the woods. Warm red blood melted and stained the snow. Ryan castrated the deer and hung its testicles from a tree, something he had learned from O. B. Eustis, who said it was a necessary act to honor the deer's spirit. Ryan separated the deer's heart, and the family ate it that night for dinner, pan-fried. The rest of the deer was slaughtered and eaten in time by the French family, by Ginny and Howard's neighbors, and by the residents of an Alpena homeless shelter. Ginny knew all the shelters in town, from her work as a drug-and-alcohol counselor and as a weekly congregant at Trinity Episcopal.

Shortly before Thanksgiving, Ginny and her daughter, Dallas, and Dallas's daughter went to New York City for a few days. Ryan stayed with Howard. The family was together at Scott's vacation house for Thanksgiving. Then came Christmas, New Year's Eve hot on its tail. Michigan won every game it played, until its final one. Howard had always been a Michigan State guy. Alpena was Spartans country.

Ginny didn't think Howard would make it to another Christmas. She could see the river from her living room, and it always gave her pause. There were times when Howard said he would walk into it by way of goodbye, and others when he said he'd never end things that way. Just before Thanksgiving, Howard went missing for a couple of hours, and Ryan's first thought was to check the river. Scott and Ryan found their father, through his tracking device, wandering in the woods. The footprints in the snow were in imperfect circles.

One way or another, his end was coming. Ryan knew Alpena. He knew a day would arrive when a small group of old-timers would gather in the name of his father and say nice things about him, meaning most of them. Howard had tried to do some good in his house and beyond it. Everybody would agree on that. He had tried to rise above his own dark clouds. He had tried to help Ryan. When Ryan needed a guide, a shepherd, a father, Howard was there.

Ryan arrived at the Alpena golf course for the Alpena City Open along with Mark Baldwin. Their friendship came from their shared love for golf and out of Ryan's Monday Q account. Mark was caddying because Howard could not. Howard was there to see them off. It wasn't easy, but he got there.

"'Play well,'" Howard said. He still had a loud voice. He was calling out to his son, a few feet away from him. "Remember that?"

Ryan remembered that. It was from one of their father-son road trips.

For the short length of a tiny exchange, clarity had revisited Howard French. Ryan's father had stopped time and turned it back, put his disease in remission. In four words, Howard shared with his son everything he could share and needed to share. For a moment, Howard was right there, and that was good enough. Ryan headed to the first tee, and his father stayed behind.

On the day after she turned twenty-three, I asked Pratima if she could picture her life at thirty, when she would be starting, in Sam's accounting, a phase of life he called Implementation. She could.

"I think I'll be married, with children, living in Nepal, owning my own business," she said. She imagined her first child being a girl.

There was a liveliness to her voice. There had been times when she sounded not quite defeated but on her heels, worried about what might come next. On this day, there was none of that.

I asked Pratima if she had a sense of how golf would fit into her life at thirty.

She saw herself as a member at Royal Nepal, playing regularly there and elsewhere, introducing the game to her children, teaching the swing to young people who encountered obstacles on their way to the first tee. Those obstacles made Pratima the golfer and the person she had become. "Golf will always be in my life," she said.

Pratima was predicting a period of growth for golf in Nepal. "Golf would be good for Nepal," she said. "In Nepal, people are late for everything. In golf, you have to be on time. Golf taught me that."

The conversation went in that direction for a while. Then Pratima said, "Everything I've learned, I learned through golf."

Trevino likes to say, "Golf made me." He doesn't say it casually, and he's not referring to the material things golf has given him.

That's a theme for a lot of us, golf as a teacher. Roberto De Vicenzo, the great Argentine golfer, won the British Open, a tournament Trevino won twice. They played in hundreds of the same events over the years. De Vicenzo was as refined and intelligent as a person could be, even though he never made it to seventh grade. He once said, "My seven-iron is my professor." Trevino knew and admired De Vicenzo and understood that observation.

"Golf teaches you how to act, how to respond, how to respect different kinds of people," Trevino said once. He was talking to a reporter whom Trevino knew well, a golfer and a Texan. Trevino is not trusting by nature, but if you're a golfer and a Texan, you have a chance. "Golf teaches you about the world and about life. Golf teaches you how to act and to react. I know people here who have never left Dallas County, and I could have been one of them. But I had golf, and that let me see the world." See the world and learn something from it. See the flight of your ball and learn something from it. See yourself under pressure and learn something from it.

On the spring day I turned thirty-one, Christine and I were staying in a house called Frogwell Barn, deep in southern England, on the eve of the Benson & Hedges International, a flashy stop on the European Tour. I was there as a caddie. Nick Faldo, David Feherty, Bernhard Langer, and Vijay Singh were in the field, as was my man, Peter Teravainen, a Yale-educated, profoundly frugal American golfer who played the European Tour. I had found steady work as Peter's caddie, and he was bankrolling (not lavishly) the extended honeymoon Christine and I were on.

Peter was an original. On one memorable late-winter night in 1991, as the European Tour lurched its way from Spain to Portugal, Christine and I were on a packed, smoke-choked overnight caddie bus, organized (used loosely here) by a Scottish caddie known as Turnberry George. (Yes, I had married a girl who *liked* being on an overnight caddie bus.) There was—and nobody was surprised—one and only one player on the bus. Peter's first goal, on a weekly basis, was to make more money than he spent, and the overnight bus ride helped put him on the right side of his ledger. The border to Portugal wasn't open when we arrived, so we ate Petit Écolier cookies and Valencia oranges while we waited. Christine watched the sun come up over a barren farm field.

She turned thirty-one half a year later, when we were staying in a farmhouse called Whitekirk Mains, in the town of Dunbar, in Scotland. That summer, the summer of '91, I had fallen under the spell of a Highlands golf teacher named John Stark, who smoked cheap cigars, stirred his coffee with a letter opener, and possessed a mesmerizing voice. He'd show me something about the backswing or the head position while putting and conclude by saying, "On you go." Those three words, in Stark's distinct burr, were planted in me.

I have heard people describe John Stark as a real-life Shivas Irons, the mystic golf teacher in Michael Murphy's *Golf in the Kingdom*. I get that. Both had a powerful surname, a terrific brogue, and a knack for getting to the heart of the matter without drawing blood. It is a measure of Shivas's generosity that he invites the book's narrator, conveniently named Michael Murphy, to a dinner gathering of golf kooks. (Pages thirty-six to seventy-one are a fever dream.) It was a measure of John Stark's generosity that he invited me to play a secret six-hole course he knew, a course miles from civilization. It had been laid out by a shepherd and, to the degree that it was maintained at all, tended by sheep. Stark, bless his soul, didn't tell me where we were going or what we would be doing when we left his cluttered pro-shop office that morning. The drive there was rough, on roads barely wide enough to accommodate his Volvo.

When Ben Hogan won the 1953 British Open at Carnoustie in Scotland, Stark was there. It was a long and winding two-hour drive from Crieff, but Hogan was one of Stark's golfing heroes. For a period, Stark was obsessed with frame-by-frame analysis of Hogan's action, believing, as many did and do, that there was a perfect position for every moment of the golf swing. By the time I found my way to Stark, he had moved on from that. He was back to his Scottish roots, and he was looking at the swing as he looked at people. The whole person, start to present day; the whole swing, start to finish. From everything I could tell, Stark thought for himself, just as Hogan did. Few things draw me more to a person than that. When I knew Stark, he favored wash-and-wear pants and seemed to have a particular fondness for a bright red pair. Under Stark's tutelage, I was a born-again golfer, happily so. To Stark, the starting point to a good swing was good breathing. I totally bought into that. But the trousers were a bridge too far.

I started 1991 as an American golfer but finished the year as a Scottish one. That summer, my first summer with my new bride, Christine and I became smitten by a remote Scottish village with an irresistible golf course, both called Machrihanish. Christine, not a golfer, walked the course with me, collecting wildflowers, placing them at night in the books we were carting around. We ate our dinners in the clubhouse and stayed for a magical week. Later I joined Machrihanish as an overseas member, put up for membership by a caddie friend with a law degree he didn't use. By then I had returned home and had a regular Sunday-morning game at the Philadelphia Cricket Club. Our foursome was always the first or second group off. We played fast, by the rules, for keeps, and without a lot of chitchat. I'd drive to the course in the day's first light, through our sleeping village (the Chestnut Hill section of Philadelphia), past a George Thomas course (Whitemarsh Valley) that once hosted a PGA Tour event, across a sprawling gentleman's farm (Erdenheim Farm), before arriving at the Cricket Club's Tillinghast course, a Golden Age classic from 1922. We would throw balls to decide partners and flip a tee to determine who would play first. We holed our putts and settled our modest debts just off the eighteenth green, after paying our caddies. It was amazing how often our matches were decided by a putt on one of the final two holes. It might have looked like American country club golf, but in our minds, we were playing the game in ways our brothers (and sisters) in the old country would have recognized. I'd be home by late morning, if not earlier, and sometimes the French toast would still be warm. We had two kids and they were the center of our lives, but Christine understood the joy I got from those Sunday games.

A public road, narrow and curved, runs through the National Golf Links of America, and on one occasion, as a callow teenager, I went from road to course and played a few late-day holes. I was on guard the whole brief while but never saw a soul. I experienced just enough of it to determine that playing irons off its firm turf and putting its heaving greens was unlike any other golf experience I had ever had.

Some years later, I was invited to play there by a lifelong member, Michael M. Thomas, an investment banker by day and a writer by night. Michael M. had various amusing takes on the game. He believed every golf club should have a reverse admissions committee by which one person per year would be kicked out of the club, just to keep all the members on their toes. I was nervous upon arrival, driving through the Macdonald Gates for the first time as a legitimate guest, and more nervous by the time I stood on the first tee. The first hole at National is a short par-4 played into a valley and up to an insanely curvaceous green. I duffed my tee shot. Also my second, third, and fourth shots. I played my fifth from about thirty yards off the green. I could barely see the flagstick. The shot went in for an unlikely bogey, and that seemed to settle me.

From there to the house, I shot three over. Believe me, I had never done anything like that. Afterward, Michael M. Thomas was under the incorrect impression that I was a good golfer. By the end of the day, I had three favorite courses in the world: Bellport, Machrihanish, and the National Golf Links of America.

When we were in our thirties and forties and fifties, Burt McHugh, my fellow golf-bum friend from the Philadelphia Cricket Club, and I would occasionally go on out-of-town golfing benders. We would travel by car around the Northeast for two or three days and play two and sometimes three rounds per day, always walking. If you have never played three rounds in a day, I'd recommend it. (You might want to put an extra pair of socks in your bag and a spare pair of golf shoes in your car.) Somewhere in the second round, I have found, you forget about swing mechanics and just play golf. The joy of the match and the setting take over. On one of these dawn-to-dusk golf days, I was one down to Burt after fifty-three holes. I would have halved the day by winning the last hole. I lost the last hole to lose two down. The sun set right on cue, and it was all good, right down to the scorecard totals.

That was at a course called Misquamicut, in Watch Hill, Rhode Island. It's a par-69 course and not even sixty-three hundred yards long, and it's all you could want, or all I would want. (The American obsession with par-72 courses that measure at least seventy-two hundred yards from the tips on vast pieces of land—the Augusta

National Golf Club course comes to mind—has not served American golf well.) When this excellent day of Ocean State golf was over, Burt and I showered in the club's employee quarters and drove home.

Burt made these trips. He's a golfer. He's all in on ball searches, he roots for you to make your putts, he always knows how the match stands, and who did what where. He plays at a brisk pace without rushing and has an appreciation for all manner of little pleasures. The night we got the day's last pie at La Strada (one of Patchogue's leading pizzerias) and used the roof of the car as our serving table. An analysis of the Bellport course, identifying the holes that seemed to bear the stamp of Seth Raynor, a Golden Age course architect. A two-hour session at the Shinnecock Hills driving range when our host was delayed by hangover. Did we care? Absolutely not. We still got in thirty-six holes that day, no sweat.

One day at National Golf Links, when Burt was closing in on fifty and I was a little past it, we started our round on the par-3 fourth hole. The hole is called Redan, modeled after a famous hole at North Berwick in Scotland. I hit my tee shot from 160 yards to four feet. I would have liked to start the round with a birdie, of course, but that first putt did not touch any part of the hole. Lacking that, I would have liked to start the hole with a par, of course, which would have matched Burt's par. (With a half shot per hole, that would have put me one up with thirty-five to play.) But my par putt was worse than my birdie putt. My first experience with the yips, the putting malady where you can't get your body to do what your mind tells it to do. Burt was only encouraging, that day and since.

One attempted fix has been to go righty on the long ones and lefty on the short ones, when I feel the yip coming on. This is easily accomplished with any legal two-way putter, such as the Acushnet Bullseye. If you've ever seen the two-way rubber-headed putters used at many mini-golf establishments, they are modeled after the Bullseye. I bought my first one in a gas-station parking lot on the Monterey Peninsula from a guy who was selling vintage putters and dinged surfboards. Corey Pavin used a Bullseye for years, and so did Payne Stewart. It has a sweet spot the size of a pinhead. I once asked Pavin if Bullseye putters had loft on both sides of the face. "Lemme guess," he said. "You're going righty on the long ones and lefty on the short ones." Turns out there is loft on both sides. Some years later, Burt went to a long-shafted putter and later cut a few inches off that shaft and went to a split-handed claw grip that he used effectively in concert with a no-release stroke. If none of that is meaningful to you, consider yourself lucky. Putting is the game within the game, and most every golfer over the age of fifty has to make some sort of adjustment while putting, some sort of concession to frayed nerves. The other option is to take two weeks off and then quit altogether.

The eighteen-hole course closest to our house is Walnut Lane, a par-62, forty-five-hundred-yard muni that is part of the Philadelphia park system. It's two miles away. Walnut Lane was designed by Alex Findlay, one of the first Scottish golfers to bring the game to the United States. That probably makes the place sound charming. It is charming, but not in the conventional sense. John Chaney, the legendary Temple basketball coach, played Tonk and dispensed wisdom there for years. (Tonk, a cousin to gin rummy, is the main card game at Walnut Lane.) The course is hemmed in by loud streets, row houses, and a vast, magnificent park. Hikers will sometimes slip onto the front nine, as the park's trails lead right into it.

I have played the course only a half dozen or so times but have dropped into the pro shop often over the years, to buy gently used ProV1s (a golf ball made by Titleist) and to inspect the barrels of wedges and putters. (I prefer secondhand equipment. It's not a money thing. I want clubs with life experience.) The clubs arrive by donation and are sold to raise money for the First Tee junior-golf program at Walnut Lane. On summer nights, you'll see a dozen or two kids—Black, Hispanic, white, many of them girls—chipping near the practice green while waiting for rides home, or heading out to nearby bus stops. American golf would be better with more courses like Walnut Lane.

The course closest to our house is a short nine-holer called St. Martins, about a mile and a half from our kitchen door. The course is part of the Philadelphia Cricket Club, and I can play it in an hour: eight short par-4s, a wedge par-3, little rough. Some of the holes date to the 1890s and were part of an eighteen-hole course where the U.S. Open was played in 1907 and 1910. The greens at St. Martins are as good as greens anywhere, for the quality of the grass and for the subtle, and not so subtle, slopes in them. The third green is a complete fascination. It swoops like an Elvis pompadour from its back-left corner to its front right. Over the years, I have described it to many playing partners as a prime example of nineteenth-century green design, proof that Willie Tucker, the transplanted Englishman behind the original course, was some kind of genius. More recently, I learned the green was built in 1963.

I play a lot of my golf at St. Martins, the site of what I like to think is the fifth major, after the Masters, the PGA Championship, the U.S. Open, and the British Open. That is, the St. Martins Spring Match Play Championship, a net event where all the participants, at least in theory, are created equal, through the application of handicap strokes. Conveniently, there is a St. Martins Fall Match Play Championship as well. It, too, may be described as the fifth major. So, yes, two fifth majors. At least, that's what we say in the Bamberger house.

In 2019, the year I turned fifty-nine, I put a new two-way putter in my bag, still committed to going righty long and lefty short. (A two-way putter also allows you to turn every curving putt into a hook putt, depending on which side of the ball you choose to play from. Many golfers find hook putts more inviting to the eye.) A problem with the design of the typical two-way putter is that it is perfectly symmetrical, with the shaft coming straight up from the putter head, without any bend. Most golfers prefer putters with offset, where the shaft is in front of the face of the putter. That is typically done with a gently curving hosel, known as a gooseneck, or something with more abrupt angles, known as a plumber's neck. In 2019, I had retrofitted (with plenty of help) a circa-1965 Ping A1 straight-shafted two-way putter by adding a modified gentle gooseneck hosel to it. That gave me a smidgen of offset when putting righty and, in a term that was new to me, a smidgen of *onset* from the left. Onset, in this sense, means the putter face is ahead of the shaft. I also inserted a muffler, in this case a small piece of rubber, between the front and back face, to eliminate the ping sound that greeted any putt (and the sound that gave the company its name). With this new contraption in hand, and putting right-hand low when I went lefty, my putting was north of mediocre. On a tiny course like St. Martins, with its devilish greens, most holes are going to be won or lost or halved based on what happens from ten feet and in.

Yes, this is all a long but necessary (it says here!) preamble to the eighteenth hole of the 2019 St. Martins Spring Match Play Championship final match, featuring your correspondent and a retired tax lawyer named Fred Gerhart, who grew up putting on sand greens in Iowa. Fred didn't hit it far, but he was relentlessly in play.

Our final hole (the ninth the second time through) was a short par-4, not even 260 yards long. We were even as we stood on the tee. My tee shot finished hole-high but thirty yards left of the green, and I would be coming in from an odd angle. Fred's tee shot was in the middle of the fairway and about seventy yards from the hole. He hit his second shot to fifteen feet and was looking at a putt straight up a hill. In other words, not a difficult putt for a capable putter. Fred was a capable putter.

I didn't want the match to go to the first hole, where Fred would be getting a shot. But given where he was in two shots, and where I was in one, he had a much better chance of making a 3, or a 4, than I did. Advantage Fred.

I inspected my second shot. The ball was in a fluffy lie, and I could see a little more than half of it. As I addressed the ball, in a trial run, my right foot was almost touching the edge of the redbrick patio that surrounds the tiny, ancient St. Martins pro shop. I realized then that there were two market umbrellas, in the up position, directly in line with the hole. I went into the shop and asked the pro if the rules permitted me to lower the umbrellas. In the down position, I would have to clear only the umbrella masts. The answer was yes, the umbrellas could come down. (Temporary movable obstruction.) That was the good news. The bad news was that the question generated mild interest in my shot and the match. That is, the final of the 2019 St. Martins Spring Championship, featuring a retired tax lawyer, age seventy-three and looking for a second St. Martins title, versus a fifty-nine-year-old sportswriter looking for his first.

Fred vs. Mike.

The fifth major.

With the aid of a hand crank, I lowered the umbrella canopies. I opened the face of my (gross commercial endorsement) circa-1990 beryllium copper black-dot Ping Eye2 sand wedge. I made a good practice swing. I made a good real swing. The club's heavy flange went right through the grass with a pleasing sound, and the club-head went left on a circle, the hands leading the face, the body rotating. My ball carried the umbrella masts by a yard or two. I thought I heard murmurs of approval from a couple of onlookers behind me. The ball pitched softly, rolled out slightly, and stopped quickly.

I put my wedge in the bag and got out my two-way putter. I had about a four-footer, slightly uphill, for a birdie 3.

Fred made a no-fuss two-putt par.

If I made my putt for 3, I'd win. If I needed two putts, we would be going to sudden death, and Fred would get his shot on one. I didn't like my chances in that scenario.

As I eyed the putt, I was ambivalent about whether to hit it righty or lefty. From the right, it would be, ever so slightly, a slice putt. So that favored the left, since from there, it would be a hook putt. But it was uphill, and my tendency was to fail to give my short left-handed uphill putts enough gas.

I went lefty. The stroke wasn't a yip, but it was, in the jargon, a total decel job, a stroke that loses speed at impact, causing the ball to slip off the intended line as it crawls toward the hole.

Pardon me, gentle reader, but I feel duty-bound to share what was racing through my head as the ball rolled meekly toward the hole:

Oh, fuck—now I gotta give this guy a shot on one.

I figured the putt had no chance of reaching.

It reached.

My ball was going close to zero feet per minute, but it did reach the hole's front door and fall in. Uphill, that never happens, gravity being gravity. But I saw and heard the ball drop, and I retrieved the ball from the bottom of the hole. Proof positive. A birdie 3. I had won the match and the St. Martins spring title.

Fred looked at me and I at him. He was wearing metal-framed glasses, a floppy bucket hat, lots of sunblock, long pants on a hot day. He extended his pale, slender hand and congratulated me without a hint of what could have been. That's golf, right there. What a gent, that Fred.

Fred's golf.

FINISHING

There's another act coming after this:
I reckon you can guess what that's about.

—Stage Manager, *Our Town*

By sixty, at the dawn of his Validation years, Sam had decided to retire as the co-chairman of Dunavant Enterprises and sell his interest to his partner, Billy Dunavant. Dunavant Enterprises was by then one of the largest private companies in the United States, with interests that went way beyond cotton. It owned resort hotels, shipping businesses, agricultural financing companies in the United States and abroad, tennis centers, and extensive amounts of real estate. The company sold nearly six thousand acres of timberland off I-95 in northern Florida that became a housing development known as the World Golf Village, where the World Golf Hall of Fame was built, with a Caddyshack restaurant (owned by Bill Murray and brothers) and a Renaissance Hotel (owned by Bill Marriott and shareholders) next to it. The sale of that land was a vast transaction by any normal standard. For Dunavant Enterprises, it was a one-line entry on a profit-and-loss statement that, year after year, showed more *p* than *l*. Sam was set and then some, but he was born with the restless gene.

His four daughters were all married or bound for marriage. Grandchildren had arrived, and more would be coming. Sam wanted his heirs to pursue their passions without worrying about making rent. He wanted to diversify his wealth and be in control of it. In his thirty-plus years as a cotton merchant, Sam had seen the production of California cotton grow by every measure: acreage, production, employment, sales. He believed that California cotton had peaked. When driving or flying between Fresno and Pebble Beach, Sam could see California farms moving away from cotton in favor of grapes, corn, alfalfa, melons, and almonds. The time to move on had announced itself.

When he retired from Dunavant, Sam wrote a letter to his colleagues that explained how a regional company with Memphis roots had spread its tentacles around the world. Dunavant believed that countries with growing populations and economies would "pamper" (Sam's word) the textile industry, and in his farewell letter, he wrote why: *History had taught these governments that revolutions are the result of food and clothing shortages. Capitalism is about capital. There are three basic types of capital—human, monetary, and raw materials. The former was in abundance in these countries, the latter two becoming increasingly available. Cheap transportation reduced the landed cost of raw materials. This newfound freedom, varying from country to country, was electrifying.*

That final word popped up regularly in Sam's vocabulary. *Electrifying.* Also its cousins: *vital, joyful, alert.*

Ending his long relationship at Dunavant wasn't simple or easy, but later, when he took stock of his years there, he saw more adventure than anything else. That and calculated risk. There were (in retrospect) comically irresponsible flights in developing countries and bus rides where passengers boarded with farm animals. There were barriers in etiquette and currency, on the streets and at higher elevations, that made you figure out on the spot how to connect with others who were everything and nothing like you. The rewards were varied. Sam (he would *never* say this) could tip generously. With Betsy, he could write big checks to the causes dear to them—and he did. He could live large. Private planes, overseas vacations, beach houses. He and a few friends bought a ranch in Wyoming the size of a county, where you could ride horses for days, seeing nothing but cowboys and cattle. It lost money year after year, but Sam loved it. He loved it all. If there was one secret to his success, it was that.

He read constantly, developing his own thoughts and theories all the while. His beat was the world. In his travels, Sam came to see that people everywhere want the same essential things: food, clothing, shelter, dignity, relevancy. People want to be needed. Understanding that made Sam better in business and better at life. He and Dunavant had had some run.

His last day was July 1, 1995. He was sixty (almost sixty-one) and knocking on the door of the rest of his life.

Sam had a friend, Stan Druckenmiller, who was a successful private investor. Following Stan's path and guidance but using only his own money, Sam started a company called Pinnacle Trading. It was not named for the mass-produced golf ball sold at Walmart and other big-box chain stores. It was a nod to buy low, sell high. A great part of Sam's success as a cotton merchant came from making big, well-timed bets on huge quantities of raw cotton. At Pinnacle, working with one of his sons-in-law, Sam would have the chance to apply that skill to other industries.

Pinnacle Trading started in Fresno and later moved to greater Pebble Beach. Dick Giddings, Sam's Fresno golf friend, had put Sam up for membership at Cypress Point, the private club a few miles up the coast from Pebble Beach. Getting into a club like Cypress or Augusta National or Seminole is a secretive and undemocratic process, and there are many more candidates than there are slots. Admission in these clubs is nominally by committee and always by invitation. You can't fill out an application. It's a cruel process for those on the outside who overvalue being inside. Sam got in quickly—he was known to many there—and soon after, Dick, in his mid-eighties, resigned from the club. He had been keeping his membership just to get Sam in. Sam and Betsy bought a house high on a hill off of 17-Mile Drive with a view of the Pacific in one direction and Cypress Point in others. If you are lucky enough to play Cypress Point and you airmail your ball crazily over its elevated eighth green, it might come to rest in Betsy's flower bed.

Sam's membership at Cypress Point enriched his life more than he might have ever guessed. It's a unique club, quiet, still, confident, and its scale is unusually small and intimate. Unexpectedly, in this new stage of life, Sam found himself making meaningful relationships with other members, with guests, with caddies and employees, and most particularly and unexpectedly, with the head pro, a tall, slender man named Jim Langley. Sam had known Jim for years. Just meeting Jim was a memorable experience for many people, the unrushed pro in the long-sleeve shirt with the beatific presence. As a guest, Sam had seen Jim often over the years, quick hellos here and there. But then Sam joined the club and got to know Jim Langley on a different level altogether.

$$\bullet \quad \bullet \quad \bullet$$

I turned sixty a few weeks into the pandemic, when its dark mystery was in full flight. Had it been a normal year, I would have been making it home from the Masters right about then, in mid-April. But it was not a normal year, and the Masters, such a reliable rite of spring, had been postponed until the fall. Most golf courses were closed, in Philadelphia and elsewhere. I hit balls in an open field one early-spring day, but it felt forced and empty. Davis Love's house in Sea Island, Georgia, had burned to the ground, destroying almost everything he owned, and we commiserated about that. I had helped him with a book years earlier, and for a long while, I'd had his family's letters and his father's notes, which I had returned. Davis believed all of that was safe at his mother's house.

I had been talking to Greg Norman semi-regularly that winter and spring, gleaning what I could about a new world golf league he was involved with. He told me bits and pieces about it, but it was cryptic. As a reporter covering golf, I had always had a good rapport with Norman. I referred to this nascent start-up as the Premier Golf League, and he said that name was wrong, but he couldn't tell me the correct one, I think because he and his partners hadn't settled on one. I asked if it was possible to get commitments from players and financiers for a new golf league during a period when there was so much uncertainty. Norman, as a golfer and businessman, was famously brash and sometimes impatient. But he said that waiting out the pandemic would not be an issue for his unnamed business partners. His confidence was striking. It didn't seem like bravado. At one point, he asked me for a list of golf writers he should invite to a meeting where the details of this new league would be revealed. It wasn't the most appropriate thing for me to do, but I did it anyhow. You need to have some give and take if you want to be a reporter in the real world.

At the same time, I was playing twenty questions with Norman, trying to figure out who might be joining his new league. I offered the name Hideki Matsuyama, the young golfer from Japan. This was before Hideki had won the Masters. Yes, Norman said, there was no golfer his partners wanted more. The underlying message was clear: The world of golf did not begin and end with American stars. Norman's own career was proof of that.

On the night of my birthday, suppertime coming, I was in my office above our garage and I could hear and smell the Mexican dinner Christine and our grown daughter, Alina, were preparing one flight down. Sliced mango and pineapple for salsa; cod, pan-fried in

217

butter; the whir of the blender turning ice into slush. In my office, Brandel Chamblee, the TV golf analyst and a pal, was visiting by way of FaceTime, offering the gift of a virtual golf lesson. He went easy on me. What worried me (my crazy sway) did not worry him, but other things did. It was a break from the pandemic for ninety minutes or so. We compared reading lists and talked about some other things. You meet a lot of incredible people in this game.

I met Jim Langley in 1993. I met Pratima Sherpa in 2022 and Ryan French in 2021. I met Sam Reeves in 2017. I met Randy Erskine, a touring pro from Michigan, in 1979. (Ryan has known about him forever, of course.) I met Byron Nelson in 1985. I was caddying for Al Geiberger at the Byron Nelson Classic, and the host was on the first tee. Al said, "Mr. Nelson, I'd like you to meet my caddie." Al knew what that would mean to me. Talk about being thoughtful. Sam told me that Al and Jim Langley were friends. Not surprising at all.

I first played golf with Burt McHugh in 1989, three years after I met his sister. In 2002, Burt and I were in the final of a clubby alternate-shot event in Philadelphia called the Silver Putter. We were leading for most of the round but lost on the last hole. In defeat, Burt was a study in golfing class. Our opponent, the guy who made the winning putt, was almost crying in victory. Burt knew what the win meant to the winners.

In the final of the 2022 Silver Putter, Burt and his partner, our mutual friend Alvaro Sanz de Acedo, were all square (tied, if you like) with their opponents on the eighteenth green. Burt had a long downhill putt for a birdie. For line, his putt was dead solid perfect. For speed, it was kinda hot. And still the ball took almost ten seconds to get to the hole. It rattled the flagstick and disappeared. Alvaro and Burt had won. One of their opponents, Chris Missett, raised his arms as if *he* had won. He trotted over toward Burt and gave him a hug. He barely knew Burt, but he was joyful in defeat, and it was easy to know why: Burt's appreciation of golf and golfers is so pure, he exudes it. You'd be happy for Burt if you knew him because you'd know that he would be happy for you. So much of life is chemical, inexplicable—strange in the best way.

A few months later, Burt and I had a perfect late-summer golf day at National Golf Links. (I am *not* reporting the gift of that day casually.) I was two down through thirty-four holes but closed with two pars to halve the match, playing as we always do (that is, getting a half shot per hole). A halved match can be a beautiful thing when the other option is losing. There was Burt, on eighteen, hand out. Burt's golf.

In 2022, Ryan French and I covered the U.S. Open at The Country Club together. We played Goat Hill Park in Oceanside, California. We played the city course in Alpena, Michigan. We drove from Alpena to Philadelphia and played the St. Martins nine-holer near my house. We played at Bandon Dunes in Bandon, Oregon. The sixteenth at Bandon Trails, a gorgeous and duney course designed by Bill Coore and Ben Crenshaw, is a long, uphill par-5. Ryan nutted his tee shot, and I could not understand why he was playing his second with an iron. I was thinking, *Hit a 3-wood as hard as you can, you might reach!* Ryan hit a 4-iron hole-high and got up and down from a greenside trap for a birdie.

He got around St. Martins in 35 shots, even par. We were joined there by my semi-regular St. Martins partner, David Morse. (David's an actor and his schedule doesn't have much pattern to it. Neither does mine.) On quiet days there, David and I will sometimes stand by a green and talk about ball position on pitch shots without ever coming close to exhausting this rich subject. David and I are close in age, and I sometimes imagine what our wives would think if they could hear these conversations. *Do they actually think they're going to get better?* Yes. That's the whole thing. We actually think we can get better.

The camaraderie. The outside air. The odd and beautiful playing fields. The unexpected emotions and scenes—Burt's opponent running over and giving him that hug. Bowling is great, but golf offers things that bowling does not. It is rooted in the quest, the march from start to finish, a thousand little decisions in between. Ball position on a sixty-yard bump-and-run shot, the fairway firm but the zoysia grass clingy.

My friend Fred Anton was a contemporary of Sam's. I played more golf with Fred than with anybody else. The whole quest thing got him out of bed early. That and his AA meetings. (He didn't take the second *A* too seriously.) I'd call him on a Tuesday night for Wednesday-morning golf, and before I got to the question, he'd say, "When and where?" (Note the order. He'd play anywhere; the tee time was more urgent.) When Fred was at Villanova in the 1950s, he and some buddies wanted to start a golf team. Fred went to the athletic director.

"What can you guys shoot?" the AD asked.

"We can break ninety," Fred said.

"Come back when you can break eighty," he said.

They started the team anyway.

Fred shot in the 70s—I saw him do it—but not often. (I could say the same for myself.) On the day he turned eighty, we played golf. We played golf the next day, too. We played hundreds of rounds together, always with something on the line. When Fred was in his early eighties, I encouraged him to move up a set of tees and play a shorter course. He had a peculiar backswing where he looked like he could topple over at the top of it, and for a big man, he was a short hitter. He dismissed my suggestion. He had no interest in moving up. His body was failing him, and we were playing less frequently. When we did play, the competitive joy that had marked our matches was gone. I was worried about him.

He lived in a ground-floor apartment on a harbor of the Delaware River in downtown Philadelphia. On a windy, gray November day, wearing a long khaki-colored raincoat, he walked off a pier (by all available evidence), into the river, and to his death. He left behind a partner, a daughter, and a son. He left behind scores of journals in his apartment, filled with personal insights into life and business, many filled scorecards, and scrawled observations about the game that absorbed him.

I don't know.

In Alpena, after Ryan and I played the city course there, we went to its driving range. My golf that day was horrendous, and I wanted to try a couple of things to leave on a good note, swing-wise. I was worried about my weight distribution at address. I know, I know: *fascinating*. Well, at least Ryan was willing to take a look.

The young golfers on the Alpena High girls' team were hitting balls, too. The day was gorgeous. A song I knew well, a live version of Hot Tuna's "Talking 'Bout You," a Chuck Berry rocker, flooded the range.

"It's amazing, how kids today find their way to old music," I said to Ryan.

How random can you get? On a driving range in Alpena, Michigan, teenage girls listening to a song I listened to when I was their age?

Talking 'bout you.
I do mean you!
Won't you give me a clue?
Trying to get a message through.

I tried to control my head-bobbing.

Ryan took in the scene and said, "The music's coming out of your car."

The windows were down, and my charging phone, once dead

but now roaring back to life, was playing a song from my high school playlist, as it had been when I rolled in four hours earlier.

About four months later, the Alpena range was frozen. Christmas was in the air, and Ryan's father was getting worse. Ryan and I were talking (and texting) regularly, and one day I asked him if he could imagine his life at sixty. It was fifteen years away for him. "I hope I'm playing golf with my kids," he said. "They haven't shown much interest in the game so far, but I hope they do at some point."

Yep. About every four years, our son, Ian, asks if I want to play nine holes. Fun when he does, but he has his own things.

I asked Pratima the same question. How did she imagine sixty? She had taken her last final of the semester and was counting down the days until Christmas. Sixty was thirty-seven years away for her.

"I'm sure I will be living in Nepal," she said. "I hope I have my own house, not a big house. A small house. In Kathmandu. But not right in the city. Somewhere quiet. With my husband. We'll have grown children. We'll have dogs. Two little white Japanese dogs. And a putting green."

She was going to spend Christmas with her American family, the Montanos, near Ojai. Christmas was not a thing for Pratima, as a girl in Kathmandu. "I'll always have two families," she said. "But Nepal will always be home."

A backyard putting green. How fun. Pratima grew up with one, beside her golf house, on the Royal Nepal course.

●　●　●

Jim Langley was the longtime head pro at Cypress Point, and he and Sam, both tall and lean and fine-haired, looked like brothers.

Jim, though, was as patient and calm as Sam was excitable. Sam was older only on paper, by three years. He was forever on a quest, for information, for insight, for improvement. Jim seemed like somebody who had found what he wanted. Part of that was his faith. He was a lifelong and devout Catholic, the religion given to him by his mother over his father's objections. In Carmel-by-the-Sea, the affluent village and shopping mecca a few miles from Cypress Point, he attended Mass weekly at the Carmel Mission Basilica, so stately and old. He found that the mission, like the club, had a sense of quietude and mystery about it. Its walled courtyards, heavy doors, and stone floors that made you want to whisper.

Jim had grown up twenty miles away, in Salinas, and was a member of the 1958–'59 Cal (the University of California, Berkeley) team that won the NCAA basketball title, defeating West Virginia and Jerry West 71–70 in the final. People who met Jim Langley at Cypress, and experienced his pacific demeanor while looking up at his tall self, were often surprised to learn about his role on Pete Newell's Cal team in that championship season. Jim was an enforcer, sent in to rough up, rile up, and wear out the other team's best shooter, then head back to the bench, a new foul or two attached to his name.

After Cal and after the U.S. Marines, Jim applied himself to golf full-time for the first time. He got good enough to know he wasn't good enough for the tour. He played in about fifty events over a half decade. By 1971, Jim and his wife, Louetta, a former Cal cheerleader, had three children, all boys. (A fourth child, another son, came later.) The father of the house was close to broke. He was loading lettuce and cauliflower boxes on train cars in Salinas to make money while trying to figure out what to do next. He wanted to work in golf.

Jim knew Cypress Point because everybody in golf, at a certain level of the game, knew Cypress Point. It was one of three courses, along with Spyglass Hill and Pebble Beach, used for Bing Crosby's annual pro-am, a tour event known for decades as The Crosby, or, even more simply and commonly, Pebble. (Almost a decade after Bing Crosby's death, the tournament's official name became the AT&T Pebble Beach National Pro-Am, but old-time pros continued to say, "You playing Pebble?") Jim had played in the tournament, and when he heard that Cypress Point's head pro was retiring after forty years, he applied for the job. He had never even worked in a pro shop. But he was desperate. The club president saw something in Jim—he saw Jim—and, on that basis, offered him the job.

Cypress Point in 1971 was sleepy, casual, patrician. The course, designed by Alister MacKenzie, the genius behind Augusta National, introduced to the golf world (or a tiny subset of it) the most memorable, fragrant, and beautiful two-hole stretch in golf, two late-round cliffside par-3s, the charming fifteenth and the sixteenth, a beautiful beast.

The latter hole was there almost before MacKenzie arrived. There's a small, dangerous teeing ground (don't fall off it), a big, inviting green, and nothing but brackish air in between, a large, cold, swirling pool of ocean water underneath it. The wind comes out of every direction. George Plimpton, in the pages of *Sports Illustrated* and later in his classic tragicomedy, *The Bogey Man*, recounted how he'd played the sixteenth hole as an amateur in the '66 Crosby, his brooding pro (Bob Bruno) looking on. He took a 3-wood from his wheezing caddie (Abe), handed the woolen headcover to him, and heard the spectators on hand "stir and fidget." They didn't know that 3-wood was Plimpton's layup club, as he looked to take a shorter route to a more welcoming bit of earth well short and left of the green. Not that the layup was easy.

After those write-ups and others—*SI* captured Plimpton's not-going-for-it moment with a photo—the hole became even more famous. But Cypress was so low-key in Jim Langley's early years there that when tourists dropped by, wanting to see "the Plimpton hole," he'd either point the way or escort them there himself.

In the time line of Jim's life, one dark date jumps out: November 12, 1987. It was a Thursday, and it started pleasantly. Jim and his boss, Bill Borland, the club's well-liked president, were driving north to the San Francisco Golf Club to play in a tournament there. They were on a notorious stretch of Highway 101 known as Blood Alley, south of San Jose, in a new Ford. Borland was driving. (Once Jim could afford them, and he could by then, he drove only Cadillacs.) Borland did not know that the fuel gauge was defective, and the car ran out of gas. Jim was fifty and powerful. He was pushing the car off an exit ramp when he was struck by another vehicle. Jim went rolling down a ravine. It took Borland and the other driver ten minutes to find him—Jim was forty feet away and unable to speak. Borland held Jim's head as they waited for an ambulance. Jim was drifting in and out of consciousness.

Jim had broken both legs, punctured a lung, dislocated both shoulders, and had extensive nerve damage. He was in the hospital for a month. He had twelve surgeries and lost the use of his right arm. His circulation was poor after the accident, and his body ran cold. He wore long sleeves every day, and the tiny space heater in his small, cramped office was always on full blast.

"I worried I had lost some of my manhood," he told a writer years later. "Here I am, with only one good arm and two bad legs, wondering how I can protect my wife and children." But he carried on. He started calling his right hand "my silent partner." He shook hands with his left. In the club's many afternoon lulls, he would practice. After a while, he could break 90 on good days, using a right-handed club in his left hand. He said his teaching improved after the accident because he started to emphasize rhythm over every other aspect of the swing. He said his life improved because he developed an even greater sense of gratitude, which he expressed through prayer and in his caring, observant everyday manner. Jim Langley had become the Lou Gehrig of golf. Not in scale—Gehrig's "luckiest man" speech reached millions—but for the impact he had on people, Sam among them.

Jim had material needs, as all people have material needs. He saw the things money could buy beyond new Cadillacs. In the company of his members, he was surrounded by immense wealth. But Jim believed he had more than he needed, and more than he wanted. He refused to charge for lessons. He gave away his shop merchandise to charity groups staging auctions. He became a benefactor to some of the caddies. His values and manners seemed to come from another place and time. He always used honorifics when referring to members. Clint Eastwood would say, "Call me Clint." He remained Mr. Eastwood. Mr. Tatum (Sandy Tatum, the former president of the USGA). Mr. Reeves. Sam didn't like it or want it, but he respected Jim's wishes.

Before the accident, Jim played pickup basketball regularly, in indoor gyms. He was a careful eater, a moderate drinker, a paragon of fitness who never climbed on a gym machine in his life. After the accident, his exercise became walking. What he liked about walking was that it gave him time to think, too. He arrived at the club early each morning and walked from the driving range to the tee on the fifteenth hole, the first of the two oceanside par-3s, where you can smell the swirling kelp below you. He used a golf club as a walking stick. He'd walk from fifteen to the house just as a golfer does, except Jim would have rosary beads in his good left hand. His office was in the back of the pro shop beside the first tee.

Only a few people at the club, most of them caddies, knew the sorrows in the head pro's life. (Among the members, Sam surely knew more than most.) Jim's own father, an accountant by trade and a Protestant by upbringing, did not attend Jim's wedding to Louetta because the ceremony took place in a Catholic church. The first of the couple's four sons, Brett, played basketball in high school and at college and, in time, became the head pro at Pebble Beach. But his life was derailed by addiction. Jim saved the sorrows of his life for his church.

Every morning, on those walks, Jim would stop near the fifteenth tee, say a prayer, and throw a ball into the water, almost as a sacrifice. Then one day he ended that practice. He didn't want to add more plastic to the ocean. In the vicinity of his usual resting stop, he saw an old rusting water pipe sticking straight out of the ground. It was about three feet long, surrounded by thick green vegetation called ice plant, and half-hidden by weathered, decaying logs. The pipe had no cap, and Jim started placing a golf ball on its top. The ball fit right on it, as if sitting on a tee. Jim stopped there every morning without fail, regardless of the weather. If the previous day's ball was gone—and it often was, moved by human or animal or wind—Jim would place another there. On different mornings, he'd think about different people there, but he always said a prayer for one person, an unusually tall Cypress Point caddie who went by Stork but was Frank Shea by birth.

Frank Shea's parents were founding members of the club, which opened in 1928. But the family fortune was decimated by the Depression, and the Sheas were members only briefly. Frank had problems of his own. He was a lifelong bachelor and lived near the Elks Lodge in the heart of Monterey, five miles from Jim's house in a wooded development off Route 1. The caddie master, Joe Solis, typically drove Frank to work, and Jim usually drove him home. It's unlikely that anybody knew more about Frank Shea's pain than Jim Langley. For dinner, Frank drank large quantities of Burgermeister beer. Jim would have one with him and call it a day.

In Jim's era, many head pros at elite American clubs avoided contact with the caddies, another nasty example of country club classism. Jim was the opposite. One of his sons was a caddie at Cypress, and Jim knew he could have been one, too. The professional caddie needs three things: cooperative legs, a sense of humor, and the empathy gene. Jim qualified, and he knew what it was like to need a job. He didn't forget. There were caddies at Cypress looking to reclaim a former life, or find a new one, and Jim helped where he could. The caddies at Cypress were allowed to play the course on many afternoons, and that ball on the water pipe was a symbol—it was there if they needed it, and Jim was there if they needed him. Jim gave quietly, broadly, and regularly. It would be impossible to say how much he gave away, but it was likely in the millions. He gave away more than he saved. But he needed to share.

This long entrance ramp into the life and times of Jim Langley may not sound like it has much to do with Sam Reeves, but it has everything to do with Sam Reeves. Jim Langley's values matched and enhanced Sam's values. Sam took one lesson from Jim but didn't take a second when he realized that Jim would not take a payment from him, as he would not from any member. In Sam's rounds with Jim, Jim played bogey golf with his right hand in his pocket. When they went out for dinner, Jim often ordered fish— easier to cut with one hand. They got to know each other gradually, over time. Sam visited with Jim almost every time he came to Cypress, and those visits numbered in the hundreds. Every time Sam won something at Cypress, and he won often, he had longer visits with Jim. Sam won the club championship four consecutive years. He won senior titles, member-guest tournaments, other events. He had his own little golfing get-togethers. After these events, the contestants and others would typically gather in a fenced-in clearing between the fourth hole and some maintenance buildings for what the club quaintly called a "picnic," with picnic tables, a well-stocked bar with a bartender, and a barbecue. A dozen or so times, Jim stood with a piece of hardware in his left hand and congratulated Sam for winning an event. There were silver plates, silver cups, and silver vases that went from Jim to Sam. In the clubhouse, you'd see Sam's name, and scores of others, in gold paint on dark-stained wooden boards. An oasis of civility. Another world. But what drew Sam to Jim so powerfully was not all that gentility. That was in the club's DNA. What drew Sam to Jim was his faith, his drive, and what he overcame on a daily basis. He inspired Sam.

Jim held the course record at Cypress, 63, though not by himself. Others had shot it, including Hogan. Jim had the one-handed record, too: 81. For the length he was hitting it, par was 90 or higher; 81 is an astounding score.

On the day he shot that 81, Jim was playing with his three oldest sons, all of them in the golf business (a club pro, a course superintendent, a caddie). Jim's caddie that day was Vince Lucido, who, like his Uncle Joe, the caddie master, had spent his life at the course. Jim liked being surrounded by all that course knowledge, and he leaned on it. The round began in the fog, but by the time they made the turn, it had lifted, and they played home through a benign wind. Jim hit a good tee shot on fifteen, short of the green. The group—four players, two caddies—walked past Jim's pipe, his Frank Shea shrine. He got up and down for par there. The sixsome (if anybody was going to count caddies in this tableau, it would be Jim) made its way to the sixteenth tee. Vince handed Jim a club, just as Abe the caddie had done with Plimpton years earlier. There were six nervous people on the tee, plus any golfing gods in the vicinity who might have been stirring and fidgeting. (Sandy Tatum liked to call Cypress Point the Sistine Chapel of golf. It's a bit much, but that's golf for you.) Jim had a career round going, and his tee shot on sixteen was going to make or break it. If one ball goes in the ocean on sixteen, a dam can burst. Lawson Little, in the '52 Crosby, made a 14 there.

Jim smoothed a one-handed, 170-yard driver to a safe patch of green, mown terra firma. He pitched on with a 9-iron. Two putts later, he had a bogey 4. The first rule of breaking 85 is to play from the tees that are appropriate for you. Jim played from the everyday men's tees. The second is to start and finish with the same ball—in other words, no penalty shots. Jim did that. (On fifteen and sixteen, he had kept his ball dry.) The third is to make all the putts you should make, those from three feet and in. And Jim did that.

After that 4 he made on sixteen, things still could have gone bad for Jim. That's golf. Finishing is difficult, and things can always go awry. That's why short putting is mentally draining—only bad things can happen. (You're *supposed* to make your short putts.) But when Jim picked up his ball out of the hole on sixteen, he was over the hump. He made a 5 on seventeen and a 5 on eighteen. Both are par-4s on the scorecard, but they played as par-5s for Jim. His one-handed 81, when you think about it, is more remarkable than his course-record-tying 63, even though that score is staggeringly good. But there are, at any time, thousands of golfers good enough to shoot 63 at Cypress Point. It's hard to imagine five players with enough strength and skill and discipline to shoot 81 with one hand. (Nick Faldo, in his prime, would have been one of them. He could hit 140-yard rising draw shots with a 7-iron with one hand. But there can't be many others.) One last point: Not all the most important rounds of golf played—Johnny Miller's final-round 63 at the 1973 U.S. Open at Oakmont, for instance—are played on TV. Not even close.

In September 1987, Pope John Paul II, the skiing pope, came to the Carmel Mission Basilica, Jim's home church. Dick Telles, a San Joaquin cotton grower, a devout Catholic, and a close friend of Sam's, invited Sam and Betsy to the mission to see the pope under the big tent—that is, in the nave itself. (Dick and his wife, major donors, had four tickets, and this was a sold-out show.) Sam was thrilled. He liked this pope. Many did.

As John Paul II made his way down the basilica's main aisle toward the pulpit, he was surrounded by security people, the cardinal of Majorca, various deputies, a photographer, mission officials. The church was packed to its fire-code allowance. The pope kissed congregants but generally kept moving. The atmosphere was borderline pandemonium.

When the pope was almost at the altar, he made eye contact with a tall, white-haired man on his left. The pope stopped and shook Sam's hand. Sam did not know why. He had been to the Vatican but had never met a pope. Sam felt a distinct power from him, to be in his presence, but he did not freeze. Sam told the pope that he appreciated his global view of the world's problems, a theme in many of his encyclicals, which Sam had read. The pope, in his Polish-accented English, said something affirming back to Sam. He then turned to the Majorcan cardinal beside him and instructed him to give Sam a small silver crucifix.

Some years later, Sam told Jim about his experience with the pope that day at the mission. He described how the pope, after his homily, went into an anteroom. Mirth runs through Sam, and he recounted how he asked a member of the entourage what the pope would be doing in there.

"He's going to pray," the robed brother told Sam.

Sam, in counterpoint: *Really? He's had a long day already. I bet he's going to nap!* The pope was sixty-seven.

In Sam's telling of the story to Jim (and others), the robed brother then placed an eye in front of a large old-fashioned keyhole, looked through it, and said, "The pope is on his knees. He's praying."

Jim laughed at the telling. He and his wife, Lou, had been at the mission for the pope's visit. There was a massive crowd outside, but they were under the roof. Two of their sons were there, too, as altar boys. Jim knew the anteroom and its dark wooden door. He knew every inch of Carmel Mission.

Two months later, Jim was pushing a car with no gas off the road when another vehicle struck him. The accident. The accident that started a new chapter in Jim's life.

Jim Langley retired from Cypress Point at the end of 2005. He was hired on the basis of one main qualification, his personality, and that was the foundation of a career that lasted thirty-five years, in good times and bad. He was ambivalent about retirement, but Lou was eager to see the world while they could. Jim was made an honorary member of the club but seldom used it. He died in 2013 at age seventy-five, his health compromised by the accident.

Throughout golf, Jim Langley had a reputation few did for being steady, ethical, and generous. His funeral service was at the Carmel Mission, and it was packed with caddies, Cypress Point members, club employees, family, Cal teammates, church friends, loads of other club pros and touring pros. There was a small silver crucifix in his coffin, the one the cardinal gave to Sam at the pope's behest. Jim's wife and their four sons and spouses were in the front pew. The oldest son, Brett Langley, the club pro, died five months later. Addiction, in the end, took its toll.

When Jim retired from Cypress, *Golfweek* published a profile of him. The writer of the piece, John Steinbreder, thought so much of what Sam told him for the story that he wrote out Sam's words on a heavy personal notecard and secured it, by way of a pushpin with a red bulb, to an antique map above his desk. The notecard was surrounded by ocean.

Jim has a life of joy, which is remarkable when you think of what he has gone through. Joy, you understand, is different from happiness. Joy is an inward peace, a sense of contentment and acceptance of life and what it gives you. And while pain may be inevitable, suffering is a choice. Jim has pain but he chooses not to suffer. Rather, he gives, and he inspires as a result.

• • •

My mother, Dorothy Frank Bamberger, died a few weeks before the virus that paralyzed the world washed ashore. She was eighty-eight. She was born in Hamburg, Germany, and had come to the United States with her family on the *Queen Mary* in 1938. Forty years later, I graduated from high school. I was on the masthead of the *Red & Black* and was the captain of the Patchogue-Medford High School golf team. The paper was published sporadically, and the golf team was no great shakes, but we had a lot of fun, putting out the paper, trying to make bogeys. My mother, in her gentle and indirect way, put me on a path (no training wheels) to the paper and the golf team. A great mom. Just like yours.

My father died two years later, at ninety-four. He came to the United States from Hamburg, too—in 1940. In other words, late. My parents knew each other in Germany and grew up on the Upper West Side of Manhattan together. My mother's family, the Frank family, helped the Bamberger family get out and get in. My father wasn't tall, or close to it, but he had powerful legs, lines of striated muscle running up and down them. At eighty-eight, he was strong in every way, but then he fell while on a bike. He had stopped, on the wide promenade between Gracie Mansion and the East River, to take a photo, and he and the bike toppled over. (No helmet. Wear a helmet, people!) He wasn't the same after that, and after Mom's death, that became truer yet. Still, when he was in a small hospital in the Bronx, getting near the end, my brother and I joked about his excellent color. He had a big window in his room, and the winter sun streamed through it. In the hospital lobby, there was a framed photograph of Pope Francis, smiling warmly. My father would have liked that.

He never played a round of golf in his life, but he owned an E-Club, my little invention. Once, my father and I were in St. Andrews at the same time on separate trips, and we had the urge to find an open field and hit balls. This was a first. (The power of St. Andrews.) I kind of showed him the grip and put down coins for where his feet should go.

"Okay," I said. "Now address the ball."

He stepped on the coins, looked at the ball, and said, "Hello, sir."

Joe Bamberger's short experiment in golf.

That was in 1991, the year Christine and I followed Peter Teravainen around Europe, the year John Stark took me to Auchnafree, the secret six-hole shepherd's course in a Scottish dale, the year Christine and I rented a flat in St. Andrews for a fortnight.

In 2022, the Open was played at the Old Course, the muni between St. Andrews Bay and downtown St. Andrews. It's played there every five years or so. I've been to, I don't know, maybe two dozen Opens—I feel no need to count them. In 2022, Cam Smith of Australia shot a Sunday back-nine 30 to catch and pass the 54-hole (and the 63-hole) leader, Rory McIlroy. Usually, the Old Course is closed for play and open to walkers on Sundays, by an edict from Old Tom Morris, the course's caretaker. But an exception is made for the Open. The weather that Sunday was a bad break for McIlroy. There was, unusually, barely a breath of wind. Without wind, and with the course slightly soft, Smith was able to play a series of bold and aggressive shots coming in. The 30 he shot, coming home.

Afterward, during a crowded press conference in a big white tent, a reporter asked Smith if he had any plans to join Greg Norman's LIV Golf tour, by then up and running.

"I just won the British Open, and you're asking about that?" Smith said.

FINISHING

Six weeks later, Smith announced by press release that he was joining Greg Norman's LIV Golf tour. He didn't say this in the press release, though he could have: *Yeah, it's Saudi oil money, but there's too much of it to pass up*. Whatever.

As a reporter covering golf, I was required to care on some kind of professional basis, but deep down, I didn't. I found it all unfortunate, greed run amok. Professional golf, in my experience, had never looked grubby before, but now it did. Money, money, money. Blech. Charl Schwartzel was in the first wave of LIV sign-ups and won the first LIV tournament, earning—I don't know, and I don't care.

A month or so before the British Open, I had played in an open myself, the two-day National Hickory Championship at a nine-hole course in Foxburg, Pennsylvania. It's truly open. Anybody can sign up for it. I went there from the Memorial Tournament, Jack Nicklaus's event. Most of the chat at the Memorial was LIV-LIV-LIV, and I found myself looking forward to Foxburg. As it turned out, the hickory clubs I'd brought to NHC didn't qualify. They were from approximately 1910 and were too young by about a decade. (The organizers had spare clubs that I could use.) The men were required to play in hats and ties. You made your own tees by pinching a little sand from a small pile, and a long drive for me went maybe 150 yards. I shot 108 and 109 and thoroughly enjoyed it. I never heard anything about LIV golf the whole time I was there. Not one mention of Bryson DeChambeau.

The thing that makes an Open at the Old Course in St. Andrews so special is that it plays out in the present and relives the past at every moment. The Old Course got its name in 1895, when the course next to it, the New Course, opened for play. The course that Rory McIlroy and his brethren played was the same one Old Tom played and maintained. It's accurate to say that the Old Course evolved, by nature, through the centuries, but it's also accurate to

235

say that Old Tom shaped the first and last holes from his mind and with his own hands. Those two holes were good then, and they are good now.

What made the biggest impression on me at the 2022 Open was Lee Trevino. He was back twenty-two years after he'd played his final Open, also at St. Andrews. He had returned to attend a dinner for former Open champions, to play in a four-hole exhibition, to receive an honorary degree from the University of St. Andrews, and to work the range. His vitality was astounding. One afternoon, he was showing Jon Rahm how to play fast-rising bunker shots.

A young American touring pro, Brandon Wu, was nearby. Wu had played at Stanford, met Sam Reeves along the way, and they had become friends. When the 2019 U.S. Open was played at Pebble Beach, Wu stayed with Sam, made the cut, and was presented with his Stanford degree as he came off the final green on Sunday.

I called Sam and painted the scene from the Old Course practice area, Brandon Wu over here, Lee Trevino over there. I could hear the excitement in Sam's voice. He knew, chapter and verse, how Wu had played his way into the Open by way of a Sunday 67 and a sixth-place finish in the previous week's Scottish Open. Sam knew all about Trevino, the two U.S. Opens, the two PGA Championships, and the two British Opens he had won, and the four Masters tournaments he skipped in his prime, because he didn't like the club or the course.

"Love Trevino," Sam said in his clipped way. "The way he steps into the shot."

The exhibition of various champions was on the Monday before the tournament started. It was four holes, the first and second out and the seventeenth and eighteenth in. Trevino played with Tiger Woods, Rory McIlroy, and Georgia Hall, the English golfer and the winner of the 2018 Women's British Open at Royal Lytham. On the rectangular putting green, next to the first tee, Trevino and Woods compared putters while waiting to play.

"Did Santa Claus tee off yet?" Trevino asked Tiger.

John Daly, with his ample stomach and luxurious white beard. St. Nick with a cig.

"No, he's in this group," Tiger said, motioning toward the first tee. Daly, Nick Faldo, Louis Oosthuizen, and Zach Johnson had gathered on it, waiting to play. All four of them had won the Open at St. Andrews. What a sight. Trevino, Tiger, McIlroy, and Hall followed them. Another terrific sight. Golf does a good job of keeping its past alive.

Trevino was wearing black pants and a pink shirt and hit a driver off the first with a black-and-pink shaft. He hit a low burner and said, "That'll run for twenty minutes."

On the seventeenth tee, Nicklaus joined the group, and Trevino demonstrated a wedge shot that Nicklaus had fatted fifty-one years earlier, when Trevino beat him in a playoff to win the U.S. Open at Merion. Second shot, ninth hole.

"Did I hit one of those?" Nicklaus asked.

"The sod covered the ball up!" Trevino said.

Rory and Tiger were shaking with laughter. "They weren't even born yet," Nicklaus said.

"That's why I was showing them," Trevino said.

The next day, there was an elaborate, formal ceremony in an ornate auditorium called Younger Hall at the University of St. Andrews. Nicklaus was made an honorary citizen of St. Andrews, as Bobby Jones and Benjamin Franklin had been, and Trevino was given an honorary doctorate. "Golf has been my whole life," Trevino said from a lectern, wearing his black academic robe. Barbara and Jack Nicklaus were seated behind him. "I have devoted my entire life to this game. It is the only thing I know how to do." He talked about winning the first tournament he ever played in, the

Texas State Open, in 1965. He won on the first hole of a two-man playoff and earned twelve hundred dollars. He was playing for money, no question about that.

I was sitting in the auditorium's upper deck. My friend Jaime Diaz, the golf commentator and writer, was sitting in front of me. We were both hanging on Trevino's every word. Trevino noted, diploma in hand, that he had never played an amateur tournament in his life. He needed money, and pro golf was there, offering a payday. But all these years later, here was Trevino with his PhD by way of golf. From my seat, it seemed like golf meant more to Trevino than his livelihood, and I'm not diminishing the importance of that in the slightest. (Those first four letters—the *l*, *i*, *v*, and *e*—didn't get there by accident.) But it seemed like Trevino, that day at the University of St. Andrews, was saying what Roberto De Vicenzo had once said about his 7-iron being his professor. De Vicenzo said that to Jaime, by the way. Jaime got the quote. I think golf was Jaime's professor, too.

Christine joined me in Scotland a few days after the Open. It was her first time in Scotland since we had last been there, in the summer of '91. We started in Edinburgh, and one week after Open Sunday, we were in St. Andrews. The giant leaderboard above the grandstand on the first hole was still up, Cameron Smith's name atop it. The course was closed, in keeping with the Sunday tradition.

I had arrived in St. Andrews two weeks earlier. One of the first people I saw that day was Sheila Walker, the great-great-granddaughter of Old Tom Morris. She was a retired medical librarian who lived in the second-floor flat where Old Tom lived, in a stone building beside the eighteenth hole; I had met her on a visit seven years before. She and I stood on a North Street sidewalk—Sheila was walking home from the grocery store—and she told me about the masonry work being done in the graveyard at the St. Andrews Cathedral, where Old Tom and his son, Young Tom, were buried. It was her great-great-grandfather who said, "If you dinna need a rest on the Sawbath, the links does."

On the Sunday after Cam Smith's Sunday, I went for a jog on a pathway between the Old Course and St. Andrews Bay. Christine was at our hotel. A kid, maybe four, on a bike that looked like a little motorcycle, was tearing down the pathway directly at me. He wore a round, snug helmet like soldiers wore in the first world war and aviator goggles, and he gave me a massive head nod, athlete to athlete, local to local. Later that morning, I drove to Gleneagles for the final round of the Senior British Open. The last time I had been there, I was caddying for Peter Teravainen in the Scottish Open. I was thirty-one then, and suddenly I was sixty-two. It's true, what old people have said forever: It goes too fast.

The next day, Christine and I drove to Auchnafree. The course was primitive in its prime, and it hadn't been played in years. There were sheep all over the many hillsides, and we shared the narrow dirt road with others. The rain was intermittent. The river by the road, the Almond, was high. I looked for a boulder I had seen years earlier, one that paid tribute to John Pollock, the shepherd who laid out the course and knew the twelve thousand acres surrounding it as well as anybody. As I climbed one hill, the grass beneath me lush and damp, several sheep scattered, but one did not, and as I got closer, I could see why: It was a ewe protecting a dead lamb, I guessed her own. I never found the boulder. On our way out, I pulled the car off the road, walked down to the Almond, and took a drink from it out of cupped hands. I wasn't worried. John Stark drank out of that river for years while fishing for salmon or while playing each year in the Auchnafree Open. Of course, he was adding the river water to his whiskey, so maybe that's different.

• • •

In the early 1990s, almost twenty years after Melvin Hemphill's death, Sam found a new golf instructor, Butch Harmon. Sam once met Butch's father, Claude, famously the pro at Seminole *and* Winged Foot, and the winner of the 1948 Masters. He was a golf prodigy as a child, and the game always seemed easy to him. But all that had little to do with Sam's path to Claude's namesake son, E. Claude (Butch) Harmon, Jr. It was Butch's success with Clay Spears, married to Sam's daughter Sandy, that got Sam to Butch.

As his daughters married, Sam liked to say to the new arrivals, "You marry into the Reeves family, you work on your golf game." Clay knew what he was getting into. He was a good athlete but, tragically, a 92-shooter. Clay and Sandy were living in Houston, and Butch Harmon was teaching at Lochinvar, an elite men's club. Sam knew from the TV broadcasts that Butch was working with Greg Norman, then the best player in the world. That's always a calling card for Sam: the best at anything. (A common word for him is *exceptionalism*.) At Sam's urging, Clay went to see Butch. Within months, he was breaking 80. Sam was awed by the improvement. "Sambo ain't no fool," he told Clay. He got himself in line for a lesson.

One lesson with Butch turned into a long series of them, and from there came a late-round friendship. In his sixties, Sam had made two new and close friends, Jim Langley and Butch Harmon. Both were golf pros, but in personality, they could not have been more different. Butch was profane, funny, and assertive. He ate his steak so rare it was practically mooing, drank expensive wines, told one comical story after another, wasn't a churchgoer. Jim Langley was his opposite in almost every regard. Sam was, too.

But Sam was drawn to Butch's drive. Butch, like Sam, had gone into his father's profession and taken it to places it had not been. The obstacles in Butch's life weren't obvious to most people, but Sam could see them readily. He could also see how Butch had risen above them. But that came later. The starting point (of course) was Butch's expertise in golf.

Butch was a savant. He could watch Sam make three swings, observe his ball's flight pattern, and make a series of necessary and minute adjustments to his grip, stance, and takeaway. He didn't believe in the makeover. He believed in proven fundamentals and incremental improvement. Sam was all in, and their relationship was off and running.

Sam saw that private Butch and public Butch were two different people. At group dinners, while giving clinics with his brothers, in broadcast booths at golf tournaments, Butch was onstage, and he was good at it. Butch was like Lee Trevino: The bigger the crowd, the more gregarious he became. But when the stage lights were off and Butch didn't have to show off for anyone, he was a different person. Sam knew both and liked both, but was especially drawn to private Butch. That Butch was always looking to learn something. How do corporate boards work, and hospital boards and admissions committees and securities markets? Sam knew worlds that Butch did not. Butch had lived lives, plural, that Sam had not. Sam liked people who had learned about life by living it. They were good for each other.

Growing up as the son of the head pro, Butch was almost a country club kid, but only almost. Being the son of Claude Harmon at Winged Foot was like being the minister's son. You're on display, and whatever you do, it won't be good enough.

Butch went to college (Houston), left for Vietnam, saw death at close range, and came home to a country that did not thank him for his service. He got himself on the PGA Tour, barely, and saw how hard it was.

"I see you're leading the tournament," Claude once said to Butch.

What are you talking about? Butch was DFL.

"Oh," his father said, "I must have the paper upside down."

The power-of-positive-thinking movement had not reached Claude Harmon.

There were six Harmon kids, and Claude's wife, Alice, managed everything on the domestic front. With a husband who had two jobs in two states, there was a lot to handle. Alice died in 1970, at fifty-two, and Claude was never the same.

Butch was a young husband and a young father, trying to play for money. He was spending more than he was making. Though he had grown up surrounded by affluence, now he had nothing but his name, and he didn't want to trade on that unless he had to. With mouths to feed, he had to. He taught golf to the king of Morocco, as his father had before him. Later, and anonymously, he drove tractors on golf courses under construction. He worked at golf courses in Iowa and Texas. His first marriage ended. His second marriage ended. He remarried his first wife. That didn't work out a second time. He spent a lot of nights sleeping on a sofa at his brother Dick's house in Houston, trying to sort through his life. He was drinking too much.

Butch knew hundreds of people in the game. His three brothers were successful club pros and teachers. So were many of his father's former assistants. But Butch didn't want to ask for help.

And then his phone rang. It was Jeff Sluman, former winner of the PGA Championship, inviting Butch to join him at a tournament in Japan in late April 1990. Sluman took lessons from Butch's brother Craig, the head pro at Oak Hill in Rochester, New York, Sluman's hometown. Sluman had a second plane ticket and a spare bed in his hotel room. Sluman played poorly over the first two rounds, as did Davis Love III. They had just made the cut. Butch was on the tee with both of them. Davis's father, a noted teaching pro, had been an assistant under Claude Harmon at Winged Foot—

a meaningful link. Love's swing that day in Japan was a mess, and he knew it. Butch was looking at him but not saying a word.

"What?" Davis said.

"You really want to know?" Butch said.

Davis said yes, and Butch did not hold back. He didn't like Davis's grip, his transition, his attitude, or anything else. Davis took it all in. Butch got Davis in better positions in one session. Other teachers could have maybe done that. But what Butch really gave Davis was the sum total of his golf and life experience. Davis was a different golfer on the weekend, finished third, and started singing Butch's praises, not only as a golf technician, though there was that, but as a true coach.

Word travels fast in golf. Within a year, Greg Norman was working with Butch. You'd hear Butch's name mentioned during the tournament broadcasts, and you'd see his name in the golf magazines. Sam sent his son-in-law, who lived in Houston, to see Butch, and then went to see Butch himself. Earl Woods called Butch, looking for the best teacher for his seventeen-year-old son, Tiger. Earl had no money, but that didn't stop him. He and Butch were both Vietnam vets, and they spoke the same language. Butch had a fox-hole mentality, and so did Earl. Sam was around all this golfing exceptionalism. It was intoxicating.

What Butch taught Sam was right out of the Melvin Hemphill school. It was proven. Claude Harmon would have recognized it, Ben Hogan would have recognized it, Gardner Dickinson, a student of Hemphill's and a disciple of Hogan's, would have recognized it. Make a big, rhythmic turn with your lower body, like you own the dance floor. Lift your left heel (you righties). Get your left pocket behind the ball. Start the downswing with your left hip. Clear *hard* and go left on a circle. If you do all that, you can't swing too fast. You can control distance with a dozen little things, but the swing is the swing. A serious golf swing requires its greatest speed *at impact*, in Butch's teaching and really all teaching. But Butch emphasized speed. Without speed, you were just slapping at it. You build speed gradually on the downswing, just as a large rock tumbling down a steep hill gathers speed. Speed was not power, not a function of brute strength. "If the game required power, all the best golfers would be bodybuilders," Butch told Sam. They weren't. Tiger was 140 pounds, if that, and he could kill it. Sam was hanging on Butch's every word. Tiger Woods was winning U.S. Amateurs, and there, on TV, was Butch, right at his side. Sam's guy was Tiger's guy. Who wouldn't love that?

Butch was giving Sam swing thoughts and pep talks he could use for the rest of his life. In the name of creating speed, Sam would swing a headless shaft so hard you could hear the whirring two ball piles down. Sam's quest for better golf doubled as a time machine. He was a kid golfer again, and Butch was the one guy who knew how to work the machine's many knobs. They were having a good time, and Sam was generous in every way. Butch had an older brother for the first time in his life. Each was good for the other.

Butch was getting married, and he wanted Sam to be his best man. Sam knew that Butch had found the right woman in Christy. Butch adopted Christy's son. When Cole Harmon was looking to attend grad school to study history, Sam was there to offer guidance. Sam was like Cole's uncle.

When Sam turned seventy, Butch caddied for him in a four-day pro-am in Scotland, the Dunhill Links Championship. Sam played with one of Butch's students, Adam Scott. It's impossible to buy a present for Sam, but this was a present you couldn't buy. The weather was nasty, cold, windy, rainy. September in St. Andrews.

"Damn, Butch, we been out here for four days, and you ain't taken a piss yet," Sam said.

"What?"

"You haven't urinated, brother."

"I've got on four layers of clothing—how in hell am I gonna take a leak?"

"Okay, then," Sam said.

They marched down the fairway through the wind, Sam's slender bag on Butch's back. They were playing in.

"Where did that come from, anyway?" Butch asked. Like, who would notice such a thing?

"Just observing ya," Sam said.

Sam saw Butch in ways others did not. Sam observed.

•   •   •

From Auchnafree, in that remote Scottish glen, Christine and I drove north, and the next day we toured Balmoral Castle and its estate, smack-dab in the middle of nowhere. I should say we toured a sliver of it. The estate is fifty thousand acres, and only part of the first floor of the castle is available for public viewing. Balmoral (per Christine, my tutor on royal matters) is the privately owned summer residence of the Windsor family, and our late-July date was the last day the estate would be open to paying visitors in the summer of '22. The owners, most notably Queen Elizabeth, would arrive soon for their summer holiday. After many years of making the trip, they surely had a better route there than ours, on the A939 from Blairnamarrow. It's a hilly and narrow road through long stretches of wilderness. Drive on the left.

Then you get to Balmoral, or the parts that we saw, and it's like an arboretum. As Christine and I walked some of the trails and paths, I was surprised to come upon a charming nine-hole golf course. A woman who had just finished playing told me that the course is actively used, not only by royal golfers and their guests but also by the estate's employees and their family members, my source among them. The course was empty when I walked the short length of it, checking out its little greens, its wee tee boxes, its modest traps. I kept thinking that somebody would chase me away, but nobody did.

Beside one of the traps was an itty-bitty sign that read NO DOGS IN BUNKERS, THANK YOU. Other animals had not gotten the message, based on the available evidence. Balmoral could double as a wildlife preserve. (In the movie *The Queen*, there's a memorable two-minute scene, set in a Balmoral dale though shot elsewhere, where Helen Mirren shoos away a giant stag being pursued by a hunting party.) I took the liberty of raking one of the Balmoral bunkers, chiefly to see what it was like. It was like raking a bunker anywhere else with a lightweight rake with plastic tines. I do think I felt a heightened responsibility to get it right.

About six weeks after our visit, Queen Elizabeth died at Balmoral. I was driving on the Pennsylvania Turnpike with Ryan French when the breaking-news report of her death popped up on his phone. "All right, great lady, but, you know, ninety-six," Ryan said.

I could relate. For all of Christine's interest in Elizabeth and Diana, I could barely keep Harry and William straight. But after our visit to Balmoral, especially after reading many of the superb postmortem write-ups on the queen's life and times, I felt like I was finally starting to get it. She was more than the queen of England to her people. She was their mother, a selfless person always doing what was best for them. She represented Britain at its best because she had a true value system, as Britain did, without being haughty about it. That's a neat trick. You know the phrase *It's all good*? If Queen Elizabeth ever heard it, which seems unlikely, it could not possibly have meant anything to her. She had standards. Good was good.

Golfers have standards. There's a right way to mark a ball and a right way to rake a trap. There's a correct place to stand when somebody else is playing a shot. There's an appropriate way to acknowledge victory or defeat. Yes, some of it is ridiculous. (You do *not* have to take off your cap to shake hands, it says here.) Some things have evolved sensibly. (Shorts. Hallelujah!) But having standards—an accepted rule book, a code of conduct—makes golf golf.

For decades, this was the first paragraph of the *Rules of Golf*:

Golf is played, for the most part, without the supervision of a referee or umpire. The game relies on the integrity of the individual to show consideration for other players, care for the course, and to abide by the rules. All players should conduct themselves in a disciplined manner, demonstrating courtesy and sportsmanship at all times, irrespective of how competitive they may be. This is the spirit of the game of golf.

I have admired that paragraph for a long time and have reread it frequently. I wish the game's governors, at the R&A and the USGA, had left it in place. But you could also say that every golfer is a governor of the game.

Sam Reeves has thought a lot about this subject. He'll tell you that every golfer has to help keep the flame, but you can't be so hidebound about the whole this-is-how-we-do-it thing that you repel others from coming in. What makes the Montell Jordan song so good is the party breaking out all around it.

This is how we do it
All hands are in the air

Sam saw the queen-golf connection. At his home in Pebble Beach, he followed the reaction to the queen's death. He watched as 250,000 people stood in line for hours for the chance to pay their respects, and there was no jostling, no breaking of the queue. The queen's code was civility, and her people were honoring it. As for the hundreds of millions of people around the world who watched her funeral on TV, Sam saw that as the greatest expression of respect for a deceased person in his lifetime, and an excellent use of modern technology.

"Queen Elizabeth didn't chase the last wind that just blew in," he told me. "She had what all great leaders have, in every field. She believed in the people she led, and they in turn believed in her. Everybody could see her dignity. People all over the world picked up on that. In everything she did, she somehow conveyed her belief in people. Now, how can a leader do better than that?"

Golf, we agreed, was in a precarious place. Over the years, it had benefited from principled leaders. Old Tom Morris. Bobby Jones. Joe Dey of the USGA and, later, the PGA Tour. It had charismatic pros from varied backgrounds—Arnold Palmer, Seve Ballesteros, Tiger Woods—who took the sport to new places. One generation set the tone and paved the way for the next. Golf's code, forever, has been civility.

And then came the summer of '22 and the emergence of LIV Golf. Greg Norman and his mega-rich Saudi backers dropped a money bomb on golf and, along the way, exposed its fault line. Golf became a free-for-all, all these golfers in their tourwear looking like a bunch of oiled-up wrestlers. Everybody getting whatever they could as fast as possible.

Can I get another crack at that? *Professional* golf was in a free-for-all. And not even all professional golf. More like two hundred men, those who stayed and those who left, most of them rich already, aided and abetted by their agents.

But a shrill and overwhelming noise was rising with this revolution, and it was making you wonder: Would *their* pursuit of bigger paydays, their sudden willingness to break with tradition, do anything to diminish the joy we—you, me, Sam Reeves, Ryan French, Pratima Sherpa, and millions of others—get from *our* game?

For me, no. For Pratima, Ryan, Sam: no, no, no. I'm pretty sure I can make a good guess about you.

Tiger Woods was inducted into the World Golf Hall of Fame a few weeks before the 2022 Masters. As many of us walked into the hall that night, the question of the evening was whether Phil Mickelson had been suspended by the PGA Tour because he had aligned himself with this new competing golf league and was recruiting others to join it. The whole thing was crass. Then Tiger stepped up and stopped time. He spoke for about fifteen minutes, without notes, and most of it was about the golf he played as a kid. He described meeting another golfer in Mr. Cordova's seventh-grade Spanish class. He talked about waiting for 4:12 p.m., when his father's shift at McDonnell Douglas ended, meaning they could go to the course. He recalled how he hunted for balata balls at the Navy course not far from his house. He remembered being driven by his mother to junior tournaments.

"I know that golf is an individual sport," Tiger said as he wrapped up. "We do things on our own, for hours on end. But I didn't get here alone."

Beautiful.

This beautiful game.

I'm happy for soccer, for *fútbol*, that it has one short, powerful phrase—*the beautiful game*—attached to it. Field, ball, kids, water bottles for goal markers. It's beautiful. You don't come by golf's playing fields and equipment so easily. Still, there are many paths to the game, and there are more now than ever before. Sam Reeves and Pratima Sherpa started on simple nine-hole courses. Any kid could play the public course in Alpena, Michigan, where Ryan French first played. They all had people to help them get started, and you do need that in golf. Tiger said as much as he closed out his induction night. Sam, when you think about his golfing life, was launched into the game on three separate occasions. His first start, in Thomaston, Georgia, as the skinny white kid playing with the older Black caddies. Then his second, playing Army golf at Fort Jackson in South Carolina, Melvin Hemphill presiding. And his Act III golf, with his two new golf mentors, Jim Langley and Butch Harmon. In Jim, Sam had an example of how golf can enrich every aspect of your life, even when you're beyond your physical peak. In Butch, Sam had a teacher and a friend who understood that the golf dream does not die.

Please indulge me, but here, once more, with feeling, are my big three. Mr. Greenlee, my eighth-grade gym teacher. John Sifaneck, my high school golf coach. My mother, finding those clubs at the Salvation Army on Main Street in Patchogue.

If you're looking to start and can't find clubs, drop me a line. It would be my pleasure to help. It's the least I can do.

After Balmoral, I went to Machrihanish alone. (Paris called for Christine.) Machrihanish, the village and its namesake golf course, is an Eden for me, and a true north. It's in southwestern Scotland, at the bottom of a peninsula called the Mull of Kintyre that protrudes off the Scottish coast and into the Irish Sea like a child's pinkie. It's as remote as it sounds. Belfast is the closest big city, but you have to cross a sea to get there.

Christine and I first heard about Machrihanish one winter night shortly after we were married at the home of Jim and Harriet Finegan, who lived in Villanova, in close proximity to the Philadelphia Country Club. Jim was the chairman of an advertising agency in Philadelphia and would race out of his downtown office to squeeze in nine holes during his extended lunch break. He wrote beautifully about golf. As far as I know, he was the first American to write about Machrihanish, which he did in a piece for the USGA publication *Golf Journal* in 1982. For the story, Jim and Harriet rented a house near Machrihanish, and Jim went around the windswept links repeatedly, avoiding the sheep that roamed the course. The course was laid out by Old Tom Morris in 1879, but Old Tom noted Mother Nature had done most of the work before he arrived. Jim was playing a course that had barely changed in a hundred years. *The sea is sometimes in view and sometimes shut off by the great dunes*, he wrote. Does that not make you want to go? The highlight of the piece is a visit Jim and Harriet received from their son John, who had been working as a counselor at a camp for needy kids in Belfast, at the height of the Troubles. The last time Jim Finegan and I went out for lunch, some months before he died, John helped his father into the car, securing his seat belt before gently closing the passenger door.

In my rounds, in the summer of '22 at Machrihanish and at a course down the road called Dunaverty, I played only with Scots. That was only out of happenstance, but a lot of my life relies on happenstance. One of the Machrihanish games was in a two-ball with a man exactly my age named Tommy Blue, a retired roofer. I had interviewed Tommy once by phone, about Paul McCartney's connection to the Mull of Kintyre, but at Machrihanish we were meeting for the first time. He had played the course and lived in its vicinity all his life.

In the mid-1960s, McCartney bought a sheep farm in Machrihanish—you can see it from the golf course—and after he married Linda Eastman, they added to the farm and spent long summer breaks there as their family grew in number and height. In 1977, McCartney and his band Wings recorded a folk ballad called "Mull of Kintyre" at the farm. Tommy, at the age of seventeen, was one of the musicians on the recording, which became an unlikely hit in Great Britain. Linda was there during the recording, pregnant with her son Jamie. Some years later, Tommy Blue was back at the farm, doing work on McCartney's slate roof.

"Do you remember me?" Tommy asked.

"Your face does look familiar," McCartney said.

"I played the bass drum for you on 'Mull of Kintyre.'"

"Then that's it then," McCartney said in his singsong way.

Tommy and I had a good match and a fine time. There's something about being in the company of people who are very near you in age, I find. It relates to how time shapes you, almost to the day. We were just comfortable together. Machrihanish was one of the few courses Tommy had played in his life. There was a new course a few miles away called Machrihanish Dunes, but Tommy had heard it was grueling and difficult and it held no interest for him. I got that, completely. Still, I went over there. It was way too hard for me. But you might like it.

Tommy and I compared family notes. We were both well into our married lives. We each had a son and a daughter. Tommy's wife, Marjorie, had health issues that restricted their travel and kept Tommy close to home, but they managed as best they could. They would soon be celebrating their son's wedding, many months after the actual ceremony, the party postponed because of the pandemic.

How golf promotes intimacy is a marvel. At the end of our round, I felt a closeness to Tommy that I cannot express. We had shared a fine round on a superb course with meaningful conversation on a breezy summer day. That's a lot.

Have you ever watched the footage of the Beatles, on the rooftop of Three Savile Row in London, singing "I've Got a Feeling"? Four minutes of magic. At the start of their second take, McCartney waves his left hand in Lennon's direction and smiles at him. It's like he's bringing in the whole world while reaching out to an old friend. It was the band's final concert. Casual, slapdash, eternal, great. Nobody knew that wrenching ends were coming for John, for George, for Linda, for the keyboardist Billy Preston. But they had that moment, all of them, on that roof. That's how I feel about some of my golf games, including that one with Tommy Blue. We had a game and a moment that came and went, but that round is not going anywhere, not in my mind.

Sam Reeves and I met through a mutual friend, Brian Roberts of Philadelphia, when Sam was eighty-two. Sam had recently become the oldest person to make the cut, walking every round with his pro partner Nick Watney, in the AT&T Pro-Am at Pebble Beach, the old Crosby tournament.

A couple of weeks after that tournament, Sam and I were sitting at a beach club in South Florida, where Sam has a winter home. Our plan was to go bodysurfing. (My best sport and in Sam's top two.) We were wearing bathing suits, talking about the human capacity for redemption, and looking at the gray and uninviting surf. I should say Sam was talking about the human capacity for redemption. I wrote a short piece about our visit that ran under the headline THE TAO OF SAM. That was our start.

We still haven't gone bodysurfing together, though Sam, as I type this and with eighty-nine on his horizon, gets in the ocean regularly. He likes the salt water on his skin and his feet on the ocean floor, lifted by a power far greater than his own.

You'd be hard-pressed to find a serious person with a greater sense of fun. There's a looseness about Sam, in how he walks, how he talks, how he thinks. We were once having lunch on an outside patio at Cypress Point. Condi Rice was one table over. Sam said hello, and Ms. Rice said, "Sam, can I visit with you? There's something I'd like to ask you." So charming and Southern.

After lunch, cookies to go for dessert, Sam said, "I don't know what she wants, but whatever it is, the answer is yes." I laughed. My friend Fred Anton, in any kind of similar situation, would have said the exact same thing. Fred and Sam were both born in 1934.

Sam has a lot of moves. He has the warmth gene, the curiosity gene, the genes for connection, organization, efficiency, and intimacy. He begins his phone conversations with "Hey." He's sometimes moved to say "I believe in a just God," and often becomes emotional when he does. Sam will speak with powerful and depressing candor about mankind's capacity for cruelty, the human instinct to control. He doesn't name names, and doesn't need to.

Golf tests control as few things do. Your control of your emotions. Your control of your swing. Your control of your golf ball, to the degree you can. You get over your ball and you make your swing and the next thing you know your ball is in the air, propelled by you but now with a life of its own.

Be the right club TODAY.

If I had to get Sam's life view down to a single sentence, I'd say this: We all have failings, large and small, and we all can improve, with guidance and love.

At Christmastime, Sam and Betsy rented a house in Eleuthera, in the Bahamas, for their daughters and sons-in-law and their twelve grandchildren. Sam was getting in the water every day. We were talking regularly. One day, our subject was Sam's close relationships with caddies.

Sam's interest in caddies started at the beginning, at the Thomaston Country Club, and never dissipated. He liked the idea of not being out there alone. (I've known many golfers who felt differently.) He liked the idea of having expert advice. (I've known many golfers who felt differently.) He was fascinated by the life and times of Old Tom Morris, a caddie who made good. "Before Old Tom, there were no pros as we know them," he said. "The caddies were the pros, except they were like puppets for the rich, and when the caddies had their tournaments, they were just instruments for betting purposes.

"But then Old Tom—and his son, Young Tom—changed all that. They financed themselves. They were entrepreneurs. They risked their own capital. They maintained courses, built greens we still play today, designed courses we still play today. How amazing is that? They lifted themselves, and that was not easy to do then.

"But at the same time, they held on to these Calvinistic ideas about what golf is. That there are rules that you have to follow. That it takes discipline to play golf correctly, that it takes a work ethic to improve at it, that you earn what you get in the game. And when the Scots brought golf to the United States, that matched up with our constitution, with our basic tenants. Now, maybe that's under threat right now. I don't know.

"You see Trevino out there, teaching Tiger what he knows, teaching Charlie. He has this need to connect. *I* have this need to connect. Golf connects us. Connects us to everything. The ground, the air. Our hands to the club. Each other. Dick Ferris and I, as you know, played in a tournament when he couldn't talk or eat solid food—his ALS—and *still* he wanted to play, and we did. We played, and we played our asses off, and we won!"

I did know about it. The event is called The Swallows. It's a handicap event, but still—golf for three straight days. Two men in their eighties. Dick Ferris was a close friend of Arnold Palmer's and the former chairman of United Airlines. He was eighty-four when he won that event with Sam. He died nine months later.

At the awards ceremony, Sam did the talking, because Dick could not. "The external friendship is what we see, but the internal is what we all gather here for," Sam said. Dick was wearing a puffy coat on a cool afternoon. As he neared his end, his body shook all the time, except, miraculously, when he had a club in hand and was making a swing, and when he was holding on to something with two hands. Somebody handed Dick the trophy, and he lifted it as high as he could.

I raised Bing Crosby's name with Sam. He had met him. Sam and Betsy started making annual trips to the Crosby shortly after they moved to Fresno in 1962. At their first tournament, they watched Jackie Burke, Harvie Ward, and Jimmy Demaret play at Cypress. It was raining, and many spectators had their umbrellas up. On the thirteenth hole, Betsy realized that the man standing beside them, wearing a rain hat and a long khaki coat, was Bing Crosby. They said hello, talked with him some, but didn't linger. The man had a tournament to run.

"Do you know about Bing's last round of golf?" I asked Sam.

He knew there was something there.

"What is it?" Sam asked.

In 1977, Bing had gone to Madrid to play golf for a few days. He played with friends at a stately course on the outskirts of the city. He was seventy-four and shot 85. He won ten dollars with the help of a Spanish pro. When the round was over, he said to his playing partners, "That was a great game of golf, fellas." A few minutes later, between the eighteenth green and the clubhouse door, he had a fatal heart attack.

Great game, fellas.

Sam played the scene in his mind.

"That's amazing," he said. "That is *amazing*."

About the Author

Michael Bamberger was born in Patchogue, New York, in 1960. After graduating from the University of Pennsylvania in 1982, he worked as a newspaper reporter, first for the (Martha's) *Vineyard Gazette*, later for *The Philadelphia Inquirer*. After twenty-two years at *Sports Illustrated*, he is now a senior writer for the Fire Pit Collective. He lives in Philadelphia with his wife, Christine.

Author email: mfbamberger@aol.com

Avid Reader Press, an imprint of Simon & Schuster, is built on the idea that the most rewarding publishing has three common denominators: great books, published with intense focus, in true partnership. Thank you to the Avid Reader Press colleagues who collaborated on *The Ball in the Air*, as well as to the hundreds of professionals in the Simon & Schuster audio, design, ebook, finance, human resources, legal, marketing, operations, production, sales, supply chain, subsidiary rights, and warehouse departments whose invaluable support and expertise benefit every one of our titles.

Editorial
Jofie Ferrari-Adler, *VP and Publisher*
Carolyn Kelly, *Assistant Editor*

Jacket Design
Alison Forner, *Senior Art Director*
Clay Smith, *Senior Designer*
Sydney Newman, *Art Associate*

Marketing
Meredith Vilarello, *Associate Publisher*
Caroline McGregor, *Marketing Manager*
Katya Buresh, *Marketing and Publishing Assistant*

Production
Allison Green, *Managing Editor*
Benjamin Holmes, *Senior Production Editor*
Alicia Brancato, *Production Manager*
Joy O'Meara, *Interior Text Designer*
Ritika Karnik, *Desktop Compositor*
Cait Lamborne, *Ebook Developer*

Publicity
David Kass, *Senior Director of Publicity*
Katherine Hernández, *Publicity Assistant*

Subsidiary Rights
Paul O'Halloran, *VP and Director of Subsidiary Rights*

The author also wishes to express his gratitude to the entire staff at Avid Reader Press, and to two editors with whom he has worked for decades, Mark Godich and Beth Thomas.

AVID READER PRESS